Friends and the Vietnam War

Papers and Presentations from

A Pendle Hill Conference

Bryn Mawr College, Pennsylvania

July 16-20, 1998

Edited by Chuck Fager

Pendle Hill

All essays in this book, unless otherwise noted, are copyright © 1998 by the respective authors, and all rights are reserved by them.

Cover design by Sandy Overbey, Qubic Communications

ISBN No. 0-87574-931-3

Published by Pendle Hill
338 Plush Mill Road, Wallingford PA 19086

http://www.pendlehill.org

Contents

Thursday, July 16, 1998

Daniel A. Seeger: Introduction	1
Lou Schneider: Conscientious Objection: Reactive or Forewarned?	7
"War Stories": A Panel	
John Bach	28
William A. Eagles	40
Jay Worrall, III	46
Charlie Bonner	49
Beth Taylor	58

Friday, July 17, 1998

Joint Plenary Presentations: "If I Knew Now What I Knew Then"	
Lynne Shivers: Vigils, Speeches and So Much More	68
Movement Life Line	79
Jack Patterson: Modes of Friends' Witness, As Practiced Individually and Corporately, During the Vietnam War Years	93
"Peace Witness War Stories": A Panel	
David Hartsough (mass demonstrations)	122
Anne Morrison Welsh (The Sacrifice of Norman Morrison)	126

Saturday, July 18, 1998

Gordon Browne: On Being Conformed to this World
    (The impact of the Vietnam War on the Religious
    Society of Friends)   149

Jeremy Mott: From Protest to Resistance – The Quaker
    Peace Testimony During the Vietnam War   167

Kathleen Hertzberg: Canadian Friends – Trying to Serve God
    in the Spirit of Christ   187

"Corporate Effort War Stories": A Panel

    Liz Yeats (Draft counseling)   204

    Ken Maher (Underground Railroad)   210

    David Finke (Military counseling)   214

    William A. Eagles (Quaker House, Fayetteville, NC)   221

Sunday, July 19, 1998

Panel: "But What Canst Thou Say?" Personal Reflections of
    Three Generations of Quaker Peace Activists   226

    Bronson Clark (World War II Resister)

    Max Carter (Vietnam War CO)

    Garrett Colgan-Snyder (1990's CO)

    Chuck Fager (Moderator)

Peter Goldberger: Conscience, Citizenship,
    and the Road Ahead   258

Monday, July 20, 1998

Arthur O. Roberts (EFI): The Vietnam Era and the
    Evangelical Quaker Community   276

Bruce Birchard (FGC): It Was a Hard Time, and Friends Were There	295
Johan Maurer (FUM): Was there a War Going On?	306

Additional Comments:

Daniel E. Ensley	332
Marion Anderson	336
Carlie Numi	340
Tom Rodd	341
Carl Stieren	342
Chel Avery: A Letter to the Organizer of the Next Event on the Subject of Friends and the Vietnam War	352
About the Presenters and Panelists	362

INTRODUCTION:

The original inspiration for the gathering which is described in this book actually occurred at another event sponsored by Pendle Hill. In November of 1996 we convened the alumni of Civilian Public Service Camps to lead a reflection about the meaning of the CPS camp experience for those who participated. We wanted to reflect upon, and to appreciate, the significance of the lives of leadership and of service which grew out of the CPS camps, lives which did so much to guide not only the evolution of the Religious Society of Friends and of Friends' organizations in subsequent decades, but which also significantly helped to shape and form the wider movements for social change in society as a whole.

The experience of that gathering was an enchanting one, a quite mysterious and marvelous blend of historical documentary, vigorous debate, searching spiritual inquiry, and family reunion. The proceedings of that conference are recorded in the book *Friends in Civilian Public Service*, also published by Pendle Hill.

Now it happened that at the November, 1996 gathering of CPS alumni there were three or four Vietnam War-era activists in attendance. They were deeply touched by what transpired, as was anyone privileged to be present. Before the CPS gathering was over, we were receiving urgent suggestions that a similar gathering be held focused upon the Vietnam War era.

I have to admit that we at Pendle Hill hesitated for a long time about this. The situation regarding the alumni of anti-Vietnam War activism is obviously not analogous to that of CPS campers, and we were uncertain that there was the same sort of common thread that would make a gathering cohere. The group of enthusiasts from the Vietnam War-era who had actually experienced the

CPS gathering was small; the question was whether they represented any definable group. Chel Avery, whose magnificent staff work is at the basis of the present report, began an exploratory and consultative process.

What Chel discovered is that there was, indeed, a constituency of people who felt an urgency to begin the process of documentation and reflection upon the experience of anti-Vietnam War activism. But the urgency had a different coloration about it than had been the case with the CPS camp alumni. Aspects of the CPS camp experience were known and understood: the criticism of the peace churches for collaborating with the War Department in operating the camps had already been aired; the differences between those who had found in the camps a positive life-transforming experience and those who had been so offended that they had rebelled and left the camps was known; the experience of spouses was familiar; many of the impressive outcomes of the camp experience had been related in some place or another. The urgency in the case of the CPS camp experience was one of time. It was felt that there was a need to get this panorama into view in one place, and to collect first-hand experiences, while significant numbers of the participants were still available to contribute to the process.

For obvious reasons, the element of time is much less a factor when the matter of anti-Vietnam War activism is in view. We picked up a different sort of urgency. It was as if something haunting and unresolved had been left unexamined for too long. So, with the help of an excellent committee and Chel's planning, we proceeded to organize the gathering of which this book presents an account. It was much more an excursion into unknown territory, much more a reflection on unsolved dilemmas. We are grateful for all who gathered to participate in this adventure. I am sure the efforts they made to understand our experience, to tease out meanings from it, and to assess learnings for the future, will be valuable to anyone interested in the struggle for peace.

One hundred years ago, the decade of the 1890's provided two occasions for reflection by the establishment-oriented historians of that era. The first occasion was the great Chicago World's Fair, held in 1893; the second was the diamond jubilee of Queen Victoria in 1897. To the official mind of those days, a retrospective look at history had a great simplicity. Everything had converged in the establishment of North Atlantic civilization's ascendancy, with its capitalism and its colonialism, over the rest of the world. This was the consummation of a process which had begun 400 years earlier with Columbus' transit of the Atlantic and Vasco da Gama's voyage to the coast of India. History, viewed in retrospect at that moment in the 1890's, appeared to have resulted in the attainment of a stable state. It seemed quite plausible that the global ascendancy the West had attained was going to be permanent.

As we look back over the succeeding century's two world wars, countless regional wars, world-wide economic depression, Russian Revolution, the progeny of other revolutions the Russian Revolution spawned, the Cold War, and the breakup of colonial empires, it is amazing how naive the perspective of the historians of the 1890's seems. For within twenty years of Queen Victoria's diamond jubilee the overriding conflict of our own tragic and bloody century had been defined. As one pundit put it: the specter of communism was haunting Europe.

Yet, after all the horrors and humiliations of the twentieth century, here we are in the 1990's, and the landscape looks strangely similar to that of the 1890's. The Vietnam War seems to have been, with all its pain and tragedy, merely the last spasm in a titanic conflict. The feared heap of falling dominoes has not arrived at our own door; rather, it is the huge effort at social transformation based upon the theories of Karl Marx which now lies everywhere in ruins. The communist experiment was certainly one of the most spectacular commitments of thought and labor ever devoted to the logically planned improvement of human life – an effort at social transformation which was expected to be matched by nothing less than the transformation of human nature itself, an effort that at once challenged us, bewildered us, and frightened us. Yet it seems to have collapsed before our very eyes.

At the same time, in England and America, the Thatcher

and Reagan administrations set in motion an unprecedented redistribution of wealth away from working people and the poor to the already rich in two democracies. The theory seemed to be that rich people will work harder if they get more money as an incentive, and poor people will work harder if they get less. This bizarre redistribution of wealth is a singular achievement! And now, instead of the specter of communism haunting Europe, the specter of capitalism haunts the globe. And what is most eerily reminiscent of the attitudes of the 1890's, the pundits of the 1990's have proclaimed the victory of the European/American political and economic systems, and some have even announced the end of history.

The other day I heard on National Public Radio an interview with the author of a recently published book in which she gives account of her upbringing by countercultural parents during the 1960's and 1970's. As I recall the interview, she describes how her father felt that they were living at an enormously significant moment in history, a moment when a world transformation was about to take place, a moment which demanded all we could give to it in order to make the desired changes come about.

The words described a feeling, a passion, I can well remember. The fact that her father was explaining to her why he had become what we now would call a deadbeat dad, why he had neglected her, is, in a certain sense, both ironic and very relevant. The protest era was indeed one in which the world was turned upside down: an undeclared, constitutionally illegitimate war in which so many lost their lives; criminality in the White House; loss of faith in the institutions and traditions which define our country. Yet the outcome of it all seems to have fooled everyone. Was the administration naive in fearing the communist threat? Were the protestors naive in feeling that a special moment in history had arrived which held revolutionary possibilities?

While there is clearly much in the capitalist spirit that is enterprising, socially productive, and laudable, there is also much that is immoral, socially damaging, and reprehensible. The free play of market forces can provide needed discipline; it can also produce chaos and many victims. Socialism and communism were invented because capitalism can be very offensive. Greed and the desire to make a fast buck do not necessarily lead to benefits for society. The fact that communism has failed does not necessarily mean that capitalism has succeeded. We suspect that the self-complacency of the 1990's will prove as short-lived as that of the 1890's.

This, at least in part, accounts for the sense of urgency about reflecting on the Vietnam War period and the protest movement which Chel, in her explorations, picked up. There is a temptation to look back on the period in a mood of cynicism, because the historical situation has so changed as to seem to render the feelings and experiences of that time to have been strictly a passing phenomenon, and perhaps even illusory.

But we also suspect that we should look back on the time as a source of hope because so much was learned and experienced that will be relevant to a future in which history will not, after all, have come to an end, but a future in which the issues the Vietnam War epitomized will rise again in some form. Learning, preserving, and reflecting upon that experience is a vital responsibility we owe to such a future. With this in view, we have collected here all the contributions of the resource persons at the Friends and the Vietnam War Conference who were able to submit to us written versions of their presentations.

The fine committee which helped us prepare the event reported here wisely determined that for an initial conference it would be useful to focus on the Vietnam War years in the experience of Friends as individuals and the Religious Society of Friends as a community. It would clearly have been unwise to try to be too undefined in what we focused upon. The topic could open up whole universes of possibilities. But perhaps it is not presumptuous to suggest that if, as I personally believe likely, there is future need for an awareness of the experience of the Vietnam War period, it is the Religious Society of Friends, and perhaps the other peace churches, which are apt to provide the thread of continuity between that future time and the past. So it is important that we Friends undertake some careful discernment and take stock of our experience. I am grateful to all those whose participation made the following study possible. I am confident that it is a valuable contribution to Friends' search for a faithful peace witness.

Daniel A. Seeger

Based upon welcoming remarks at the Pendle Hill Conference
Friends and the Vietnam War
Bryn Mawr, Pennsylvania
July 16, 1998

Opening Plenary Presentation: Lou Schneider

Conscientious Objection: Reactive or Forewarned?

The canonical stated purpose of the military establishment is to close with the enemy and kill him. I have put this in the singular to convey a certain poignancy of feeling that goes infinitely beyond statistics. In the Amsterdam apartment where Anne Frank and her family hid to escape the holocaust the tourist visitor upon entering faces a sign on the wall: "Six Million Jews were not killed in the holocaust. A Jew was killed Six Million Times." When put this way one can begin, but only begin, to grasp the enormity of the brutality of war in our century, indeed a century of war.

This is the one hundredth anniversary of the Spanish-American War, in which the United States launched itself into an epoch of militarism and imperialism throughout the world: The Spanish-American War, World War I, World War II, the Korean War, the Vietnam War, and the Gulf War.

At this time 81 years ago the fiercest and bloodiest battle of World War I was already deadlocked in the fourth month at Verdun. Over a period of nine months a German and French soldier was killed 750,000 times. I went there 30 years later on a beautiful summer day. It was a peaceful pastoral scene. But I could discern the contours of collapsed trenches and mounds of earth blown up by bombs leaving craters now all covered with grass. When the United States went to war against Germany in 1917, the American Friends Service Committee, just recently established, sent over 400 relief and reconstruction volunteers to France. One fourth of them were conscientious objectors furloughed from the army to the American Friends Service Committee. In addition to providing 2,500 families with hospitals, schools, new and rebuilt houses, and agricultural supplies and equipment in the Verdun district, the AFSC workers planted 2,500 trees, mostly fruit trees, to rehabilitate the place where the battle had raged. As I turned away from the battlefield I felt that I was leaving a scene once filled with agony beyond my comprehension but also that I was leaving a scene that had become a forgotten experience.

I am brought up short every time I read these lines in the 1947 Nobel Peace Prize Committee's citation of the American Friends Service Committee and the Friends Service Council (Britain): "It is the silent help from the nameless to the nameless which is their contribution to the promotion of brotherhood among nations." Everyone whose life has been sacrificed to war and everyone who has been maimed psychologically and physically has been a person with the unique identity of personhood as well as a name. These persons are not a blur of the nameless. They must not be abandoned to obscurity.

Persons and only persons are endowed with consciences. Governments have policies and laws and the courts' interpretation of the law. Governments do not have consciences. Government policies are based on national interest or, put more bluntly, self-interest.

Conscience is an inward knowledge of right and wrong. Conscientious objectors to war in their opposition to the military hold this knowledge with conviction. Conscience with the infusion of conviction and commitment to finding alternatives to violence infuses the witness with an innate integrity. Other individuals of course have the right to their opinions about this witness. Does government have the same right?

In this century of conscientious objection, our government has assigned to itself in Selective Service legislation and administration the right and power to judge the sincerity of conscientious objectors and their witness without itself having the innate capacity and, I would argue, the constitutional right to do so. We are indebted to those conscientious objectors who have endured imprisonment in their unqualified challenge to this unwarrantable intrusion by government.

While I attribute "that of God" to persons, it does not follow that I attribute that quality to government functionaries when they retreat behind the mask of office and become beyond reach as persons. In the struggle of conscience against officialdom there is always a disequilibrium of power which arbitrarily threatens the free exercise of conscience.

George Fox and 21,000 other Friends suffered death, jailings, and brutal beatings for conscience' sake. Some 420 died in prison. At one time there were as many as 4,200 Quakers in prison in England. On one occasion George Fox, himself having been imprisoned, encountered Oliver Cromwell riding in his coach in Hyde Park. Fox rode up to the coach on horseback and pleaded with Cromwell to desist from his persecution of Friends. The next day they met at Cromwell's house to talk further. Fox, sensing that he was not getting through to Cromwell, finally said to him that he should "lay down his crown at the feet of Jesus." In other words, until you drop the mask of government you can neither acknowledge nor understand the force of conscience.

I began with the classic definition of the role of the military: to close with the enemy and kill him. The military and those who serve its purpose will never be hospitable to conscientious objectors. This was put to me by none other than General Hershey, who directed the Selective Service System during World War II. Immediately after VJ day in August of 1945 I went to Selective Service headquarters in Washington to make a strong case for discharging all CPS men at once. This fell on deaf ears. In the spring of 1946 we went again to make the same plea. After an hour of unproductive discussion General Hershey asked leave to say one more thing: "The problem you Quakers have had for the last 5 years is that you have been trying to put a square peg into a round hole." That sums it up. At time of war there can be no easy accommodation between the government and conscientious objectors unless they remain free to exercise their freedom of conscience.

In 1650 George Fox was offered a commission in the army to gain his release from prison. In refusing he said, "I live in the virtue and life of that power that took away the occasion of all wars." Ten years later the first declaration against war was made by a *group* of Quakers. "We do testify to the world that the spirit of Christ [substitute conscience] which leads us into all truth will never move us to fight against any man with outward weapons, neither for the Kingdom of Christ nor for the Kingdom of this world."

Between these first utterances by the original Quakers and the creation of the American Friends Service Committee in 1917, two and one-half centuries later, untold numbers of Friends endured persecution by the State.

While conscientious objection to war with a commitment to finding alternatives to violence is essentially a personal stand, an inalienable birthright, an institutional counterpart has taken place. In the main, two strains of Quaker testimony and witness converged to achieve this: conscientious opposition to war and a concern to render humanitarian service for the relief of those suffering from the ravages of war. Just 24 days after the United States declared war the American Friends Service Committee was launched on April 30, 1917.

In the Selective Service law of 1917 the only provision for conscientious objectors was exemption from combat service. This exemption was provided *only* for members of recognized peace churches. On arrival at a mobilization center the men had two options: noncombatant service in the army or imprisonment for refusal to accept noncombatant service. In practice, in some cases the law was actually more broadly interpreted to cover those whose opposition was not based on religion.

There was considerable variation among local boards in this matter. Men whose objection was found to be *sincere* were eligible for furlough from the army to various forms of alternative service. About 1500 men who were examined by a Board of Inquiry were recommended for farm or industrial furloughs. Four hundred and fifty men served prison sentences in the Disciplinary Barracks at Fort Leavenworth, Kansas.

About 58,000 men were given noncombatant classification. In camps and prisons there were serious hazings, beatings, immersion in latrines, and solitary confinement including shackling. Although these were later commuted, there were 17 sentences to death. Ninety-nine men were furloughed to the American Friends Service Committee to engage in war relief work in France. Their experience as conscientious objectors was a liberating one in association with the AFSC.

After the end of World War I, the United States returned to a voluntary military despite efforts by some to impose universal military training. Although the United States was not yet in World War II the Selective Training and Service Act was enacted in September, 1940. The Friends War Problems Committee strongly argued at legislative hearings for complete exemption for those men found to have *sincere* convictions against all forms of compulsory service. I note here that both the government and Friends were attaching weight to the sincerity of conscientious objectors. This raises questions to which I wish to return later.

Friends were unsuccessful in achieving complete exemption. After much negotiation with the Selective Service system it was agreed that the American Friends Service Committee, the Brethren Service Committee, and the Mennonite Central Committee would accept drafted conscientious objectors in camps and units under their administration to work under civilian direction in projects of national importance without pay and at no cost to the government. The first Civilian Public Service camp was opened on May 15, 1941, six months before the United States declared war.

Time does not permit an extensive review of the complexities which ensued during the next five years of the CPS program.

I believe that two major experiences of the AFSC had a direct bearing on the readiness of the AFSC, however reluctant, to engage in the CPS program. These were:

(1) World War I relief and reconstruction work in Europe involving furloughed conscientious objectors without government interference, and

(2) the volunteer work camps for young people during the Great Depression years. One notes in passing here that it would be over six months before the US entered the war and both the

government and the AFSC presupposed that there would be conscientious objectors who *would* declare themselves in the event of war.

Over 10,000 men were assigned to CPS. Over 4,800 other men were convicted and sent to prison for violating the Selective Service Act – 3,500 of them were Jehovah's Witnesses.

Before the end of the war in Europe the AFSC had already published a candid and critical report and appraisal of the CPS program, with recommendations for changes in the Selective Service Law and its administration. In the main these were to provide full recognition of conscience by making *sincerity of conviction* rather than religious training and belief the test of conscience; and assignment of conscientious objectors to work of unquestioned value and urgency commensurate with their vocational skills including foreign relief work.

The orientation of the Selective Service System to conscientious objectors is reflected in a 1942 statement of policy: a conscientious objector ceases to be a free agent and is accountable for all his time, in camps and out, 24 hours a day. His movement, conduct, and actions are subject to control and regulation. He ceases to have certain rights and is granted privileges instead. These can be restricted or withdrawn as punishment. He may be moved from place to place for the convenience of the government regardless of his personal feelings or desires. Should the assignee's conduct indicate that he is not a *true* conscientious objector he may be referred back to his Local Board for reconsideration as one improperly classified.

When the war with Japan ended, the AFSC decided in the fall of 1945 that in the future it would not again participate in the administration of a program such as Civilian Public Service.

Unfettered voluntary service is adventurous, dynamic and innovative. When subsumed under conscription and made compulsory it is blunted and eventually sapped of its vitality. Coerced service is an oxymoron.

The CPS program never achieved the early expectations for it. Conscientious objectors in camps, units, and prisons were marginalized with no opportunity to move beyond objection to positive and constructive achievement of the socially valuable service of which they were capable.

Nevertheless, when history assesses the cumulative witness of conscientious objectors in this century, is it possible that the massing of men – 10,000 men – in opposition to World War II may have widened the public's tolerance if not its approbation of conscientious objectors to war?

When I was developing my own position as a conscientious objector before World War II, I was intrigued by a line from Ralph Waldo Emerson. He wrote in one of his essays, "Conscience is essentially absolute but historically limitary." In other words you can push your views and witness to an extreme thereby inviting such strong resistance as to be virtually suicidal. Better to pace yourself and build acceptance one step at a time.

Nonetheless conscience *is* essentially absolute and to acquiesce in limitary impositions is to deny its fulfillment.

With apologies to Emerson and John Woolman I offer this celebration of conscientious objection to war: There is conscience which is essentially absolute and which in different places and ages hath had different names. It is, however, essentially absolute and proceeds from within. It is deep and inward, confined to no forms of religion or excluded from any, where the heart and mind stand in perfect sincerity. Even though the state may threaten conscience by intrusive efforts to judge its sincerity, it is never inherently limitary and cannot be subjugated.

Men are still required to register for the draft. There undoubtedly will be a ground swell of conscientious objection if and when the draft should again be activated. Throughout this century of conscientious objection great emphasis has been placed both by the government and various conscientious objector counseling services, including the AFSC, on the pivotal importance of establishing one's *sincerity* to the satisfaction of government review boards. Put in the context of a Universal Military Training and Service Act, conscientious objection is regarded as an aberrant attitude and conviction. By what standard is the government qualified or competent to judge the sincerity of conscience? I should say none.

Since World War I Selective Service laws have placed conscientious objection in the context of religion. Religious training and belief are still by law components of the government's consideration of the sincerity of a conscientious objector. The first amendment of the United States Constitution states that "the Congress shall enact no law respecting the establishment of religion or prohibiting the free exercise thereof." Does Selective Service law put the government in the position of prohibiting the free exercise of conscientious objection to war– namely, our exercise of religion? Is this the basis for undertaking renewed efforts in the courts to remove the government from the role it has arrogated to itself to be the arbiter of conscience?

With the end of the Korean War the AFSC gradually became concerned with Southeast Asia. Very few Americans had any idea of Vietnam. I may have been the first person associated with the AFSC to have visited Vietnam in October, 1954, three months after the defeat of the French at Dienbienphu by Ho Chi Minh's forces. With American support the French had continued to resist Vietnamese claims to independence.

For the next twenty years, through the Eisenhower, Kennedy, Johnson, and Nixon administrations, the United States entangled itself in disastrous policies. These strengthened the resistance of the Vietnamese people to the various corrupt, reactionary and inept Saigon regimes. By 1965 the United States began directly to wage war by bombing North Vietnam and the Vietcong in the south with no firm or reliable support from South Vietnam on which it could rely.

At the end of my visit to Saigon in October, 1954, I wrote in my report to my colleagues in Philadelphia, "For 9 long years, 1945-1954, Indochina and Vietnam have been approached from a military point of view and it has resulted in a political and military shambles." I remarked that in its efforts to hold the state of affairs together the United States was holding a rope of sand. In the previous year the United States had distributed $55,000,000 to several political and military factions, some for assistance to refugees from the North, to little avail. All the while time was running out.

Refugees were arriving in the South at the rate of 10,000 a day with no provision being made for them. I myself watched for hours the disembarkation of thousands from US troop ships which had brought them south from Haiphong. I rode with some of them in US Army trucks north on Highway #1 which then was only a dirt road. One hundred feet of clearing of the jungle on either side of the road had been made for security reasons. Each truck stopped just beyond where the previous one had unloaded its passengers – no shelter, no clean water, no facilities.

After the tortuous events of the next twenty years I am haunted by what I wrote at the end of my report. "And now for *the* question. What should *we* do?

This had been partially answered before I left Philadelphia. "We don't have the money or the personnel, given our involvement in postwar Europe, the Middle East, and Korea. We don't sense a concern rising from the general public or among Friends." This notwithstanding I had visited Vietnam anyway. The division of North and South had not yet become a full scale war. I saw endless opportunity for community development. It was too easy to say that there are no funds and no volunteers while time is running out.

As early as June, 1955, I presented testimony before the House Foreign Affairs Committee in support of contributions from the Foreign Economic Aid Program in the reverse order of its priorities of 80 percent military aid and 20 percent non-military economic aid. I stated that the real enemies in Southeast Asia were poverty, disease, malnutrition and illiteracy.

By 1965, the escalation of the war by the United States was calamitous for the civilian population throughout Vietnam: contamination and defoliation of wide ranging jungle areas which also destroyed rice crops by herbicide such as Agent Orange, "pacification" measures including torching of whole villages and forced evacuation to "strategic hamlets," dropping grenades in tunnels sheltering women and children, bribing children to reveal hideouts and torturing prisoners to reveal information.

After investigation of the needs in South Vietnam by an AFSC Team the AFSC launched a program in Quang Ngai to manufacture at the lowest costs and then fit prosthetic devices for the severely crippled followed by physical therapy. In 1967 there were estimated to be 3,000 amputees in Quang Ngai Province alone, with additional casualties every day. In one of the early months as many as 50 protheses a day were achieved with a goal of 200 a month as soon as possible. A first class device was being turned out for as little as $4.50. Metal was being used from salvaged military equipment including downed airplanes. Trainees became skilled technicians working alongside skilled workers.

We also developed a Child Day Care Centre for refugee children up to six years. Every day 75 children came for recreation, a good meal, milk, vitamins, a bath, clean clothes and a rest period.

Meanwhile the AFSC Board authorized an approach to the North Vietnamese to seek a visit to Hanoi to explain Friends' opposition to war, specifically the Vietnam War, to describe efforts we were making for the prompt withdrawal of the American military from Vietnam, and to have the opportunity to render humanitarian aid in the North. Early in November, 1965, I carried a thoroughly prepared and voluminous presentation of these proposals to Paris with the names and biographical data of three Friends who would undertake such a mission to Hanoi.

Mai Van Bo was the only diplomatic representative of the North Vietnamese still in Western Europe in Paris. We had been told that he would be quite approachable and open to receiving our request. He was very gracious. After an initial greeting he expressed his deep appreciation of the Friends Peace Testimony and his profound regard for Norman Morrison who in the days just previous had immolated himself in Washington. He said that all Vietnamese were deeply moved by this and asked me to express this to his widow. I visited Anne immediately upon returning home.

We did not receive a response from Hanoi to this first overture. However, as time went by it may have been a significant first step.

Opposition to the war developed rapidly and with such intensity that an unprecedented question was raised for the AFSC to confront. Strong dissension within various quarters of the AFSC emerged in regard to our humanitarian work in South Vietnam. Our work in South Vietnam had begun in 1966 with the approval of the South Vietnam government. Was this collaboration with a government at war with its own people and with the overwhelming support of the United States government undermining or compromising the AFSC's antiwar efforts at home in the United States? Did the service undermine the integrity of our opposition to the war? Should we terminate this work and, presumably, render our efforts to stop the war unimpeachable? Or would our remaining involved in meeting the needs of those suffering the fierce ravages of the war inform our outrage at the war and thus enhance our witness?

Our Quang Ngai team raised the same question for itself in October, 1967, and came to this view: "We speak in the context of our direct daily involvement with those victims of this war with whom we work. We are confronted every day with the suffering of these victims of war. We are ever mindful of their need and are called upon to respond to it.

"Many of our team express concern lest our program...be linked too closely with the US and R.V.N. military pacification efforts. We strongly urge the AFSC to treat the belligerents in this war impartially and to interpret our Quang Ngai program to them in this light. We would wish to reiterate at all points of opportunity Quaker opposition to any and all war.

"Weighing all of this we feel that more good is being achieved by our presence here than withdrawal at this time would accomplish.

"We need to always be seeking to know what is right in agonizing questions from our involvement here in Vietnam; but human need is central to our reasons for being here and we cannot easily turn away from this service."

The AFSC Board wrestled with this question and in early 1968 decided to continue in Quang Ngai and to continue efforts to send aid to war sufferers in North Vietnam. This was in keeping with AFSC's commitment to work on both sides of a conflict if at all possible.

By the end of the war, seven years later, the Quang Ngai Rehabilitation Centre had treated over 5000 war injured civilians, particularly amputees.

One year after the visit to Mai Van Bo in Paris the AFSC received a Department of Treasury License to ship medical supplies to "any destination in Vietnam." Shortly afterwards the department changed its policies and said that henceforth it would not grant licenses. The issue was that impartial observers were not allowed to accompany relief shipments to observe their distribution. Feeling that additional shipments were needed, the AFSC decided to proceed without licenses even though this would be in violation of the Trading with the Enemy Act of 1917.

The commitment was made with sober awareness of legal action being taken against the AFSC and its officers as well as withdrawal of our tax exempt status. Our Quaker constituency had been canvassed about this and there was clear support to go ahead. A shipment was made but no retaliatory action was taken by the government. In 1969 an AFSC representative, Joe Elder, was able to accompany a shipment of $25,000 worth of open heart surgery equipment to Hanoi.

By the end of the war in 1975 the AFSC since 1966 had sent over $2,000,000 of humanitarian aid to all sides in Vietnam including areas controlled by the Provisional Revolutionary Government in the south. Beginning in 1969, shipments to North Vietnam and the PRG in the south were received during visits by AFSC representatives. The supplies included such things as 100 tons of acrylic yarn, $75,000 worth of screw making machines, fish nets, agricultural equipment such as heavy duty walking tractors and school supplies.

In July, 1975 licenses were again denied, simply for political reasons, even though our government had committed itself to postwar aid. On November 10, 1975, over 2,000 AFSC persons nationwide vigiled on the issue, including 250 of us in front of the

White House. Although the President would not see us we left over 2,000 forms signed by vigilers addressed "For the President." We were joined by the leaders of six other religious groups. The administration withdrew its objections. This was only one of a number of AFSC and other Quaker vigils convened throughout the war.

In December, 1970, in preparation for my first visit to Hanoi, I wrote to every family of every American prisoner of war of whom we were aware. I said that I would be going to Hanoi by January first and would be happy to carry letters to their loved ones. When I left Philadelphia I carried a suitcase bulging with over 500 letters to American POW's. When I arrived in Hanoi for a three-week visit I told my hosts that I had brought the letters and hoped that they would receive them for delivery to the men. The next day they came to me and said, "Please, may we have the suitcase." Three weeks later at the airport for departure as I was about to climb the steps to the plane they handed me a parcel wrapped in brown paper. In it were 80 letters from POW's to their families. Seventeen were from men about whom there had been no report since their disappearance and who were not on any POW list.

When Stewart Meacham, Secretary of the AFSC Peace Education Division, left Hanoi after a visit, the North Vietnamese asked him if he would accompany a POW whom they were releasing, which he did. These were extraordinary conciliatory gestures.

When given the opportunity we pleaded with top administration officials to end the war. During the heightening of the war in the years 1966-1968 I was with Stewart Meacham on one occasion when we went one Saturday morning for a long talk with Secretary of State Dean Rusk. He and Stewart had been college roommates. The beginning of our meeting seemed unusually propitious, with greeting of "Hi, Stew" and "Hi, Dean." But Dean Rusk didn't hear us. Later, much later in retirement, he reflected that he had misjudged the determination of the Vietnamese people and the patience of the American people. This is what we, from our own experience, were trying to get across to him.

When Richard Nixon took office in 1969 we immediately sought to see him. He referred us to Henry Kissinger, then his National Security Advisor. Over a period of nine months we met with him three times. I was a member of the last delegation to meet with him. A few weeks ago Channel 12, Public TV, ran a series of profiles on Presidents Kennedy, Johnson, and Nixon. The station invited me to state in 45 seconds after a two and a half hour program about President Nixon what his impact on the Quaker religious community had been. I identified myself as now retired from the AFSC and then said, "In 1969 we met at the White House with Henry Kissinger, who spoke for President Nixon. We were there to urge the speedy end to the Vietnam War. We were told that this would risk an overwhelming adverse negative reaction from his political right.

"Thus over the next 5 years of his administration 25,000 more Americans and countless Vietnamese were needlessly sacrificed. I was appalled that he would hold all of us hostage to domestic politics. Richard Nixon should be seen as a war criminal."

Throughout the war the AFSC issued public statements informing the public of our views and activities. A number of timely newspaper ads were published, notably one as early as October, 1966. After reviewing the background of our rising concern, the AFSC announced that it would be undertaking nine steps. Among them were: opposing the war and offering humanitarian aid on all sides, encouraging resistance to the war, encouraging and supporting conscientious objectors, and exploring the concept of conscientious objection to the violation of international law and crimes against humanity.

On Monday, the day after the outrageous Christmas bombing of Hanoi, we started to compose an ad for publication in the NY Times and the Washington Post called *"Make Your Own Peace."* The idea was that the government wasn't making any effort to make peace so people might do what they could to send a message of peace. By Thursday the text was ready for publication in Sunday's edition, one week after the event. The response was most reassuring – hundreds of thousands of dollars to expand our humanitarian work in Vietnam.

The AFSC also published books composed by working parties of knowledgeable people. Among these were *Peace In Vietnam* in 1966 followed by an updated and enlarged edition in 1967, *In Place of War*, and in 1979, *The Police Threat to Political Liberty*.

Although surveillance of the AFSC by government intelligence agencies predated the Vietnam War, this was greatly extended during the war. Telephone lines were tapped and mail was intercepted. In the early seventies public disclosure of such activities led the AFSC to create a Program on Government Surveillance and Citizens' Rights. Under the Freedom of Information Act the AFSC requested and received over 13,000 documents relating to AFSC activities and many of its personnel, some of it going back to the 1920's. AFSC's peace education, antiwar activities, and draft counseling were increasingly targeted. At the end of the sixties one of the key so-called "Key Activities" listed for possible Counter Intelligence Program disruption by the FBI was the Peace Education Secretary of the AFSC.

In 1976 the AFSC issued a public statement calling for the abolition of the CIA and the Internal Security Division of the FBI. It also called for elimination of "illegal wire tapping, mail interception, burglaries, cover-ups, surveillance and infiltration of lawful groups, use of *agents provocateurs*, investigation of dissent and dissenters...and the maintenance of political dossiers on citizens and groups exercising legitimate rights."

It was my privilege to present testimony based on the public statement at a Senate Hearing. When Senator Garn asked me if I realized how peacefully we all slept at night because the CIA was watching over us the only response that came to mind at the moment was to say that he must have information to which I was not privy. He did not elaborate.

During the Vietnam War there was a rising concern over the payment of federal income taxes, a large portion of which were devoted to war expenditures. Two of our colleagues requested the AFSC not to forward to the government that portion of their taxes withheld, approximately 53 percent, which would be used in support of the war. The AFSC agreed to their request. Instead of not forwarding those funds, the AFSC forwarded an equivalent amount from its own general fund, and requested the government to reimburse us for that amount since we were in complete sympathy with our employees in their concern based on First Amendment principles. When the Internal Revenue Service refused to reimburse us we took the matter to court.

The Federal District Court in Philadelphia decided in our favor, saying that we not only should be reimbursed, but that the government had a variety of other methods of collecting taxes than relying on an employer who was completely identified with its employees in their conscientious conviction. The IRS appealed the case to the United States Supreme Court, which ruled against us, Justice William O. Douglas dissenting.

At the invitation of the Democratic Republic of Vietnam I represented the AFSC in Hanoi at the celebration of their National Day on Sept. 2, 1975, 30 years to the day after Ho Chi Minh had declared Vietnam an independent nation. When I left Hanoi these were my reflections:

"The most moving experience of joining the people of Vietnam in their celebration of this National Day was to understand with feeling their deep happiness that freedom and independence had been redeemed. After struggling to emerge from decades of colonial domination and war the mood of the people was one of jubilation to be sure but tempered with a deep and quiet dignity that surrounded the celebration with a certain serenity. One sensed that the people regarded themselves as having achieved not only national sovereignty but the restoration of their integrity as well. One also sensed the deep feeling of relief that the long years of fighting had ended. For the first time in over twenty years families divided between North and South were experiencing the sweet joy of visiting and becoming reunited. Despite the heavy burden of postwar problems the people are approaching the future with a light heart.

"The United States is regarded as having both moral and

political responsibilities to fulfill its commitments to the reconstruction and development of Vietnam. In insisting on this as well as the normalization of diplomatic relations the Vietnamese people are neither vindictive nor retributive.

"In a conversation with Pham Van Dong, Prime Minister of the DRV, he remarked that in his treatment of these obligations in his address to the country on September 2nd he spoke not of the past but of the future only."

Throughout the Vietnam War the AFSC undertook humanitarian service on both sides of the conflict. We supported a broader range of conscientious objection than in previous wars. We were altogether open in our opposition to the war both in the United States and in Vietnam. We advanced proposals for ending the war. We appealed to the public to support our humanitarian aid. We further appealed to the public to join us in protesting the war. We published books and pamphlets about Vietnam and its history. We expanded our conscientious objection to include tax refusal and shipments of aid in violation of the law. We made numerous representations to successive administrations to end the war. We presented testimony to congressional committees. We joined others in demonstrations against the war and we held our own discrete vigils.

What did we overlook? Could more have been done?

A more tormenting question now follows before all this experience becomes an abandoned experience. How should Friends now be more actively engaged in efforts to sustain opposition to war and to expand the scope of opposition to war? After a century of conscientious objection to war which is still a living memory for many of us, should we be able to discern unexplored frontiers for extension of our efforts to curb war?

There is now no significant peace movement in the United States. There hasn't been a draft in over a quarter century. Does dwindling immediacy necessarily neutralize us? Can there be a continuance of witness informed and enlivened by past experience?

War is brutish. Throughout this century it has been a searing experience. It leaves nothing to the imagination. We who are committed to finding alternatives to violence need all the imagination we can muster. Do our reflections on the Vietnam War sharpen our wits as we stand on the threshold of tomorrow?

One can't review the history of the Vietnam War without wondering "What if?" Ho Chi Minh declared Vietnam an independent nation on Sept. 2, 1945. What if, then, the United States had recognized that declaration?

What if! Think about it. Could speculation about this have a bearing on approaches to future contingencies?

Each generation is entrusted with the safekeeping of civilization. It has been in our hands for the time being but only for the time being. The onslaughts of war and barbarism have revealed how fragile it can be. Has the way we took up the witness against war in this century strengthened the Peace Testimony? Have we strengthened the Peace Testimony within the Society of Friends? Has our witness sensitized society to the critical need to search for alternatives to violence? Does the heavy reliance on armament and military posturing give a false sense of security and inhibit society from giving any serious thought to this question?

The Vietnam era is defined by explicit actions by Friends which took the Peace Testimony beyond a long-suffering, undiversified stance against war. With this precedent, is conscientious objection the impetus for strategizing innovative initiatives appropriate to the times? Is this a function of conscientious objection? Does a critical appraisal of actions taken during the Vietnam War have any relevance to how we would address prospective crises?

When war threatens, is there a pragmatic extension of conscientious objection which strives to be effective not only in opposing the war but also in preventing war? Or is the integrity of the witness alone, without any consideration of efficacy, its own reward?

Will the expanding access to nuclear war capability and other sophisticated military technology have so changed the nature of full-blown war as to make obsolete the traditional roles of soldiers and conscientious objectors? Will the next war be over before it starts? Will conscription as we have known it be overtaken by events? Will conscientious objection have been left in the enshrouding dust?

Persevering witness to the Peace Testimony has lapsed during the last quarter century. Unprecedented and ceaseless military preparedness proceeds without interruption. Meanwhile, with no war and no draft we allow conscientious objection to be marginalized. Can Friends, forewarned by the experience of generations of conscientious objectors, enliven the Peace Testimony during quiescent intervals? Can we project ourselves beyond the celebration of the record of past endeavors?

Going or Not? "War Stories"

A Panel

July 16, 1998

John Bach

William A. Eagles

Jay Worrall III

Charlie Bonner

Beth Taylor

"War Stories" #1 – Draft Resistance and Prison

John Bach

First, my thanks for all the work done by Chel Avery, Trish Roberts and the many others whose names I don't know for all their work in putting together this conference. Rarely have I been part of anything so gracefully and efficiently organized.

And second, may I say how impressed I was with the remarks by Lou Schneider and Dan Seeger this afternoon. I am so very proud to be associated with the likes of these gents, and I hope they may say the same about me ten minutes from now. We'll see.

And finally (by way of introduction), like everyone else here, I am happy to be in attendance. I mean this in the sense of the early description of Friends as "Happy, Content and Always in Trouble." So I confess that I am also content (politically and spiritually) to be in your midst and I hope not so much in trouble 10 minutes from now. We'll see.

I thought what I'd do in these next heroic 10 minutes would be to present some 21 separate yet related points concerning my "war story." They're enumerated and have headings. This way when I get to #11 you'll know I'm mercifully half way done, and by #21 I'll soon be thankfully seated.

My plan is to serve these little easily digestible morsels in bite size pieces which, when taken together, will constitute a whole meal – or an overview – and that you won't gag.

So hang on. It promises to be a bumpy ride through this Unified Theory of the Universe. I'll talk fast so Margaret doesn't have to beam her flashlight on me and Chel can relax her grip on the shepherd's crook.

#1: Concerning the Nature of War Stories

I'm happy to stake a claim to the term and reclaim it from popular culture and the stories and murderous myths promulgated by John Wayne, Ronald Reagan and Sylvester Stallone – to name three well documented real-life slackers in matters of conscription and real-life war. Not that I have anything against slackers in matters of conscription and war (in fact I rather applaud it); it's just the subsequent hypocrisy and rewriting of history that presents the rub, and makes future wars more likely and attractive.

For their war stories are companion pieces to misery, privation, sexual abuse and the same old dead ends. We all know what really happens: men become mercenaries, women become prostitutes and children become beggars.

No, in contrast, our war stories are really peace stories, and our companion pieces are (as Gandhi might put it) the pursuit of truth, loving means and self-sacrifice.

#2: The Lens Through Which We View These War Stories

Yes, I'll try to avoid speaking with the perspiring groans of a weight lifter: you know, so many pounds jerked and pressed, so many months served, so many stints in the hole, and so on.

Rather, may we focus upon and remember the unsure footing in that crucible, the mysteries unfolded, the contemplative and exploratory, the experimental nature of The Next Step, and the silences in between the advances and retreats.

And above all the modesty. As audacious as we were in the times which demanded boldness, our actions were basically modest and the more we remembered that the stronger and surer we were.

Camus wrote that sometimes in the human adventure it's necessary for some to die in order to assert that 2 and 2 are 4, and there is nothing more modest (or profound) than that. We said that when we said that human flesh is not meant to burn, or that this war is a huge bummer, or "not with *my* body you don't."

Now in stark contrast to all of this, here's.....

#3: The Crass Vital Statistics of This Soldier's War Story

Selective Service Violation: Refusal to Submit to Induction;

34 months and a couple of weeks served ('69-'72), which I'm told is the second longest term for refusing induction (although I fear that survey does not include Black Muslims, so I don't wear that campaign ribbon);

7 transfers;

refusal to stay in minimum custody;

2 rescinded parole dates;

a 33-day hunger fast;

3 personal work strikes;

co-editorship of an underground newspaper;

a bunch of times in solitary confinement;

a member of the 3-man inmate committee that negotiated with the heavies from the Federal Bureau of Prisons after a week-long, total and unequivocally non-violent work strike;

2 straight months in the hole as a result of that;

a guard's invitation to contact him upon release so he could introduce me to his daughter who was my age.

A year after release, I conscientiously refused to stay on parole, declared myself a free man and armed federal marshals stormed the community house where I was living at dawn and dragged me – literally – back to jail.

#4: How I Got To Where I Was and the General Outcome (In Two Sentences)

Thinking that the student deferment was both racist and classist and the means by which the ruling class protected and bought off its sons, and remembering Mark Twain's observation that he deserted the Confederacy and the South fell, I resolved to take a sabbatical from college in order to lose my student deferment, refuse induction, resist the war, and change the world.

The plan succeeded gloriously on all accounts.

#5: The Guy Who Really Sent Me To Jail

Algerian/French philosopher and writer Albert Camus, who wrote a novel called *The Plague* which is about good and evil and absurdity, and which I had the good fortune – or even better misfortune – to read in the midst of studying the humanities and in the midst of the dirtiest little war imaginable.

Something had to give.

#6: And The Kids, Too

Yep, it was those damn photos and film clips and the realization in the very marrow of my bones that there was no system of political, societal, or religious beliefs, standards, norms, or values that could possibly justify or excuse the piercing look that comes from the eyes of a six year-old girl, shedding skin like a molting bird, whose whole village and family have just gone up in napalm.

This was like adding hardener to resin to make epoxy which was more than enough to steel anyone's resolve.

#7: An Operating Metaphor (If Not Paradigm)

In the mid-sixties, a young woman named Kitty Genovese was grabbed off a street in a borough of New York, pushed into some bushes and stabbed to death. It was documented that at least 40 people had heard her screams and nobody did anything, not even to call the police. This was not illegal. It did not make one proud to be a member of this society, any more than witnessing a little agrarian country grabbed off a map and pushed into a pitiless war while again most people did nothing. Doing nothing is always legal.

#8: An Early Lesson Learned in the Process

That whatever they do to you for conscientious action is nothing compared to what you do to yourself for not heeding that call.

And more: that in the course of taking a principled stand there are always accompanying strengths and safeguards that enable one to accept and handle gracefully any future consequences.

You get stronger as you go and grow.

And thus: the miraculous process by which prison became as unnettlesome as the briar patch was for Br'er Rabbit.

#9: In the Judge's Chambers and Courtroom

My federal indictment is signed by Ramsay Clark. Twenty years later he and I joke about this.

I dismiss my lawyer as he is on the verge of winning the case on a meaningless technicality. The judge, who is a good guy, finds me "in no way insincere," but meets my eyes and tells me "the law is the law." I hear this with a German accent.

He offers me a deal. Would I accept being convicted and sentenced to alternative service? I see him washing his hands.

Later in the courtroom, during the presentencing statement, I say only "We have nothing to say to each other." This is not technically correct, of course, since he still has to impose sentence. I receive the Youth Corrections Act, and am led from the courtroom not knowing for how long I'm going to prison. Court officials tell me I'll probably do a year and then be paroled.

The rest, as they say, is history.

#10: Further Lessons Learned

As long as the flame of resistance burns, the free person can never be shackled or scarred.

And that everything you need not just to survive but to flourish, is already inside of you.

The Way *will* open. Our job is simply not to mess it up.

#11: The Wonderful Menagerie of Characters

The most common refrain uttered to myself about 23 times a day is, "Man, you can't *buy* this kind of entertainment on the street."

Bernard, a lifer who has done time on chain gangs in the South and still carries the scars, tells me, "Every time I can make do with half a step instead of a whole, and every time I can carry half a load instead of a whole, I plan to do it, and there is my victory over the Man."

And Jimmy Joint, doing life on the installment plan (in and out, in and out), says, "You know, in here the time stretches out so smoothly. I got my friends and I got my place and I do well and there is no idiot necessity to Hold Up Your End like there is on the street."

And in both cases (and hundreds more) I listen closely and nod and say I understand, but of course I don't, not fully.

[Take heart – we're half way through.]

#12: The Nature of Time

Time has weight as well as length, and it's the first, far more than the second, that determines everything.

And like unfulfilling jobs or bad relationships or public education, imprisonment is not time out of your life, but part of it, and is just as permissive of joy and growth and spirituality as any other part.

#13: Never Being Alone

There was always an immense amount of fortitude to be garnered from those who had come before; those who have ennobled our species and rescued it from barbarity. It's a glorious and honorable recitation that goes all the way back to the teacher who was handed the cup of hemlock and the carpenter from Galilee. More recently in this most violent of centuries, the resisters from the two world wars: Dave Dellinger, Larry Gara, Jim Peck, Igal Roodenko, guys who occupied some of the same cells I did; the brothers imprisoned in this country during World War One who were tortured (there is no other word for their treatment).

It was easy to conjure up the spirits of Steven Biko, Nelson Mandela, Victor Jara.

Where we were was a tribute, a gesture of thanks to those whom we admire: Margaret Fell, Lucretia Mott, Emma Goldman, the Pankhurst sisters, Mother Jones.

If I were to ask you to call out some names of people who have inspired you, chances are many would have known jail – or worse. So remembering them was a way of saying "Presente" as our comrades do in Central American struggles, or as many of our Native Americans say "All my relations" in order to invoke all who have come before and summon their strength and guidance.

And most of all, it was an honor to join those whose names and actions we will never know; those whose heroism and humanity were never illuminated or acknowledged.

You couldn't help thinking: would these elders approve, would they be proud of this course of action? And could this projection be a beacon? For that matter, could we take our cues from our victims? What would the Indochinese ask of us? That six year-old girl?

I tell you, there were times when even a barren subterranean strip cell in Lewisburg was just too damn small to accommodate all the moral luminaries and victims who visited and who were no strangers to cells.

#14: The Compilation of Gratitude and Beauty

Prison gave us a chance to meditate on all the things we had to be grateful for and to be in constant staggering awareness. To wit:
> a functioning body and superb health;
> a nonbrain-dead and inquisitive mind;
> a loving community both inside and out;
> an endless ability to be amused;
> sisters and brothers in resistance.

And by the same token we developed in that stark landscape of grimness and stupor, an awareness of beauty everywhere.

The luckiest among us still cultivate this. Such as:
- the pattern made by milk poured in coffee;
- sparks from a cigarette thrown from a moving car at night;
- snow covered barbed wire;
- the relaxed heartfelt laugh of a person behind bars.

#15: The Myth of Organizing

Many of us knew guys who told us they were entering the military to organize, and many of us listened politely, fearing the worst. Organizing in prison wasn't much easier, and I'm certain anyone who set out to organize, didn't. It didn't work that way.

Sometimes, no matter what, you can't make goodness happen beyond an individual level. And other times, for no apparent reason, situations arise, and people arise and amazing things happen, as though it were a gift from a spirit. When this happens you sometimes get to be, as Marx suggested, a midwife. I have witnessed miracles in prison, and the biggest was formation of community as the definition of freedom moved beyond what side of the wall you were on. In prison I read an interview with Jean-Paul Sartre, published in a semi-pornographic magazine (ah, the contradictions), and he said, "We were never so free as we were during the Occupation."

There was an underground newspaper in Danbury. It was called *The Shit House Press*. The editors put out a couple pages of copy in longhand, and stapled a few blank pages for additional news. Here's one entry:

"Hardly one Correctional [sic] Officer has his life together, yet they are hired to help us get our lives together. What a laugh. Like monkeys on ladders, the higher they climb the more their asses show.

"But how many of us have our lives together? How many beyond the crooks' scam?

Beyond the hustle? Beyond mistreating our women?
"Moral: monkeys change when men change first."

There were hunger and work strikes concerning issues beyond personal gain, and these involved large and sometimes entire parts of the population. Rape was stopped for an entire year in Danbury. There was a shared consciousness that this benefited everyone.

The key to these miracles, I think, is to turn all the prevailing norms upside down. So –

>don't look out for number 1;
>don't go along and get along;
>don't don't make waves;
>don't just work/consume/be silent/die.

#16: Lessons Learned, Cont.

No matter where you are, including prison, if you're not having a good time, you only have yourself to blame.

When you find yourself getting too heavy, remember to not take yourself too seriously.

It takes so very little to make another so very happy no matter how oppressive the environment.

#17: The Role of Humor and Sharing

I am standing next to a man who has been introduced as "The Most Famous Priest in the World" (to his chagrin and my amusement); and we are outside the prison visiting room after a visit. We perform a syncopated, comical, and obscene dance directed by a guard who commands us to strip, run fingers through our hair, stick out our tongues, lift our balls, and so on. As we obediently turn around, bend over and spread our cheeks, he says to me, "Keep smiling. When they get your smile they've gotten too much."

Your smile, like your life, is utterly political, and thus no effort was spared in having a good time. Birthdays were celebrated clandestinely with cakes baked in the prison bakery and spirited out to the compound in a guitar case. Snickers were melted into small vats of instant coffee, munchies procured from the commissary were laid out and shared, and musical reviews were staged. Imagine a chorus line of khaki clad troopers high stepping in the manner of the Folies Bergère or the Rockettes and singing in fractured yet spirited harmony the following, to the tune of "My Favorite Things" and with apologies to Oscar Hammerstein:

> Clanging of locks and being a number
> Frowns from the hacks and rude awakened slumber
> Cross country transfers and laps 'round the track –
> What else can you do to keep time off your back?
>
> When the goon squad throws you a-round
> When you're bleeding bad
> Simply remember your mind isn't bound
> And then you'll know you haven't been had.

None of us that I knew ever trafficked in prison commodities and alternative legal tender, but there is a gripping political dimension to being offered gifts of marijuana, home-brew, or pornography without thought of recompense in a very capitalistic culture where everything had a price. It indicated that we were doing something right, and the walls were beginning to fall.

#18: Concerning Dr. Johnson's Well-Known Remark

Yes, ol' Sam got it right. There's nothing like the threat of imprisonment to clarify a person's mind wonderfully. This works equally for regular scoundrels as well as our brand of scoundrels, although for us this worked in a positive and reinforcing fashion.

But I'll tell you and Dr. Johnson something that clarifies a man's mind even more wonderfully – and that's the prospect of being raped repeatedly in your mouth or ass.

And since we were all young and perceived to be vulnerable, we all have stories, and I'll share something of mine.

It was a full fifteen years after release that I felt comfortable enough to stand in front of a urinal in a public restroom instead of choosing a stall with a door. And even in there, much of me was, on a hair trigger level, ready to turn abruptly, pissing penis aspraying, to fight with teeth and fingernails any attacker, quite prepared to inflict maximum and vicious violence.

To this day, I can tell you between which two ribs a knife or ball point pen is most effectively thrust, or how a sharpened pencil put through an ear drum will neutralize an unrequited suitor.

It came to pass in a maximum security penitentiary that I was set up and found myself in a small cell with four fellow inmates brandishing knives. I marveled at how in an environment of constant scrutiny and limited resources men were still able to fashion weapons of such startling lethality. They wore knitted caps pulled down over their faces as masks.

I escaped by using both biological imperatives of fight and flight, and because being raped was inconceivable and just not a possibility. The threat of being, or the reality of being, or the possibility of being stabbed and killed was, in a perverse sense, what saved me.

The much more interesting and even more perverse question is not whether I was willing to die, but whether I was willing to kill to prevent being raped. And on long cross country drives or times when I'm too fatigued to sleep immediately, my mind drifts back to that cell and that question. I really don't know. I suspect I would probably put my body on automatic pilot and observe – with a mind wonderfully clarified.

And the only other thing I know is that even my most beloved elder from my home Meeting would never pass judgment on what I thought I must do to see the end of a conscientious day's work.

#19: A Point I Never Miss A Chance to Bring Up Whenever I Get Anybody To Listen To Me

That none of us (which is to say nobody I knew or knew of) ever spit on vets or called them baby-killers. Those things happened undoubtedly. The times were passionate and babies were being killed. Lots of them. But such misplaced anger was in no way a measure of our style or vision in speaking truth to power, or asking hard questions in murderous times, or enacting our Peace Testimony.

That in fact many of us were honored to work alongside vets to scream bloody murder about Agent Orange and the deplorable conditions in VA hospitals. We insisted that brothers who went to Canada and vets with less than honorable discharges be included in any discussion about amnesty.

#20: And While I'm At It

The treatment afforded to women in the anti-war movement was too many times dismissive, unjust, and lecherous. I would have my sisters know that many of us regret and repent. We live and learn and hopefully get better. This is what distinguishes us from our government.

#21: Final Lessons

There are no final lessons; just more variations of the consequences of the marvelous complexity of the carbon molecule. And that being the case, we might just as well do what we can to stay happy, content, and, as the need arises, always in trouble.

My thanks for your kind attention. I know I have been over-winded and wound up. But I wanted to get the most important stuff I know into this. This is a ridiculous notion, of course. Yet such was the passion of those times.

"War Stories" #2 – Another Story of Draft Resistance and Prison

William A. Eagles

Since a time from whence memory runneth not to the contrary, old men – and men well into their middle years – have gathered around campfires, at gaming tables, on front porches, in bars, and sitting on upturned cola crates at country stores, and told each other stories of their youth – sometimes true. Stories of exploits on athletic fields, on battlefields, with women, and sometimes of moral struggles. They have been a forgiving audience for each other, as each has needed a forgiving audience for his own story.

It is in that tradition that we are gathered tonight and I come with my story, in search of a gentle and forgiving audience.

I was raised in rural Eastern North Carolina in a community where my father's family had lived since they started it almost 200 years ago. My father believed that a citizen military, not the professionals, won World War II. My mother taught me that the Sermon on the Mount means what it says. I was raised Baptist in a small church that dominated community life.

In my elementary school class, I was the only person whose parents were both college graduates. In our family, you read the newspaper every day, did your school work, studied your Sunday School lesson every week, worked on the farm in the summer, and were expected to hold yourself to a higher standard than was expected of the world around you. My parents worked hard, lived simply, and taught my brother and me to do the same. I was very fortunate.

In 1966, I went to N.C. State University in Raleigh – like

my father, his four brothers, and my brother before me – to study agricultural economics. It was in that large land-grant university that I watched the Vietnam War grow and faced the decisions that the possibility of participating in war thrust upon me.

My religious training served me well, as did the expectation that my standards were not set merely by adopting the world's. I came to understand that I could not participate in any war. Once I recognized that fact, the steps that my convictions required of me were clear. And, with help and support of many, I took them.

I decided to apply for conscientious objector status. But, at the same time and for the same reasons, I decided much more. I firmly believed that my application would be denied, that I would be drafted and refuse induction, followed by prosecution, conviction, and imprisonment. That belief somehow made each step easier. Occasion did not arise to reconsider my decision at each step. I knew what I would do.

Dale Hoover, one of my economics professors and later the department chairman, was a Quaker and, for a number of years, clerk of the Raleigh Meeting. In the low-key way of Friends, he introduced me to the Meeting, knowing that, if open to it, I could find support and affirmation. I became an attender, and found that support and affirmation – and much more.

I applied for conscientious objector status to the Edgecombe County Draft Board – which had never found anyone to be a conscientious objector. My father had been a member of that draft board for several years before my brother became 18 in 1964. One member was from our community and knew our family well – indeed, each member knew the extended family. But, of course, my application was denied.

Although my brother was two years older than I, his conscientious objector application followed mine. It, too, was denied. But, the lottery saved him from prison. On the night the first lottery drawing was televised live, when almost everyone in the agricultural fraternity gathered around the television for each to learn his fate, I was in my room studying. I knew the lottery would not save me. It didn't.

I finished my degree and one year of graduate study. On June 30, 1971, the last day before the draft law expired (briefly), I refused induction. It was an interesting, exhilarating day. I was a summer intern at the State Board of Higher Education. I told my employer I needed the day off to refuse induction to the Army, but I would be back. They took it in stride.

Because my physical was conducted over three days and the draft law was expiring, I was the only person in the ceremonial induction room with the officer who was conducting the ceremony and the enlisted man who told me what I was to do. I stood before the officer as he read his script from a notebook on the podium.

When the time came for me to step forward, I stood still. The officer repeated his lines; I stood still.

At that point, the procedure apparently was to remove me from the room, but, as I was the only person to be inducted, he continued in place. He turned in his notebook to a tab near the back and read in great, formal detail the penalties for my refusal, repeatedly giving me opportunity to step forward. I stood still.

Finally, he asked that I remain and speak to the commanding officer upon his return from lunch. My interview with the commanding officer was brief. He did not try to get me to reconsider, but thanked me for not being disruptive. I went back to work.

With my parents' financial help, I hired a lawyer – making the mistake of selecting someone who was philosophically supportive instead of experienced in federal criminal defense. A few weeks later, the marshals awakened me at 6:00 o'clock in the morning to arrest me. I told them that my lawyer was supposed to have agreed with the US Attorney for me to turn myself in. Surprisingly, they told me to come in at 10:00 o'clock, and left.

The process moved forward to trial and conviction. Judge Butler said that I was undoubtedly the most sincere young man it had ever been his duty to send to prison and sentenced me to three years, ordering that I surrender myself a few weeks later on November 15, 1971.

I withdrew from graduate school. Mother gathered the family for an early Thanksgiving dinner. The time went quickly and

I turned myself in. After one night in the county jail, the marshals took me to Petersburg, Virginia.

My arrival at Petersburg was marked by two events. First, the sound of metal against metal as the prison door closes behind you is just as stark and memorable in real life as literature would lead you to expect.

The second took place in the area set aside for intake of new prisoners. They take your clothes and mail them home, have you shower, take photographs with numbers below your face – 34317-118 – and finger-print you. I sat across a grey metal desk from an older guard who filled out forms. He asked what I was in for; I said I had refused induction. Looking up from his forms, he said, "You aren't one of those fanatics, are you?"

I replied, "I guess I must be or I wouldn't be here."

He smiled and said, "You'll be all right." And, I knew it was true.

The next seventeen months until I was finally paroled unfolded very slowly. I worked on the farm, first as a clerk and later with beef cattle. It was the right job for me, allowing me to spend my days outside the fence doing work I liked.

I was fortunate in that, unlike many in other wars and some of my era, I seldom felt physically threatened and suffered no physical abuse. There was a group of about 25 or 30 conscientious objectors who, with a few there on drug charges, provided some feeling of community.

Many of the inmates were Vietnam veterans. Not one of them ever expressed any ill feelings toward the conscientious objectors. They knew they had been victims of the war and appeared to respect our refusal to be forced to take part.

My brother would visit one Saturday and my parents the next. So every weekend I was reminded of the support of my family. My mother wrote me every Sunday night – just as she had ever since I left for college and continued to until 1995.

My parents firmly believed that I was doing what my religious convictions required of me – and, they loved me. I frankly believed that their position in the community was such that it could not be affected by anything I did – good or bad. And I did not learn until later of the difficulties they experienced from some of the community reaction.

Of course, these stories were not all bad. One Saturday morning, Lum Eagles, my father's first cousin and contemporary, was sitting at the country store talking with other men when my parents drove by. "There go John and Lib," one said, "going to see Billy." Another opined about what I had done, disapproving of their support for me.

Lum stood and said, "It's their boy and their business," and walked out.

I was married when I went to prison. My wife had been supportive of my decision. But, she was young. Shortly after I went to prison, she left me and moved in with a man who had been a good friend of mine since high school. Her leaving, and my inability to even talk through it all with her, was the hardest part. But, my observation was that everyone's wife left – or everyone's but Jehovah Witnesses and the highest organized crime guys. I have concluded that those two groups had a tradition of imprisonment and a community of support for their wives.

I was paroled on April 16, 1973.

Life continued. I worked at a historically black college, finished the master's degree I began years before, was pardoned by President Ford, and eventually went to law school. I have been called upon to explain all this many times, to the law school, to the bars in North Carolina, the District of Columbia, and Arkansas – each place I have practiced. But, it has never ultimately been a barrier.

My wife of now some fifteen years is a judge – a gubernatorial appointment during the course of which she too was called upon to explain my actions taken long before we met. But, she was appointed and now has twice been elected.

And I still believe that each step along this road was made clear because I made the entire decision at the beginning. I knew what I believed and why.

And I am very fortunate, even blessed. For, on one

occasion in my life, I was faced with a clear choice of doing what was right or what was wrong. And I chose what was right. I did it for the right reason, knowing it would not be easy. I have never been more alive, more confident, more true to my best self.

"War Stories" #3 – My Path to Conscientious Objection

Jay Worrall, III

I was born in Walter Reed Army Hospital, Washington, DC, in the middle of World War II to a junior US Army officer from Newtown Square, Pennsylvania, and the young woman my father met while at Officer's Candidate School in St. Louis, Missouri. My father is a graduate of Haverford College, and at the end of the war he left the army and my family moved to Reading, Pennsylvania, where they joined the local Friends meeting when I was three years old. Three years later, at the beginning of the Korean War, my father was called back into the military where he stayed, still an active Quaker, until he retired in 1967. In this way I grew up in two worlds: as an 'army brat' in military communities around the world, and as a practicing Quaker who regularly attended Meeting wherever that was possible.

I finished my last two years of high school at Frankfurt American High School in Frankfurt, West Germany. Shortly after my 18th birthday I went to the American Consulate in Frankfurt to register for the draft. Considering my mixed upbringing, I registered as draft status 1-AO. Under this classification I would be eligible to be drafted into the military, but would not be required to carry a weapon. It was well known that 1-AOs were routinely assigned as medical corpsmen. In order to justify my draft status I had to write a long essay on my religious beliefs. I don't remember much of it except I talked a lot about United Nations police forces and the like. I don't think I had ever heard the words "Vietnam" at this point in my life.

The next year, 1962, I entered Earlham College in Richmond, Indiana. Nothing much of interest to this symposium happened there until sometime early in my junior year when I and some of my friends became increasingly aware of the building conflict in Vietnam. A number of us organized a series of "informational debates" on campus to engage students and faculty in moderated dialog on the pros and cons of the conflict. As an organizer I spent a great deal of time reading everything I could find on Vietnamese history and culture, and on the American involvement there. At the end of my junior year I spent a semester at the University of London, in England, where I took part in anti-war marches. At parties with English friends I would often find myself defending my country from accusations of genocide and baby killing and other horrendous deeds.

During my senior year of college I had two pressing decisions to make: what I was going to do after graduation, and what I was going to do about the draft. The two questions were inexorably connected.

As far as the draft was concerned, I went down to the draft board in Richmond, Indiana, and announced that I wished to change my classification from 1-AO to 1-O. 1-O is the traditional conscientious objector status which requires two years' alternative service instead of any form of military induction. I had to write another long essay with my application justifying my changed beliefs.

As for a life after college that would keep me out of the clutches of the military, I applied to (1) graduate school in engineering at the University of Pennsylvania, (2) the Peace Corps for teaching in Ethiopia, and (3 & 4) to two organizations that would take me to Vietnam to do my alternative service – the American Friends Service Committee (AFSC) and International Voluntary Services (IVS), the private predecessor to the Peace Corps.

This discussion is about choices. I was accepted by all of the organizations I applied to except possibly the AFSC, which wanted me to write a long essay on my religious and spiritual beliefs, and which at that time could not promise that I would go to Vietnam in any case. On the same day I was given a very generous offer by the University of Pennsylvania for a fully paid doctorate in engineering and was accepted by IVS to work in science education in Vietnam for two years. Ultimately I decided that I could become an engineer any time, but that I was called to go to Vietnam.

During training for IVS two things happened. First, I was asked if I would change my assignment from science education to refugee resettlement. I agreed. Second, my draft board in Indiana informed me that my request for change of classification was denied and I was ordered to appear for a physical examination. In the letter (I think) I was told that I could appeal by letter but that I might have to appear in person before the board. The IVS office in Saigon said that they would pay for my flight to Indiana and back if necessary.

I appealed the board's decision in what I remember as a very brief letter. I told them that my religious beliefs as stated in my application to change my draft status remained accurate, that in any case I was not a conscientious objector and morally opposed to war only if my draft board approved it, and finally that I was in Vietnam and doing something positive in a very bad place and that they had two choices. They could leave me where I was or they could bring me home and put me in prison, but I wasn't going into the military.

My application for change of status was approved on appeal.

"War Stories" #4 – A Marine in Vietnam, and After

Charlie Bonner

I was on the planning committee for this conference and I must confess that there were times during the past few months when I wondered why, since I didn't become a Quaker until some time after the Vietnam War. Those doubts have been erased today. In the course of meeting old friends and in the pleasure of making new ones here I feel very much that I am in the right place...among Friends.

I grew up in inner city Philadelphia, in a neighborhood called Kensington. It was predominately Irish-Catholic and many of the people who lived there worked in the textile mills nearby. Our family moved away from Philadelphia not long after my high school graduation and except for brief visits I never returned after that time. In 1987 the Philadelphia Vietnam Veterans Memorial was dedicated, and the Philadelphia *Inquirer* published the names of the 630 Vietnam War dead from the Delaware Valley. Kensington had the highest percentage of Vietnam War dead of any neighborhood in the Philadelphia area. In reading the list of names I was appalled to learn that fifteen young men with whom I either attended school or who lived within six blocks of me had died in Vietnam.

My father was career Navy and had been wounded during World War II. He and my mother divorced and I was raised by her and a loving stepfather from the time I was nine years old. Because of medical reasons my stepfather had served during World War II as a civilian employee of the Navy at Pearl Harbor, Hawaii.

All of the men on my father's side of the family had served

in the military beginning in World War I through the Korean conflict. Many of them made the service their career. I just knew that I would have "my war." I was militarized early. I loved airplanes and had built a model of every allied warplane from World War II. One day a kid I went to school with showed up in an Air Force uniform. I asked him about it and he told me that he had joined the Civil Air Patrol (CAP) as a cadet. CAP was a civilian auxiliary of the US Air Force. Civilian pilots flew their own planes on search and rescue missions looking for downed aircraft.

I went to a meeting with him and was hooked. The squadron met weekly at North Philadelphia Airport and had regular classes which taught us everything about aviation, from navigation to how airplanes fly. They also taught us how to wear a military uniform, how to march, stand at attention and salute.

I stayed in CAP all through high school. Each summer I spent at least two weeks training at a military base somewhere in the US, culminating, in the summer of my junior year, with a one week stay at the recently-built U. S. Air Force Academy in Colorado Springs.

There was no doubt in my mind that my life and career would be in the service. If I enlisted in the US Air Force, my CAP training was the equivalent of Air Force basic training, which meant that I would be one rank ahead of other enlistees and would not have to spend six weeks in basic. I was a good student in a good Catholic boys high school and our Congressman who lived in the neighborhood and knew our family assured me that an Air Force Academy appointment was not out of the question. The onus of being the first in my family to attend college, especially a military academy, was more than I thought I could handle, and with the wisdom of my seventeen years I joined the Marine Corps.

I had seen the movie about Marines in boot camp and their Drill Instructors called "The DI" which starred Jack Webb. My favorite high school teacher was a recently discharged Marine officer who regularly spoke of the "Corps" as the high point of his life. That was all I needed to be convinced that the Marine Corps was for me. I enlisted in February of my senior year in the delayed entry program. The recruiter led me to believe that the Marines would make me six feet tall and bullet proof, and as an additional benefit their great dress blue uniform would have women falling at my feet. He never told me that I would have to kill people.

My active duty time began in June two weeks after my high school graduation in 1963. We were required to wear a suit and a tie for our swearing in at the Philadelphia Navy Yard. We were then transported to the 30th Street railroad station where we boarded Pullman cars for the overnight journey to Parris Island, South Carolina. We would spend the next twelve weeks there becoming Marines.

The Marine Corps claims that they build men. They don't. They take teenage boys and turn them into the military equivalent of a street gang. Boot camp is not about a building of anything but about a tearing down. A dehumanizing of you so that you can dehumanize and kill the "enemy."

We arrived at Parris Island still wearing the suits and ties that we had taken our enlistment oath in. They began by marching us in the pouring rain until our civilian clothes were soaking. We were then made to strip the wet clothing off, wrap it in brown paper and address the package to our parents. Our heads were shaved and we were issued uniforms. Our names were no longer used. The Drill Instructors either called us recruit, scumbag, turd or some other unpleasant name. No radio, television or newspapers were available or allowed.

We were never alone. Every day began with reveille at 5:30 AM and ended with taps at 10:00 PM, seven days a week. If we were not sleeping, eating, marching or doing physical training, we were required to stand at attention and study the Guidebook for Marines. When it was time to take a shower, ten of us would line up naked to use a single shower head. The first in line would wet down, go to the end of the line to soap up and eventually work his way to the front of the line to rinse off. All of these activities were accomplished with the DIs screaming in our faces and with physical abuse from them. Punching and slapping of recruits was not officially allowed, but who could we complain to? The Drill

Instructors had total control of our lives. They made the rules.

Strange as it seems, it never occurred to me that I would be required to kill until they began to teach us bayonet fighting. The mantra during this training was "Kill, kill, kill," while they were teaching us to stab the "enemy" with a knife attached to the end of our rifle. To practice our bayonet skills we used a pugil stick which resembled a broom stick with padding at each end. Each of us was paired off against another recruit until one of the pair dealt a "killing blow" to the other.

I was so frightened that they would find out that I didn't want to kill anyone that I turned into a raging maniac. Though I was of small stature, I "killed" my first two opponents, so they pitted me against the biggest man in the platoon. I was so enraged by then that the DIs had to stop us and pull me off of him. The Drill Instructors loved my rage. They said that I was motivated.

I successfully completed boot camp in the fall of 1963. We were given four hours of base liberty after the graduation ceremony. Base liberty meant that for the first time in months we were allowed to walk around un-supervised, alone, and not in marching formation with other recruits. We were not allowed to leave the base. We could, however, visit the snack bar and Post Exchange (PX).

The next morning we boarded chartered buses which took us to Camp Lejeune, NC for one month of infantry training. Every Marine, no matter what his job or technical skill, was trained as an infantryman first. They taught us in infantry training how to fight and kill with rifles, machine guns, hand grenades and mortars.

My first assignment after four months of boot camp was to an infantry regiment at Camp Lejeune. There I received training in my job, which was communications and electronics. Except for the time when I was in communications school, I was deployed with my unit aboard ship either for six months in the Mediterranean or three months in the Caribbean.

The Marine rifleman is called a grunt for good reason. His is one of the most physically demanding jobs in the Corps. Everything that a grunt needs, food weapons, ammunition, is carried on his back, and his main mode of transportation is walking. Twenty-five mile marches were not uncommon. I was carrying a rifleman's load plus an additional forty pound radio. An opportunity to transfer to the 1st Marine Air Wing stationed at Iwakuni, Japan presented itself and I jumped at it.

I arrived in Japan in a snowstorm at the end of February, 1965. Our voyage from San Diego seemed to last forever. The seas were so rough during the two-week crossing that for most of the trip we were not allowed above deck because of the danger that we would be washed overboard.

My stay in Japan was not to be a long one. I was there perhaps four weeks when President Johnson ordered Marines to land at Danang, Vietnam and guard the airbase there. Not many Marines were stationed in the far east so we assumed that we would be going to Vietnam soon. I was part of a three-man radio relay team. Our communications equipment was installed in a truck with electrical generators towed behind in an attached trailer. Two weeks after the Danang landing our team along with about fifty other Air Wing personnel was loaded aboard ship and sailed from Iwakuni. No one would tell us our destination. It wasn't difficult to guess. Vietnam.

Ten days later we anchored a mile offshore from what we would later discover was Chu-Lai, South Vietnam. Chu-Lai was located thirty miles south of Danang. The only maps we had available were in French and Chu-Lai did not appear on them. I found out years later that Marine General Krulak had named Chu-Lai after the character which represented his name in the Chinese language.

Chu-Lai consisted of a sand beach. Thin pine forests began a few hundred yards inland of the beach and were perhaps one mile deep. The forest then gave way to more sand which extended about twenty miles west to the base of large mountains.

We went ashore the next day. I think that most of us expected that our landing would resemble the World War II landings that we grew up seeing John Wayne make in the movies. It didn't. Two grunt battalions from two other ships landed unopposed in small boats that morning. The grunts moved inland after their landing and we heard no reports of enemy contact. We were issued ammunition before we landed but told not to load our weapons unless we were fired upon. We were also informed that we were not eligible for combat pay, which was $65.00 per month in addition to our regular pay.

We landed late in the afternoon. Our officers did not seem to have a clear idea of what was happening next, so we dug in, two men to a foxhole, on the ocean side of the pines. This is where we would spend our first night in Vietnam.

When night fell, John Wayne wasn't in those foxholes, but a lot of frightened adolescents were. We loaded our rifles in defiance of orders. One man in each hole was supposed to sleep while the other stood watch.

We wouldn't sleep that night. Every sound that we heard we imagined was Viet Cong (VC). Sand kept trickling into our hole so we were constantly digging to keep the foxhole deep enough. Darkness was giving way to daylight when a terrible crashing and banging in the woods before us drew our undivided attention. A bulldozer was coming through the trees.

I was pretty sure that the VC didn't have bulldozers, so it must be one of ours. No one had told us but the Sea Bees (Navy Construction Battalions) had landed two weeks earlier and were building an airstrip. So much for the propaganda that the Marines were the first to land.

The task facing our fifty-man Air Wing advance party was to build the base camp, and to install countless systems and support facilities so that when the airstrip was completed the flying squadrons could begin flight operations immediately upon arrival. We had landed with thirty days' supplies. Thirty days was the time allotted for completion of our work.

The immediate problem for my radio relay team was to establish telephone communications with Danang. Due to terrain and to technical problems, the only place where we could do that was from a high sand dune in front of the camp's defensive perimeter. We were in front of the front line and with forty foot antennas rising into the air; our location was not difficult for the enemy to see.

Each of our three-man team stood an eight-hour daily radio watch. During the sixteen hours off watch we fortified our site with sand-bags and cut pine boughs to make lean-tos, which were our only shelter from the sun. We also performed whatever work that was required to assist the rest of the advance party in setting up the camp.

Water was at a premium. There was enough to drink but none for bathing. The temperature in the sun was 100 degrees or higher, and even at night you didn't stop sweating. Sleep was not part of the schedule. If you could you grabbed half-hour cat naps. Food was C-rations which were cold and eaten out of tin cans when you could find the time.

Our lives became one big disorienting blur of tropical heat, work, work, work and little sleep. Three weeks of this grueling schedule and we were completely exhausted. One night, it finally looked as if we could each get about four hours of uninterrupted sleep.

It was not to be. Two of us had just settled in when the man on watch alerted us to unusual noises in the trees about 50 yards from our bunker. My first thought was, oh no – I can finally catch up on my sleep and now the VC are messing with us. I just wanted to make those VC go away and I didn't care how. Someone threw a hand flare in the direction of the noise. The blinding light of the flare revealed a single Vietnamese man and all three of us fired at least ten rounds each at him. I had never seen a human being struck by high powered rifle bullets before and it was something I never wanted to see again. Our firing had brought the entire perimeter guard to alert, but nothing else happened that night.

My adrenaline stopped pumping after some time and I began to realize that I had just taken part in killing another human being. I rationalized that maybe my bullets didn't kill him; after all, three of us had shot at him. Why then did I feel so horrible? I was nineteen years old and just starting to learn about life, and now I was killing someone. I had no tools for dealing with this.

The next morning we found blood but no body. Apparently his compatriots had retrieved his body during the night. I was still shaken by what had occurred so with a machete I started cutting down trees. I was obsessed and cut down all the trees within a hundred yard radius of our bunker. I was determined that they wouldn't have enough cover to sneak up on us. I wasn't going to have to kill again. The mindless labor of tree cutting allowed me to numb my feelings. I had learned how to deal with the insanity of war. Don't allow yourself to feel.

I was in a few other fire fights, but usually we could not see the people that were shooting at us. I prayed often that I wouldn't have to kill anyone. Later during my Vietnam tour I sought out a Catholic chaplain and asked him why it was okay to kill in war but not at other times. He talked about the just war theory and other things, but none of his answers satisfied me. I eventually came to the conclusion that it was never right to take a human life for any reason.

I departed Danang twelve months after we had landed at Chu-Lai, and five days later I was sitting in my parents' living room in York, Pennsylvania. It felt as if I was on another planet. I had just been through a year-long experience which would affect me forever. No one wanted to hear about Vietnam, and worst of all people here were living their daily lives as if the war in Southeast Asia didn't exist. I had no way of processing what I had been through, so I stuffed it as deep inside me as I could. I still had a year left to serve in the Marine Corps and rarely did any of the other Marines talk about Nam. We each had our own horrors but we didn't talk about them.

Five years after Vietnam I married my wife Mary. We were married only a short time when one morning I found her not in bed with me but sleeping on the couch. When I asked her why, she told me that I was having a dream about Vietnam and that I had struck her in my sleep.

I was horrified because I had hurt her and also because until then I didn't know that I was having these dreams about Nam. The dreams didn't happen a lot, but it frightened me whenever they occurred. I lived my life hoping and praying that someday they would end.

It was springtime 1977 and my oldest son was to play his first-ever Little League baseball game. We lived in rural York County, Pennsylvania, not far from the Maryland state line. The opener was at a high school in Maryland. Excitement was in the air. Ten teams would be playing on five fields. There was music and the Baltimore Orioles mascot was even there. I was as excited as the kids.

Then I saw it...an Army Huey helicopter sitting on the ground. The first ball was going to be thrown from the Huey. To me the helicopter just screamed Vietnam! The anger boiled up inside me....What was that obscene killing machine doing here? I appeared normal but inside I was shaken. I hadn't stuffed Vietnam deep enough. What would I do now that it was erupting in anger?

My family has a long history of alcoholism. I became a full blown alcoholic within nine months of taking my first drink at age eighteen. In 1975, by the grace of God I survived a near-fatal drunk automobile accident. I learned to turn my anger to constructive purposes in a recovery program and developed a relationship with God through that program that led me to become a Quaker.

I attended Friends meeting occasionally in York, and after moving to Lancaster I began attending Lancaster Meeting regularly and eventually joined. Becoming a Friend felt to me as if I was now a member of a large loving family. Although I sometimes felt strange being a military veteran and a Friend I was never treated that way by Friends. I recently discovered that Samuel Nicholas, who founded the US Marine Corps in 1775, was a Quaker and is buried at Arch St. Meeting in Philadelphia. I need to find out more about him.

It is not enough to say, "war no more." The tools for nonviolent conflict resolution such as mediation need to be taught to children early. Perhaps, then, our culture's response to conflict will not be, "How can I defeat you?" but "How can we both win?"

Vietnam led me to become a pacifist and a Quaker and for that I am grateful.

"War Stories" #5 – Lost to Vietnam: Choices and Impact

Beth Taylor

On November 16th, 1965, not far from Philadelphia, my brother, Geoffrey Taylor, hanged himself in our basement. He was fourteen years old. I was twelve. According to the story my family pieced together, at his Boy Scout meeting earlier that night his Scout leaders, all veterans of World War II, took Geoff into a back room of the church basement and told him they might withhold points from his patrol because he had refused to march in a parade the week before to support the Boys in Vietnam. Geoff had not marched in part because our family was Quaker, and generations of Taylors had chosen alternative service over fighting. Now, in 1965, Geoff told the Scout leaders that he could not in good conscience march in that parade.

In those early years of Vietnam, part of what led my brother to suicide was the conflict of living in a staunchly pacifist family while admiring friends who were sons of World War II veterans. My brother was a bright, athletic, popular boy who had been student body president of his public Jr. High School. But as he entered 9th grade, in 1965, and he voiced his feelings about war during history class discussion, he was called a coward, and later a gang of boys cornered him in the hallway, pummeling him with fists and names.

We did not know what he was going through. But, looking back, there are clues to Geoff's turmoil the day he died. In the afternoon, he and I quarreled – about what, I can't remember. I finally cursed at him, which I had never done before, and he slapped me, which he had never done before. Then, at dinner before his Boy Scout meeting, Geoff argued with my father about what he should say in a speech he had been asked to give about Thanksgiving for the troop. My father wanted him to talk about my mother's family who had celebrated Thanksgivings in New England for 300 years. My brother said no, and stormed up to his room. A few minutes later he brought down the Scout Manual and announced, red-faced, that he would read straight from the book and then nobody could laugh at him.

So that night, he apparently went off to Boy Scouts feeling he couldn't be a good enough pacifist or son, and then, after his speech, in the back room of that church basement, he apparently found out he couldn't be a good enough Boy Scout either.

Geoff had been upset and fascinated by the self-immolation of Norman Morrison on the steps of the Pentagon two weeks before. Perhaps in some desperate way, Geoff saw Norman as a role model and thought that by strangling himself, he could prove something too – that he was not a coward? that he was this angry? The doctor told us that, in the moments before he killed himself, Geoff had probably lost his mind. I imagine him hearing all those voices – his Boy Scout leaders, his peers, his parents–and I hear him thinking how he can't please anyone, how he must be morally inadequate. And I hear him finally turn his fury on himself. Of course, this does not totally explain Geoff's suicide; no suicide is ever finally understood. It just sits there in our hearts, a terrible, humbling hole of pain.

My brother had been a very good Quaker, and for years after his death it was comforting for me to be as good as he had been – organizing moratoriums at George School, standing quietly in peaceful demonstrations against the war, doing guerrilla theater with Vietnam Vets in the streets of Washington to demonstrate what a raid on a village looked like. I was earnest and well-meaning and sure of my mission. Life was gritty and sad, and each boy I knew who left for Vietnam as a soldier or medic, or for Canada as a resister in exile, or for prison as a draft card burner or anti-war protester was my brother crucified, again and again and again. The young men I was drawn to seemed like my brother – smart, passionate, first-born sons who faced their moment in history with full heart, and they became heroes, or they self-destructed.

Butch Geary was tall – 6'2' and lean, with confident hazel eyes, and what his mom called "a Pepsodent smile." He was the oldest of five children in a Catholic family. His dad made nuts and bolts at Standard Press Steel, and Butch liked working on the farms of our Bucks County neighbors. He raised goats and rabbits for our 4-H Club, and when he led our 4-H Club pledge, he had that smile on his face that drove a few of us girls nuts. He was a faithful enough Catholic to serve as an altar boy at a Mass at the 1964 World's Fair. Then, he earned his way through Temple University, ran its Catholic Newman Club, tutored kids, and sang for Vietnam Vets at Valley Forge.

Because his dad had been a Marine, he was proud to do his duty for his country and go to Vietnam. He planned to come home to go to law school at Temple, and then to be a senator because he revered John F. Kennedy. On April 5, 1969, as a 2nd Lieutenant for the 3rd Battalion, India Company, of the 7th Marines, he led his men, fearlessly we are told, out of a field toward enemy entrenched in the woods, and a sniper shot him through the head. He died believing in what he was doing. But his family now says he died for a war gone awry. "We were wrong," his mother says. But, she adds, "Mr. McNamara's book" – his apologetic retrospective – "is a crime."

Tony McQuail was my brother's friend who stayed brotherly to me. 1970: Tony was Student Body President at Westtown, writing me poems. Then suddenly he was making passionate speeches against the war, writing editorials in local newspapers, and burning his draft card in public. A kiss goodbye and he was gone, to Canada.

He says now that he could not face prison; as a teenager he had been molested by an older acquaintance and he could only imagine what might happen in prison. More important, he says, he knew he could have avoided Vietnam by being a CO, but as he helped other young men in his Quaker Meeting explore the choices open to them, he became convinced that "the draft was a major tool of the war trade," and he could not cooperate with it.

After Tony publicly refused to register on his 18th birthday in the spring of 1970, an FBI agent came out to his family's farm in Downingtown. They "agreed to disagree on what were one's obligations to country and to God." The agent said he would not arrest Tony if Tony promised to register by the fall. Tony agreed. But as autumn neared, his struggles of conscience made him realize he would "have to be a tax resister as well as a draft resister."

That is when he knew he needed to find a country "less at odds" with his beliefs and values. He did register as he had promised the FBI agent, but then he flew to Canada, staying with a Quaker couple until he found a job on a dairy farm. He watched from afar as his birth date drew a high lottery number, and he waited through the months of concern until he knew he would not be drafted or indicted. He knew he could return to the US, but he says now, he felt "so much more welcome and at home in Canada." There, he says, Democratic Socialism helps the society to develop a "more humane social, economic and political culture than the society [he] left."

At the time Tony left the US, his father said in no uncertain terms, "I cannot understand this decision." But his father also finally said, "I still love you." A few years later his parents sold the china collection that would have helped finance Tony's college education; with the money, Tony bought a farm near Toronto on which he built a house and barns by hand. His Westtown sweetheart, Fran, joined him, and they married, and had two daughters. Besides running an exemplary organic farm, Tony has served as president of his township, as a trustee for his Public School Board, and as the Executive Assistant to the Ontario Minister of Agriculture. He has made a moral, productive life for himself, but to those of us who had grown up expecting him to be a dynamic leader in our community, he too was lost.

Bob Martin I met through Friends General Conference. Slightly built, wiry, he had intense dark eyes and curly reddish brown hair. He studied religion at Columbia University and then, when his number was called, he went into the Navy. Quickly, though, he found he couldn't stomach the military training for a war he did not believe in. His quandary led him to convert from Catholicism to Quakerism, and he was granted one of the first discharges from the Navy as a CO.

In 1973, when the bombing in Cambodia was stepping up, Bob joined other Quakers to witness his protest on the lawn of the White House. When they were arrested he decided not to pay the $10 to let him off the hook. So he was put in the Washington, D.C. jail. The first night he was in a relatively safe cell, but the next night they sent Bob up to maximum security. The guards disappeared and the inmates passed him around, selling him for cigarettes. He was gang-raped about 60 times over two nights before having his request for transfer acknowledged. The local Florida Avenue Quaker Meeting helped get him released, and then helped him set up a press conference to protest the rapes. When he came to visit me in Pennsylvania, I hugged him and felt how his body had calcified – stiff like hard plastic, insensitive to any more pain, unable to feel comfort.

Only recently have I found clues to the troubled turns Bob's life took after I knew him. On a positive note, he founded the organization Stop Prison Rape, Inc.; he taught comparative religion at Columbia University; and he wrote as a journalist. But his trauma clearly seared him to the point of sucking him into a double life. In the late seventies and early eighties he apparently became a drug addict and a petty criminal, spent more time in jail, where he too became a rapist. He changed his name from Robert Martin to Don Tucker to Steve Donaldson. He did sustain one long-term companionship with a woman. And, as he searched for comfort in the midst of such violence and instability, he became a Buddhist, then a Hindu, and then returned again to Quakerism. He died of AIDS in New York City in July, 1996.

My cousin Rick Thompson was a buddy of my brother Geoff's. I loved him for his goofy jokes and worn red baseball cap. I remember all of us crammed in the sunny way-back of the '57 Pontiac station wagon, to go see the Phillies or to the beach in New Jersey. Rick grew into a long, lean runner. During spring break from Westtown, he would jog the three miles to our house from his part-time job as a welder, and I would watch him eat half a jar of peanut butter at our kitchen table.

Even though he too had been raised a Quaker, he felt he could not NOT go to Vietnam. So he went as a generalist aide for the Quaker hospital at Quang Ngai. He fixed everything – tools, machines, electricity, and he learned Vietnamese so he could negotiate and run errands for the team. When I wrote him my last postcard, I was doing my European hitchhiking tour before studying at Oxford. I remember staring at the snapshot he had sent, of him standing in front of the hospital.

I stared at his grin, and long droopy mustache, and his lean, strong body in jeans and white t-shirt. How different our worlds were, I thought; what did it feel like to be in Vietnam, I asked. I never got a response. In November, 1973 Rick flew with two South Vietnamese kids to Saigon to get them settled in a special hospital for paraplegics. On the way back to Quang-Ngai, on November 17, 1973, one day after the eighth anniversary of my brother's suicide, the plane crashed into a mountain during a monsoon. The day before Thanksgiving, Rick was identified because his was the only 6 foot long charred body, surrounded by small ones.

Rick's journals show me how he had assimilated deeply into Vietnamese ways, and he felt a passionate disaffection with American culture. The woman with whom he spent his last R & R says she thinks it's very likely he would never have come home from Vietnam, other than for visits, even if he had lived. Rick is now buried next to my brother behind Abington Meetinghouse. For me, their deaths – in 1965 and 1973 – began and ended the Vietnam War.

Its aftermath is another story. In the last few years I have begun to sit down with the brothers and sisters and parents and cousins and friends of my young men. Only now, 25 to 30 years later, do most of us feel some semblance of calm. It took thirty years – sometimes rocked by bouts of depression, emotional silences, strained relationships, even alcoholism – for us to regroup, finally land gingerly on our feet and appreciate the love and family we have in our lives right now, instead of always judging it less than the lives we lost in that awful night or day so long ago.

The families of my lost young men have all changed and gone on – picked up the pieces, made choices that made sense after grief. Butch Geary's sister was a novitiate in a convent in Media, Pennsylvania when Butch was shot behind the ear in a meadow in Vietnam. That bullet, she says, shot right through her life. It was the moment through which everything from then on would be seen and judged. She, the daughter and sister of Marines, is now a liberal activist in New York State, married to a public defender. She is also the mother of three boys, and she says if there were a draft she would take her sons to Canada in a minute.

I married the man who said, "I need you to get the ghost of your brother off our pillow." I married him in part because he was willing to work in a place like city hall, to wrestle with difficult but powerful people because he knew they were often the key to doing good. Although I will always be proud of my Quaker heritage, I joined a mainstream Protestant church because the service centered on the complexities of Biblical narrative, which, in my study of literature, I had come to see as central to the vision of most writers who spoke truth to me. The young woman minister seemed to know what Sherwood Anderson and Flannery O'Connor had taught me: that we are all Christ and we are all crucified; but we can easily become the crucifiers – usually in the name of a religion or philosophy.

I have learned, I think, some things which I hope make me a more alert parent and constructive citizen. I have learned that religion, even pacifism, can be blind-sided. I have learned that a child imitates a parent even though the parent thinks she has offered the child free-choice. I have learned that some truths I once held as self-evident just aren't. And I have learned that, to truly understand an issue, one must genuinely imagine how others come to totally different conclusions.

Over time I came to understand that many people – even some who go to war – also believe that "there is that of God in every person." And I learned that to live as I once thought a Quaker should, to be proudly "in the world but not of it," sometimes inhibits one from participating in crucial parts of our democracy – in legislatures, boardrooms, and public school systems, for example.

These days I try hard to show my children that their struggles can still be helped by religion, or conflict resolution, or sports, or some kind of creative process like literature, music, or art – but that no way of doing or understanding has THE answer to confusion; nor can it protect them from pain and compromise in the future. My children teach me in return that it is time for a new set of stories; it is time to let go of old pain.

Recently I have begun to read Vietnamese memoirs and fiction about the American War, as they rightly call it. Some Vietnamese wonder why we Americans are still so focused on our grief. The war with us was one in a series for them. Grief was a familiar part of life. They prepared Rick Thompson's body with flowers and traditional wrapping so his spirit would not feel lost and it would be comforted.

I believe now Rick accepted his fate even before he died. I believe Butch almost expected a bullet. I can only hope that my brother Geoff in his lonely panic and Bob Martin in his abused woundedness have also found their peace. I know Tony is living his. It is time for each of us to accept – to forgive, to ask forgiveness – and to move on into our own separate peace.

Joint Plenary Presentations:
If I Knew Now What I Knew Then....

Lynne Shivers

Jack T. Patterson

July 17, 1998

Plenary Presentation:
Vigils, Speeches and So Much More

Lynne Shivers

I

One of my most vivid memories of the war years is about a young man fresh out of high school who wanted to do all he could to end the war. He was invited to speak about the war at a parochial girls' high school. He arrived with a puppy on a leash and announced that, in order to educate people about the nature of the war he would napalm the puppy, and he held up a container with some unknown material

Instantly, the audience erupted into cries of resistance; nuns and students rushed to the edge of the stage, begging him not to. The auditorium was in an uproar. He spoke at the mike, "You can be so upset about one puppy, yet how can you not be concerned about the hundreds of Vietnamese who suffer napalm every day?" And his speech began.

So many actions against the war were like that: highly dramatic acts, political 2 x 4's to draw attention to the issues, based on the analysis that people did not know what was happening. Friends' modes of witness or forms of resistance against the war were not usually 2 x 4's to shock people into paying attention.

In this speech, I will lay out forms of witness that Friends took, individually and corporately, as they were recorded in *Friends Journal* from 1963 through 1975. I will comment on how Friends worked with other peace organizations: co-sponsorships, coalitions, cooperations, etc. Finally, I'll lay out some of the thinking of three peace campaigns I was connected to, two of them A Quaker Action Group, and what major effects they had on the wider peace movement and ending the war.

How did Philadelphia Friends oppose the war? Early and often. The Friends Peace Committee (FPC) of Philadelphia Yearly Meeting (PYM) in 1963 produced flyers and other written materials about the war. The FPC held a vigil with speakers at City Hall the same year.

Articles appeared in the *Friends Journal* in 1963. In 1964, Bronson Clark wrote an article comparing Vietnam with the Algerian anti-France revolution. The same year, George Lakey wrote in defense of engaging with social issues. Later in 1964, *Friends Journal* published a statement issued by the Friends Peace Committee of Philadelphia Yearly Meeting on the Vietnam War.

1965 saw the AFSC send a three-month mission to Vietnam, and some members appeared on the Today show in August. On Nov. 2, 1965, Norman Morrison immolated himself outside the Pentagon, and a month later, an article he had written just before that appeared in the *Friends Journal*. Shortly thereafter, a special invitation-only meeting took place in Washington, D.C. to consider what measures the Society of Friends might take after Norman's death.

Friends General Conference, held in Cape May, invited Taylor Grant as a major speaker. (One of my most vivid memories of working at FPC in 1968 was that everyone on staff stopped work to hear Taylor Grant at 4 pm, who often spoke about the war.) At the same conference about 100 people drove to DC and sat in the Visitors' Area of the Senate, and six refused to leave and were thus arrested as an antiwar protest. At the same time, some 400 held a vigil on the Cape May boardwalk. The conference approved a minute on the war, as did New York Yearly Meeting later that year.

The same year AFSC published a booklet, *Peace in Vietnam*. It was also a cosponsor of the speaking tour of Thich Nhat Hanh when he gave his famous speech in DC on not supporting either South or North Vietnam.

Some of the people who had gone to Washington from the

Cape May Conference decided to form a new organization, A Quaker Action Group (AQAG). It officially began on August 5, 1966, with Larry Scott and George Willoughby as co-chairmen. (More on AQAG later.) But by October, AQAG was sending humanitarian aid by mail to North Vietnam without applying for a license from the Treasury Department.

The Canadian Friends Service Committee sent medical aid to the Red Cross in South Vietnam, in North Vietnam, and to the National Liberation Front.

1967 saw two AFSC visits to Vietnam, especially important since the Quang Ngai Center opened. Philadelphia Yearly Meeting passed a minute of support for peace actions, including the sailing of the boat *Phoenix* to North Vietnam from Japan. In Albany, Friends began holding a weekly vigil (Wednesday noon) which continued for two years.

In 1968, in a Philadelphia Meeting, 17 men announced their noncooperation with conscription, and draft cards were received by five Friends. Draft centers and draft counseling became a major activity all over the country. Cambridge, MA, and Orange Grove, CA, Meetings declared sanctuary.

In December, a "Celebration of Conscience" event was held at Allenwood Prison, for friends and relatives to be near men who were doing time for their conscience's sake.

By this time, it is clear that both the AFSC and AQAG had articles published in *Friends Journal* on a regular basis.

1969 saw major peace movement activities and smaller Quaker bodies taking action for the first time. Friends (and many others) attended departures of men to training camps. AFSC had a presence at the Paris Peace Talks, and in May, the AFSC held a larger vigil at the White House.

Earlier that year, a congressman had read into the *Congressional Record* a list of all the American soldiers killed in the war to that date. AQAG began reading the names as a public protest on the Capitol Steps, not knowing if participants would be arrested or not. They were. (More on this later.) The event was continued weekly throughout the summer, and dozens of groups across the country copied the demonstration, either as a legal action or illegal. Even before the AQAG demonstration, the AFSC vigil read the names in front of the White House after most of the participants had gone home.

In November, the March against Death and Mobilization against the War (as well as the Moratorium in October) were enormous national events to organize, and AFSC was a cosponsoring organization. It was at this time, too, that nonviolence training hit the big time, and about 4000 peacekeepers were trained.

Two communities were formed: Friends Resistance House in West Philadelphia, especially for families of whom one parent would be in prison for conscience's sake, and New Swarthmoor, near Clinton, NY.

In 1970, *Friends Journal* published "A Call to Resistance" signed by nine men, including Peter and Allen Blood and Jeff Keith.

1971 saw an important vigil taking place in Lafayette Park across the street from the White House, from April through August. Some arrests took place. Some Friends gave support to veterans who returned heroism medals by tossing them over a fence set up in the Capitol parking lot. Jane Meyerding and others destroyed some federal files and served prison time. Friends supported Peter Blood at the time of his trial. And more and more often, Meetings saw fit to "release" Friends from normal duties to free them to carry out conscience-led anti-war work. AQAG was laid down as Movement for a New Society and the Life Center were created.

In 1972, actions took place in Leonardo, NJ, attempting to prevent a supply ship from docking and taking on war materials on their war to Vietnam. (More on this later.) Resistance to war taxes found favor with many.

In 1973, PYM approved a minute urging amnesty for all who disobeyed laws and orders which, if obeyed, would have thrown them into war situations. In August, seven Friends ("White House Seven") protested the bombing of Cambodia by vigiling on the White House lawn.

In 1974, in a tax case the AFSC filed on behalf of Len Cadwallader and Lorraine Cleveland, a federal judge ruled that the government should reimburse the AFSC for its payment of the employees' refusal, but, on appeal, the Supreme Court reversed this decision.

In January, 1975, a conference in DC and vigil at the Capitol took place; this was the last national conference against the war. At that conference, Dan Ellsberg said in a speech that all the forms of resistance – vigils, letters, speeches, imprisonment, tax refusal, and much, much more – all of it was necessary to end the war.

The war ended in April, 1975.

II

How did Quaker organizations work with peace organizations?

It varied widely. Many times, Friends Meetings chose not to work with any other groups since often their activity grew out of the worship community of the Meeting. Cosponsorship of strictly Quaker meetings (monthly, quarterly, yearly) sometimes took years of working separately before members wanted to join with other Quaker groups. (But, Margaret Bacon points out that Friends' abolition work primarily focused on removing support of the slave system by members of the Society of Friends. Friends' modern anti-war work focuses on the wider society, not only the spiritual welfare of Quakers alone.)

But usually the question of Quaker groups working with peace groups is intended to examine working relations among peace organizations in general. The more values and working styles the groups held in common, the easier it was to work together. For example, the Fellowship of Reconciliation and AFSC would find it relatively easy to work together, whereas the Friends Peace Committee (FPC) of Philadelphia Yearly Meeting (PYM) might have more problems working with the Mobilization (against the War in Vietnam).

Early on, Quaker groups realized that they were asked to

cosponsor an event in part to add respectability and visibility; sometimes for that reason, cosponsorship was denied. A request for cosponsorship sometimes created the possibility of negotiating the conditions of the event. For example, if a march was being planned, and if peacekeepers were not being trained, one party could make cosponsorship conditional on adding peacekeeper training (to increase discipline).

When large, major, often national movement events were planned, all the cosponsoring organizations would send delegates to sit through tortuous decision-making meetings to determine which organizations would be coalition members and what the policies of the event would be. Sometimes topics were the major speakers, or the platform on which the event rested, or the presence of trained peacekeepers, for example.

After these time-consuming and usually acrimonious meetings, some people wondered if these large coalitions were worth the effort. This label appeared to make the separate organizations all look stronger. But Larry Scott analyzed they were counterproductive, thinking that all the member organizations agreed only to the lowest common denominator among them. Better, he thought, to have confederations that would last only for the duration of the event and that the agreement would be looser, less demanding on each member group. No one took him up on this, however.

FPC of PYM worked through guidelines for cosponsorship that probably are no longer followed, but they were pretty useful at the time. One guideline required that at least one staff or committee person needed to be part of the planning committee of the event, so that the cosponsorship of the FPC would not be just in name only. Another requirement was that the FPC would be required to recruit people to attend the event. If that was not possible, then no cosponsorship.

III

This section of my speech visits three campaigns I took part in, two designed and carried out by AQAG and one by Movement for a New Society. The analyses will not be exhaustive or definitive; rather, I want to identify some dynamics and consequences I think are important to consider now.

Formed in 1966, A Quaker Action Group (AQAG) was created for a few but clear reasons: "to implement a religious witness..."; "to arouse the Society of Friends"; and to combine traditional Quaker peace testimony and Gandhian nonviolent direct action. Founders believed that the war was so evil that it had to be addressed.

The three voyages of the boat *Phoenix* in 1967 and 1968 with medical supplies to North Vietnam, South Vietnam, and the NLF were designed to dramatize the point of view that AQAG did not recognize the Vietnamese people as "the enemy." Program directors had learned from earlier boat actions that so long as the little boat moved on the high seas, there was an inherent drama that would capture people's attention.

And capture attention it did. A year after the first *Phoenix* voyage, AQAG office hired one full-time staff person whose sole job it was to schedule the eleven copies of the film around the country. Whenever possible, a crew member or committee member accompanied the film as a speaker.

It was at this time that feelings arose between AFSC and AQAG. Some believed that AQAG's program might jeopardize the AFSC Quang Ngai rehabilitation center. It was true that many Friends Meetings were very open to hearing AQAG's message, and many were very closed, harboring these same fears. In fact, AQAG leaders knew that AQAG's program would polarize potential supporters because the actions were technically inviting people to break laws. But we felt it was a chance we needed to take since the laws to be broken were immoral.

My favorite memory from this time is of the story that Robert McNamara, Secretary of Defense, said that of all the peace groups, it was only Quakers he respected. Throughout the AFSC, staff people said, "Oh, he must mean AQAG"; AQAG people thought, "Oh, he must mean AFSC!" So, bad feelings developed among some people over AFSC/AQAG and, for the most part, continued to rumble unresolved.

In the spring of 1969, a congressman had published in the *Congressional Record* a list of all the American soldiers killed in battle in Vietnam to that time. A small group of peace movement pacifists in Philadelphia, including Larry Scott, Stewart Meacham, Kay Camp, George Willoughby, and David Gracie, began reading the names on Good Friday, April 4, at the Draft Induction Center, then on Cherry Street. Somehow, they were permitted to stay in the lobby at closing time. And they stayed through Saturday, with no media coverage.

Knowing then how powerful that experience was, Larry suggested that AQAG should sponsor a program of reading the names on the Capitol steps in May that year. After the first event (we did not know if we would be arrested, but we were), we realized we had a big tiger by the tail! So we decided to hold weekly readings on the steps and invite other peace organizations to recruit people to read, while we maintained control of the overall plan.

Each week attracted more people to read. We occasionally read poems by Thich Nhat Hanh in between names. Each week, people were arrested and released, since the courts were crowded with other cases. (Only repeat readers were imprisoned right away.) I was hired to be one of the on-the-ground organizers to stay in D.C., taking care of inquiries, manufacturing leaflets, notifying media people of the reading, and so on.

One Wednesday, it was my turn to phone media contacts to remind them of the demonstration. One journalist said something I could not hear. I said, "I'm sorry, I did not hear you."

He replied, "You heard me."

I said, "No, I'm sorry, I really didn't."

He paused and said, "Keep it up."

Immediately I realized that underneath the silence and apparent support for the war was great underground support for ending the war! After that experience, I never again believed the government propaganda of massive support for the war effort.

Groups all over the country, through many organization networks, duplicated this simple demonstration of the reading of the names in downtown parks, in front of city halls, legally and illegally, throughout that summer and beyond. Many Americans began to think that war is not one massive indivisible event, like a slab of iron; it consists of thousands of individual lives that are connected to millions of other individual lives.

Identifying each person killed in Vietnam was the centerpiece later that year in the March Against Death, when each person's name was placed on a piece of cardboard, which in turn was placed inside a coffin in front of the White House, as people marched by for more than a day. I can only imagine that the sculptor of the Vietnam Wall was sensitive enough as an artist that she picked up this different awareness of how we had come to see "war" and chose to represent, once again, all the individual names of the war deceased on the memorial.

By 1972, AQAG was no more, and many of those committee members and staff people had formed Movement for a New Society (MNS) and, locally in Philadelphia, the Life Center community. That winter, one of us received a phone call from a crew member of a supply ship then in Rhode Island. He begged us to try to prevent the ship from sailing with war supplies to Vietnam; the ship would next dock at Leonardo, in northern New Jersey, to take on more supplies.

Some MNS members had learned to handle canoes the previous summer, when trying to prevent a ship from loading up with military supplies in Philadelphia, on its way to Pakistan. So, the canoes came out again. Once at Leonardo, eighteen canoes were tied together and successfully blockaded the ship from docking at the end of railroad tracks bringing supplies to dockside. But the ship kept on trying and eventually succeeded, and other actions took place there, including people sitting down on the train tracks and being arrested.

Steve Cary, then head of the Peace Education Division of the national AFSC office, attended one of these demonstrations, and allowed himself to be arrested. Later, he proposed to the AFSC board that it co-sponsor and help organize such activities all over the country where an AFSC office was near any of the nine more official debarkation points for war supplies to Vietnam (coastal ports and airports). The board agreed, thus supporting a campaign which included civil disobedience for only the second time in its history.

This recounting and reflection have led me to see the relationship of the AFSC and AQAG in a new perspective: instead of competing against each other for attention, support, and funding, I now see that the two organizations helped each other do their different work more successfully. People feared loss of support because they analyzed that the peace movement and support were small, weak and limited. But if we view the peace movement and supporters as potentially unlimited, and that everyone is potentially a supporter of movement activity, then organizations need not fear the loss of power so desperately.

My speech has had three main sections.

First, I have tried to lay out witness to and/or to end the Vietnam War, at least according to *Friends Journal*'s records. Reviewing this history can help us prod our memories to reveal more insights and new perspectives. I hope that you will add to this "Movement Life Line" during the conference so it will be a fuller history than it is now.

Second, I examined the various ways that some Friends' organizations related to peace organizations during the war and what some of the difficult issues were that arose.

Third, I invited the conference to examine three nonviolent action campaigns, two of them carried out by AQAG, in order to shed some light and possibly new thinking about the divisive "bad feelings" some Friends harbored between AFSC and AQAG.

I repeat my thesis that in many instances, because they were two different organizations, they helped each organization do its distinct work more successfully.

Shortly after I joined my current Friends Meeting, an older member who was active as a CO in World War II told me twice that he thought people resisting the Vietnam War had such a good time, as opposed to what he experienced. I was stunned, since my living memory of resisting the Vietnam War was mostly painful, angry, and stressful (sure, some fun). I finally told him of my perception and told him why, and he never suggested his viewpoint to me again.

I'm very grateful for this conference, for the chance to speak this morning, and for the chance to revisit the war resistance efforts that framed so much of my thinking.

Thank you.

MOVEMENT LIFE LINE

The Movement Life Line was initially designed by Bill Moyer. Usually, the Life Line is developed in an interaction between the facilitator of the event and participants of the workshop – they are the ones who suggest events to be listed on the Life Line. Thus, at the end, participants "own" what they see on the paper. It was only because of time constraints that I did not suggest we do this at Bryn Mawr.

Furthermore, there are two more steps to this process that we could not include: one was naming highlights of the war and how there might be cause and effect relationships among war events and movement events, and these would be represented by arrows sweeping from one event to the other.

Finally, participants are asked to reflect on their work and offer any new insights on their overall experience. Always people offer new insights since they have almost never had the opportunity to "see" the whole event as this experience offers them. But we sort of did that throughout the conference.

– Lynne Shivers

Movement Life Line – Or, What (Some) Friends Did During the Vietnam War
Initially written by Lynne Shivers

1963

Events in the Movement:

Philadelphia Yearly Meeting (PYM) and its Friends Peace Committee (FPC) produced flyers, held a vigil at Philadelphia City Hall.

Events in the War:

Self-immolation of Buddhist clergy in Vietnam.
Coup d'état and assassination of Diem and Thu.

Movement Life Line, *continued*

1964

Events in the Movement:

--Bronson Clark wrote a *Friends Journal* (FJ) article comparing Vietnam with the Algerian revolution.
--George Lakey wrote a FJ article on social engagement.
--FJ published a statement approved by Friends Peace Committee & Philadelphia Yearly Meeting on the war.

Events in the War:

Lyndon Johnson was elected US President.
Gulf of Tonkin crisis took place.

Movement Life Line, *continued*

1965

Events in the Movement:

–AFSC sent a 3-month mission to Vietnam.
–Norman Morrison immolated himself at the Pentagon on 11-2-65.

Events in the War:

Large numbers of marines were sent to Vietnam.

Movement Life Line, *continued*

1966

Events in the Movement:

–AFSC booklet, *Peace in Vietnam* was published.
–Taylor Grant was the main speaker at FGC in Cape May.
–A small group left for Washington to protest an escalation of the war. Some of them sat in at the Visitors' Gallery and got arrested. This later helped to form A Quaker Action Group (AQAG).
–Canadian Friends Service Committee, AQAG and many individuals sent humanitarian aid to North and South Vietnam or the NLF.

Events in the War:

Just before the Cape May Conference, Haiphong harbor was heavily bombed.

Movement Life Line, *continued*

1967

Events in the Movement:

--AFSC sent two visits to Vietnam, especially since the Quang Ngai Rehabilitation Center opened.
--PYM minuted its support for peace actions, including the sailing of the *Phoenix* with medical supplies from Japan to North Vietnam.
--Albany, NY, Meeting began a weekly anti-Vietnam War vigil that continued for 2 years.
--Draft resistance grew in numbers and forms of actions.

Events in the War:

The war continued.

Movement Life Line, *continued*

1968

Events in the Movement:

–In a Philadelphia Meeting, 17 men announced noncooperation with conscription; 5 Friends received draft cards.
–Draft counseling and draft centers were major activities and concerns around the country.
–A "Celebration of Conscience" was held just outside the Allenwood Prison to be near men imprisoned for their conscience's sake.
–Both AFSC and AQAG published in FJ on a regular basis.
–Richmond Conference on Conscription issued a strong statement supporting resistance (representatives from many yearly meetings).
–Pendle Hill (George Willoughby, facilitator) held a conference on nonviolence training.

Events in the War:

A major offensive by North Vietnamese forces during the Tet holiday in January. Eugene McCarthy, Robert Kennedy campaigned; Nixon won the presidency.

85

Movement Life Line, *continued*

1969

Events in the Movement:

–Many Friends attended departures of inducted men leaving for military training camps.
–AFSC kept a presence at the Paris Peace Talks and held a large White House vigil in May.
–The AQAG Capitol Steps Campaign lasted from May through August. This meant weekly readings of Americans killed in Vietnam.
–October: Moratorium: large DC demonstration.
–November: larger DC demonstration; about 4000 peacekeepers were trained.
–Two communities were formed: Friends Resistance House (Phila.) and New Swarthmoor (Clinton, NY)
–Many Friends turned in draft cards at a meeting of Young Friends of North America (YFNA), following a speech by Bob Eaton.

Events in the War:

The war continued.

Movement Life Line, *continued*

1970

Events in the Movement:

–FJ published "A Call to Resistance" signed by 9 men, including Peter and Alan Blood and Jeff Keith.
–Three-day sanctuary at Ann Arbor Meeting took place at the time of Peter Blood's arrest.
–Trials of many resisters became opportunities for witnessing.
–Jane Meyerding destroyed federal draft files and served a prison sentence.
–In separate actions, so did Susie Williams, DeCoursey Squire, and Joan Nicholson.

Events in the War:

US troops invade Cambodia.
Students were killed at Jackson State, Mississippi, and at Kent State University, Ohio.

Movement Life Line, *continued*

1971

Events in the Movement:

–A vigil took place in Lafayette Park across from the White House, April-August.

–Some Friends helped veterans in a protest action when the latter returned heroism medals by throwing them over a fence on the Capitol grounds.

–More and more often, Friends Meetings "released" Friends to do special work, often war related.

–AQAG was laid down, and Movement for a New Society (nationally) and the Life Center (in Philadelphia) were begun.

–Many Friends were arrested during the May Day "Shut Down the Capital" demonstrations.

Events in the War:

The war widened as a result of the bombing of Cambodia.

Movement Life Line, *continued*

1972

Events in the Movement:

–The Leonardo, NJ campaign took place; this often involved sitting on train tracks to block shipment of arms.
–Tax resistance grew.

Events in the War:

    Watergate break-in took place.
    McGovern was nominated, but Eagleton was discredited.
    Nixon announced peace just before the election and was re-elected.
    Hanoi was bombed at Christmas.
    The US government threatened to use atomic weapons in Vietnam.

Movement Life Line, *continued*

1973

Events in the Movement:

—PYM approved a minute urging amnesty for all who disobeyed laws which, if obeyed, would have thrown the people into war situations.

Events in the War:

At the Jan. 23 Peace Agreement, it was agreed that US troops should leave Vietnam. Nixon authorized carpet bombing of North Vietnam.

Movement Life Line, *continued*

1974

Events in the Movement:

−An AFSC tax case was filed for Len Cadwallader and Loraine Cleveland. The US District judge ruled in their favor, but the Supreme Court reversed the decision on appeal.
−Over the summertime, replicas of "tiger cages" were placed outside the Capitol to draw attention to the conditions for political prisoners in South Vietnam.

Events in the War:

Nixon resigned.

Movement Life Line, *continued*

1975

Events in the Movement:

A January conference and vigil took place in Washington, D.C., putting into place a strategy for ending the war: stop bills (financing the war) from passing through Congress.

Events in the War:

The war ended in April.
NLF and DRVN forces took over all of Vietnam.

Plenary Presentation:
Modes of Friends' Witness,
As Practiced Individually and Corporately,
During the Vietnam War Years

Dr. Jack T. Patterson

Lynn Shivers utilized a typology provided by Gene Sharp to recollect the actions of Friends during the period of the Vietnam War itself – 1963-75. I would like to take a different approach, one that attempts to look at Friends' witness during the Vietnam War era in the context of earlier Friends' understandings of their witness during wartime, and how these understandings gave scope and shape to the concrete activities that flowed from them. Specifically, I'd like to look at some of the assumptions, principles and methods promoted by Friends in the period preceding the Vietnam War to see how these may have evolved when challenged by the kind of conflict Vietnam represented.

I plan to do this by utilizing a 1954 publication with which many of you will be familiar – *Speak Truth to Power* (which I will refer to throughout simply as *Speak Truth)*. I will then look at how one or two of the key understandings of *Speak Truth* played out during and since the Vietnam War.

I. THE WORLD WAR II EXPERIENCE AS BACKGROUND – 1941- 45

Speak Truth was the product of World War II – that is, the lessons of World War II applied to the Cold War context.

The modes of Friends' witness during the war were to:

1. Express their principled opposition to all wars, and American entry into that war, on the ground that the war itself was a greater evil than any supposed gains could justify, and to promote the belief that the war would fail to deliver the "Four Freedoms" it promised, indeed that the seeds of a new war would emerge from the ashes of the old.

2. Reject the dominantly held view of the enemy, Germany, Italy and Japan, as so absolutely and irredeemably evil as to require nothing short of total vanquishment and unconditional surrender.

3. Provide direct relief and support for war sufferers and the persecuted in Europe and Asia, as well as Japanese citizens interned in the US as an expression of common humanity encouraging a nonvindictive spirit.

While self-consciously pacifist, the World War II generation accepted, in the words of Charles Chatfield, the "politics of relative influence" based on the insistence that ends and means have a reciprocal effect.

However, in contrast to many of their predecessors, they generally also accepted the necessity of force. They shifted their objection from coercion *per se* to violence. They explored the possibility of coercive nonviolent action being used politically and were encouraged by the seemingly successful struggle for national independence by the Gandhian movement in India, and the effort underway in the early fifties to use nonviolence and passive resistance to oppose racial apartheid in South Africa.

It must be remembered that "nonviolence" and "direct action" were not then the household words they became through the later civil rights and antiwar movements. Strong currents still opposed or were acutely discomfited by pacifist involvement in politics, regarding its truth as transcending the partisanship that politics required. The Gandhian movement for national independence in India had been very coercive in its confrontations with authorities and some pacifists were reluctant to admit coercion or force of any kind as a part of genuine nonviolence.

The impact of the CPS generation was disproportionate to

their numbers Having viewed themselves as largely "irrelevant" to one of the most profound human upheavals in history, sitting in prison, building fire-lanes in forests, or doing other useful but not dramatic work, many later committed themselves to active peacemaking and became the backbone of expanded efforts at home and abroad to relieve suffering and to address the causes of war. They would never sit on the sidelines again.

II. THE COLD WAR EMERGES AND THE PERIOD OF "NEXT STEPS" – 1945 - 52

Beginning in 1949, the AFSC published a series of studies to stimulate discussion of foreign policy issues. These included *The United States and the Soviet Union* (1949), *Steps to Peace* (1951), and *Toward Security Through Disarmament* (1952).

All assumed that "reliance on military power" is so integral in the policy of every major nation that the most practical approach to peacemaking is to suggest specific next steps to reduce tension and thereby move gradually away from the reliance on force (*Speak Truth*, iii).

Yet while the outline of an alternative policy was clear – namely, how do we encourage the US and others to move away from reliance on military power and simultaneously pursue the good ends of social development – it was even more apparent that actual American policy had continued to develop in the opposite direction. Why?

A. *Speak Truth to Power:* A Friends' Alternative to "Next Steps" – 1952 -1954

In answering that question, the authors broke with the "next steps" gradualism embraced by most liberals and most Friends, including the AFSC, and put forward the boldest argument against war and for pacifism before or since.

They argued that the basic reason for our failure to carry forward the constructive programs Americans largely agree are necessary to peace lies in the "nature of our present commitment to violence" (*Speak Truth,* 14). It is the "nature of modern war" to "bend all to its needs" and this was extended to preparation for war as well. While originally conceived as a "limited commitment," and continually justified in those terms, its limits are illusory and always recede as approached. Thus, the never-ending treadmill and insatiable appetite of the military component.

This was the paradox. One could not balance a simultaneous commitment to military power and social progress – seeing each going forward together. It was illusory to believe that a country could simultaneously arm for war and at the same time carry out positive programs at home and abroad for peaceful development.

The commitment to the former, it argued, would inevitably lead to the compromise and undermining of the latter.

The "truth," then, that is to be spoken to "power" is that a renunciation of violence is necessary to escape the paradox faced by those who would employ violence to achieve their ends. So what can be done?

The stated goal of *Speak Truth,* found in its subtitle, "A Quaker Search for an Alternative to Violence," was to advance a genuine alternative.

But before an alternative could be advanced, a critical question had to be addressed that lay at the heart of Cold War deterrence thinking and the dominantly military solutions promoted – namely, who is the enemy?

B. The First Essential: The Enemy Redefined

In a controversial chapter, "The Enemy Redefined" the authors argued that the "first essential" to a pacifist analysis required a "redefinition" of the enemy – that is, a new understanding of what needed to be opposed in the present power struggles between the US and USSR.

The dominant view in the West, and certainly in the US, was that Soviet Communism was the great evil abroad in the world and that it was the prime responsibility of the United States to wield its vast power to protect mankind from its destructive influence" (*Speak Truth,* 26).

While the members of the working party were agreed that such a world view was simplistic and dangerous, as it led to the dominance of military solutions in response, they were divided on how to deal with the exaggerated tendency to view evil as a monopoly of one party to the conflict. We can now see that this disagreement had parallels amongst Friends and others during the Vietnam conflict.

The issue was whether and how to deal with the Soviet Union. One tendency believed that evil, and good as well, were part of the human condition and as such could not be regarded as a "geographical problem." As Milton Mayer suggested, "The Devil is not a travel'n man," that is, "he's not in Germany or Japan one day and in Russia the next, he's in all of us." This tendency viewed the Cold War as the product of colossal misunderstanding gravely complicated by military rivalry.

The alternative view held that the Cold War was essentially justified, although often dangerously exaggerated. To be taken seriously, any credible message to Americans would have to recognize that reality without exaggerating it. It's important to confront the reality of evil as expressed in totalitarianism, but it needs to be done, and can be done, nonviolently.

The resolution of this dilemma was viewed by some as representing a compromise, while to others it represented a true "consensus," in the best sense of Friends, that improved both positions.

Evil, it was agreed, cannot be regarded as a geographic problem. Without "overlooking the evils of communism, we still reject the devil theory in history....Indeed, in all the great conflicts of history, each belligerent has tended uniformly and insistently to attribute a monopoly of evil to the other" (*Speak Truth,* 27). The real enemy is not the Soviet Union but the false values by which the East and West alike have lived: lust for power and control over others, and the inability of power to set limits for itself; the violations of human personality and infringements on its freedom and dignity; the "practical atheism" of a pervading materialism and secularism; the spreading cult and practice of violence and the poisonous doctrine that ends justify means.

The recognition of humanity's "common guilt and common nobility" is the necessary frame within which a non-military approach must be worked out. This is the first "pacifist essential" for an alternative approach.

C. The Second Essential: An "Alternative to Violence" and "A Choice With Hope"

But how do you oppose tyranny, homegrown or abroad, without becoming that which you oppose? The only way, they concluded, was to confront evil with new and non-military means. This was the second "essential."

They began by citing "field after field" in which pacifists and non-pacifists had sought to give practical demonstration to the effectiveness of love in human relationships (abolition of slavery, the campaign for women's suffrage). While the examples given were primarily "domestic," the authors sought to explore their implications for international affairs by citing encouraging examples in the international arena, including the independence struggle in India and the nonviolent resistance campaigns then underway in South Africa.

In a chapter entitled "The Politics of Nonviolence," they outlined what they regarded as the practical meaning of an acceptance of the nonviolent approach.

Such a policy would have serious consequences:

* There would be revolutionary changes within the US itself.

* The US would give its support to the "great social revolutions, which are both a major problem and a major hope of our time." (Policy would be freed from its preoccupation with the military power struggle.)

* The US would devote its skills and resources to the "great

programs" of the UN and with the full participation of the "receiving peoples."

* The US would get rid of its military establishment–unilaterally if necessary.

The nonviolent policy it outlined would have three dimensions (a stool with three legs):

(1) unilateral disarmament, if other methods fail, as a response to the threat of nuclear war enhanced by an out-of-control and fundamentally uncontrollable arms race;

(2) massive nonviolent civilian resistance in case of international aggression. This would involve both non-cooperation with the invading Army, while maintaining good will toward the individual invading soldier. There would be no individual acts of violence, no matter what the provocation.

(3) major changes in foreign policy would flow from a commitment to unilateral disarmament and preparation for civilian-based nonviolent defense.

If you find yourself thinking this approach unrealistic and requiring something just short of The Second Coming, you are not alone. The immediate response to these proposals on the part of critics, some pacifist and many non-pacifist (including some of the most eminent political thinkers of the day: Dwight Macdonald, George Kennan, Erich Fromm, Lewis Mumford and Hans Morgenthau), was to express admiration for the moral clarity of the call for sanity but to essentially find the prescription, the nonviolent alternative advanced, as irrelevant to the immediate threats and the real choices confronting policy-makers.

Clarence Pickett, chafing under the criticism from some pacifists, said, "It is interesting that in most of the replies that come in, pacifists find greater difficulty in accepting the thesis of the power of good as against evil than do those who are not pacifists" [Pickett response to Levering, August 8, 1955].

D. Witness and Relevance

Can pacifists, a tiny minority, ever influence public opinion and governmental policy enough to effect significant change? The authors said "Yes, let's try."

The entire effort of *Speak Truth* was to assert and argue the relevance of pacifist analysis and solutions to international issues. While the proof of relevance in the international arena was judged weak by many, the confidence of the authors in the potential for nonviolence to address the central conflicts of the age was undiminished and bold. An early draft declares, "pacifism is the key idea of our age, an idea whose time has come" (May, 1954 "Suggested Outline for Working Party Study").

In a final chapter called "The Politics of Time and the Politics of Eternity" they declared:

"Our truth," derived from the "politics of eternity," is an:

"Ancient one: that love endures and overcomes; that hatred destroys; that what is obtained by love is retained, but what is obtained by hatred proves a burden. This truth, fundamental to that position which rejects reliance on the method of war, is ultimately a religious perception, a belief that stands outside of history." *(Speak Truth*, iv)

The final arbiter of this truth is an "inner sense of integrity" rather than demonstrable results.

If ever truth reaches power, if ever it speaks to the individual citizen, it will not be the argument that convinces. Rather, it will be his own inner sense of integrity that impels him to say, "Here I stand. Regardless of relevance or consequences, I can do no other."

Still, it may be that the most significant and lasting impact of *Speak Truth* lay in formalizing and legitimizing an activist role for pacifists in political affairs. Its uniqueness lay in its determination to gather that action around the "normative principles" of pacifism and its practical expression in nonviolent action. Some were later to express regret that that door had been opened.

III. *SPEAK TRUTH TO POWER*, THE INTERVENING YEARS – 1955-1963

Speak Truth was published forty-four years ago and a decade before the Vietnam War.

    A. How, specifically, if at all, did its message inform the work of Friends in response to the war in Vietnam?

    B. In reappraising our experience of Friends' witness, can we learn anything that helps illuminate our current situation and the choices ahead?

In general, its analysis of the "military paradox" held up well!

Speak Truth asserted that it was illusory to believe the claims made for the desirability of simultaneous military strength and positive programs to carry out the peaceful intentions and high aspirations of Americans. The commitment to the former, it argued, would inevitably lead to the compromise and undermining of the latter.

This fundamental indictment of American foreign policy seems to have been largely substantiated by succeeding events. The trends predicted by *Speak Truth* were realized, often beyond the authors' expectations.

    1. In spite of episodic disarmament efforts, the arms race continued to accelerate. The language of the negotiators changed from "disarmament" to the reduced expectation of "arms control." Little of either was realized even as the "Cold War" was gradually transformed into an uneasy "detente" between the US and the USSR.

    2. As the consequences of direct and deadly nuclear warfare between the superpowers became clear, and as opportunities for expansion arose, the "Cold War" was transferred to new areas, the emerging former colonies of the Third World. "Containment" policies were ineffective, even irrelevant, when confronting internal challenges to Soviet power in Hungary, Poland, Berlin, East Germany and Czechoslovakia. Indeed, under "detente," the

scene of challenge moved from Europe to the seemingly less threatening arena of the colonial and newly independent countries of the Third World.

Korea, Vietnam under the French, Cuba, Algeria, the Dominican Republic, and preeminently, Vietnam, once again became the unexpected testing ground for containment policy, rather than the Europe around which it had been fashioned.

The principal test of containment policy obviously came with American involvement and eventual withdrawal from Vietnam.

3. Domestically, *Speak Truth* argued, the US will come more and more to resemble that which it opposes. *Speak Truth* predicted that "emotional engineering," the planned development of the mass mind, would be necessary to achieve the degree of national unity necessary to persuade Americans to send their young men to fight a war on the other side of the world, simply because a rational application of power demanded it. Military requirements, in the name of defending democracy, would rely increasingly on techniques originally employed by totalitarian regimes. One can see a straight line from the "secret" (from Americans) wars in Vietnam and Cambodia, to the Tonkin Gulf Resolution, and eventually to Watergate and the widespread surveillance of American citizens and their voluntary organizations, including the AFSC. The Great Society's "War on Poverty" was lost in the paddies of Vietnam.

IV. FRIENDS AND THE VIETNAM WAR – 1963-1975

What happened to the two "pacifist essentials" described in *Speak Truth*?

A. The Problem of the "Enemy" and "Evil" in the New Anti-War Movements

The greatest challenge to Friends' witness during the Vietnam War lay in its understanding of the "enemy" and the nature and location of "evil."

Initially, the view that the West was complicit in the very evils it deplored in communism led in the late fifties and early sixties to the attitude widely held by American peace leadership – a "pox on both your houses." This view was prevalent among activist Friends.

From this, it was easy to transfer optimism to the emerging nations of the Third World, which were expected, presumably because they had not yet been corrupted by the materialistic values of the West and East, to be the conscience of all humanity ready to bring moral and other pressures to bear on the superpowers to end a suicidal arms race, and to cooperate in a global venture to address the issues of poverty and underdevelopment.

This "Third Camp" view was dominant among Friends and prevalent in the Aldermaston marches in Britain and in American efforts to secure a test ban on atmospheric testing. This view was promoted by the Student Peace Union (SPU), which essentially disappeared in the wake of Students for a Democratic Society (SDS). Most peace efforts in the US assumed an American capacity and motivations on the part of both public and government to act in the interest of peace if convinced the risks necessary could be taken without jeopardizing national security.

Both "Third Force" and "Unilateral Initiatives" approaches shared an assumption that peacemaking required the defining of "common ground" among opponents and others affected directly and indirectly by preparation for war. Finding "common ground" or "common interests" was not only required by the method but came closer to expressing human reality, the way things really were, than the pretensions of the doctrines of East or West.

This contrasted with the view promulgated by Secretary of State John Foster Dulles in the early fifties. As a part of the emerging operational definition of containment, Dulles insisted there was no possibility of "neutrality" in the Cold War and that countries in the developing world must decide to be with the US or against it.

Ironically, by the end of the sixties, resistance to the argument that there is no "middle way" had yielded among large portions of the growing anti-Vietnam War movement to the view that, in any case, "middle ways" were inherently suspect and the possibility of constructing "common ground" was sharply reduced.

By the 1970's, the earlier emphasis on reconciling adversaries had been replaced in major sectors of the anti-war movement and the Left by an understanding of conflict that precluded "middle ways" as efficiently as Dulles had earlier on the Right. The essence of political life became "choosing sides," the question being "Which side are you on?" Those who remained pacifists found the climate increasingly inhospitable to actively expressed and distinctly pacifist perspectives.

This new perspective of the "enemy" represented a profound shift from the mid-fifties, when the most difficult issue was how to deal with the Soviet Union. In the mid-sixties, for many active in the civil rights movement and the new efforts to oppose US policy in Vietnam, the central question became how to deal with the US. The "new left" emphasized exposing the true character of the US and charging it with failing to fulfill the very values on which its culture had presumably been based. It was a short step from first- or second-hand experience with racism in the civil rights struggle to projecting a sense of disillusionment about other domestic issues. And from that it was easy to assert that a debased society at home could hardly be expected to behave differently abroad. In the words of Pogo, "We have met the enemy and he is *US!*"

For many, this meant the United States was as capable of the same evils as our foes. *"US"* in this instance could be viewed in the spirit of *Speak Truth* in which "the recognition that the evil is in Humankind is the basis and the only basis upon which an effort to reach a peaceful settlement (of the Cold War) can be saved from the fatal corruption of self-righteousness" (*Speak Truth*, 34). For others *"US"* came to be understood as defining the United States, in the instance of the Vietnam War at least, as the enemy to be opposed. The Cold War view turned upside down.

In its more thoroughgoing political expressions within the anti-Vietnam war coalitions, the US came to represent the "monopolization of evil" that *Speak Truth* had sought to warn against when applied to Soviet communism.

The tension inherent in this distinction was to become problematic among Friends as well as the larger public!

To the extent that "anti-Americanism" came to characterize, or was seen to characterize much of the effort to end the war, it became more difficult to define the "common ground" on which a majority of the American people could be united. Historically the peace movement has been most effective when it appealed to the "common ground" of democratic values it shared with the American majority, and least effective when it engaged in actions which expressed alienation from and hostility towards American society.

In a major study of polling statistics during the Vietnam War, entitled *Vietnam and the Silent Majority: The Dove's Guide*, the argument is made that there were, as of 1970, two currents of anti-war feeling in the United States. The first was college-educated and in the vanguard of public protest (though the majority of the college-educated were found to be "hawkish" relative to the whole population). The second were those at the very bottom of the education spectrum – people who had not gone beyond grade school.

Both groups were found to be the most consistently "dovish" of any population segment. Yet there was almost no meaningful communication between the two. The campus-centered peace movement, the study asserted, was almost entirely unaware of the second current and tended to assume that the 30 percent or 40 percent of the public reported in opinion polls as favoring rapid withdrawal were all part of their entourage. But while those in the second current were quite consistent in their opposition to the war, they were even more intensely negative about "Vietnam War protesters" and anxious to disassociate themselves from views and behaviors they regarded as anti-American and unpatriotic. The researchers concluded:

"It is likely that the fringe of the peace movement which has placed such a stamp on antiwar protest has done a great deal to impede the development of more urgent peace sentiment in the sectors of the population where it is numerically most impressive" (*Vietnam and the Silent Majority*, 64).

This is perhaps too harsh a judgment, but in any serious reappraisal we must be as bold in confronting our own actions as we might wish "the brightest and best" to be in facing theirs.

Further evidence this may be so came in 1970. The most dramatic breakthrough in anti-war sentiment came after the invasion of Cambodia and the shootings at Kent State. Then protest spread for the first time beyond the "leading" universities and colleges whose students were largely drawn from the upper middle and upper classes who had formed the vanguard of anti-war sentiment from the mid-1960's to over a thousand other colleges and universities, whose student bodies more accurately reflected "middle America" in composition and, not surprisingly, in attitudes. The researchers concluded that "it is fair to say that they (the latter) have supplied the very backbone of popular support for the war throughout the whole period" (*Vietnam and Silent Majority*, 58).

It may be that anti-war coalitions, like the Mobilization to End the War, in which student political radicals from the leading schools where cultural and political alienation predominated, were less effective in tapping and motivating antiwar sentiment among the less elite majority of non-leading schools and their graduates than the Anti-War Moratorium. The latter's tone was less strident and emphasized a view of the war as a violation of American values that could be ended if Americans insisted on a reaffirmation of those values. Large numbers of Americans were offended by what they viewed rightly or wrongly as the "unpatriotic," "anti-American" tone and message of the "new left" anti-war movement. These found a more acceptable avenue of expressing their opposition or misgivings about the war, doing so in a manner that did not require a repudiation of American values and, in effect, a repudiation of themselves as a people (*Vietnam and Silent Majority*, 58).

It is possible that, had the redefinition of "enemies" proposed in *Speak Truth* prevailed in anti-war efforts during the Vietnam period, some of the excesses that too easily lent themselves to distortion by the administration and which repulsed so many middle Americans, might have been minimized. "Common ground" might have been found earlier, leading to the majority needed to end or restrain American military involvement.

B. "Enemy" as "Oppressor"

Another shift occurred that influenced the message and methods of many Friends.

During the sixties the intellectual "elites" and their attentive publics among the readership of the influential journals for which they wrote, brought about a significant change in understanding about the world. While the majority of Americans still organized their worldview primarily around communist and anti- or non-communist camps, the main watershed for the intellectual elites became the division between the developed and developing countries, the "rich and poor," the "haves and have-nots." It is not surprising that those who accepted this watershed division in their worldview were also those who were likely to oppose American engagement in Vietnam.

It was a short step for many to locate the "structural" or "systemic" relations between the developed and developing nations and to conclude that the wealth of the former was at the price of, and resulted in, the continuing poverty of the latter.

This approach had at least three important effects on the way resolution was sought.

* First, while in the past peace efforts had focused on the Soviet-US encounter, the concern now shifted from "peace" to "justice" between developed and developing countries, and within those countries.

* Second, the question of "What is to be done?" then begins with the question "Where does justice lie?" After that determination, the question of whether it should be pursued violently or nonviolently is considered.

* Third, one must distinguish between the "oppressed" and the "oppressor," and must identify with the first, seeing an adversary in the second.

There is no question that viewing conflict through the lens of "oppressed/oppressors" did create a framework through which valuable insights were gained regarding the broader range of interests being served through foreign policy.

Knowledge of US complicity in the origins of the Cold War was an important corrective to "devil theories" which had placed blame exclusively on the Soviet Union. And important sectors of the intelligentsia and portions of the broader public now became aware in varying degrees of the manner in which economic interests, often through the operation of multi- or trans-national corporations, influenced or controlled the destiny of whole nations and influenced American foreign policy.

C. The Second Essential: An "Alternative to Violence"

Earlier I identified the alternative proposed in *Speak Truth* as a "Three-Legged Stool" consisting of:

1. Unilateral Disarmament
2. Civilian Nonviolent Resistance
3. Changing National Policies

What happened to each before and during the Vietnam era?

Unilateral Disarmament disappeared from the agenda of most peace organizations as the Vietnam War increasingly absorbed limited energies.

Civilian nonviolent resistance, *Speak Truth*'s answer to the question "What would you do if...?" suffered a similar fate. In 1966 the AFSC published a working party report entitled, *In Place of War: An Inquiry Into Nonviolent National Defense* (Grossman, 1966), as an effort to detail methods of civilian resistance. It was perhaps the wrong book, but more probably came at the wrong time. The subject seemed remote for those whose attention was then consumed by the question, not of national defense of one's own borders, but rather of guerrilla and counter-guerrilla war in

Vietnam. *In Place of War* was virtually our last word on the subject.

For the most part, peace and anti-war movements in the US have shown little interest in the potential of civilian resistance despite the writings of a growing number of peace researchers that have given us the opportunity to understand the breadth of its practice in many diverse settings, from the distant past until this moment.

That left the third leg, "Changing National Foreign Policies." The third leg of the "nonviolent triad" was the call for a significantly different American foreign policy that would be made possible by the adoption of the first two policies, unilateral disarmament and civilian resistance. It's clear that from the beginning of American involvement in Vietnam, the central focus for pacifist and non-pacifist opposition became the third dimension, trying to influence and change American foreign policy and seeing that policy as the primary instrument of interaction between the US and the world. As with the earlier coalitions between pacifists and non-pacifists in the early 1950's, the foreign policy agenda agreed upon during the Vietnam War had little or no distinctly pacifist content.

With two essentially pacifist legs dormant and the third leg without pacifist content, the "secularization" or "politicization" of pacifism was complete. The foreign policy changes promoted were largely indistinguishable from those of many other liberal political organizations with which pacifists comfortably found common cause. The "eclipse" of the pacifist dimensions made this transition possible, and for the most part unnoticed, even within pacifist organizations. Perhaps the perception among some Quakers that AFSC had become "too political" was the result of this reductionism.

D. What Might Have Been

How might we have mounted a clearer pacifist witness that challenged not only the Vietnam War, but war itself? I would like to suggest that in addition to the two legs in "eclipse," there were some "missing" legs that, had they been there, might have given more clarity to Friends' witness during the war.

First, in reading *Speak Truth*, there is little analysis of power, as it would be more popularly understood during the 1960's and '70s. While certainly aware in general of the suffering of many oppressed people in colonized nations, including those newly independent, the authors of *Speak Truth* did not address the issues later raised by the enduring quality of that suffering.

Had they done so, it is probable that their beliefs would have led to a parallel argument to the proposition that the commitment to organized mass violence inevitably corrupts constructive efforts and therefore must be renounced. They might also have argued that the commitment to defend "structural violence" or institutionalized injustice in which gross disparities of wealth and power are maintained is likewise ultimately illusory and corrupting. Such a commitment would result in the progressive undermining of the lives and values of both those who benefit and those who are victims of those disparities.

By not having a pacifist analysis of "structural or institutional violence," Friends were left to absorb the lessons of the academic and activist Left without the restraints imposed by 'love' to regard all, oppressor and oppressed, as both part of the human community.

Second, they might have provided a critique of the violence inherent in "just revolution." They might have addressed the role of the commitment to violence in revolutionary social change movements and armed struggle or "wars of national liberation" to overturn repressive regimes. Since liberation struggles became prominent in foreign and even domestic policy agendas, through most of the sixties and seventies, this was a critically important issue left largely unaddressed and unanalyzed.

While the Left, including the pacifist Left, has produced important insights regarding the corruptibility of "repression" and "counterrevolution," there has not been a corresponding effort regarding "revolutionary violence." Arguments have been made (Gordon Zahn, Gene Sharp, Mulford Sibley and others) to the effect that militarization of a struggle for change distorts the ends sought, with the victors often taking up the very policies and practices of repression earlier directed towards them, including the same prisons, interrogation methods, and control of press and movement. These arguments, if made at all, are generally made following the conclusion of a conflict rather than in the course of a revolutionary struggle. There may be several reasons for this, most notably the belief that such advices are of little importance when one is largely in agreement with the goals of a particular revolutionary struggle and, simultaneously, part of a society viewed as complicit in maintaining support for oppressive governments.

By not having a convincing analysis of "revolutionary struggle," many Friends and others found it easier to let go of the tension inherent in trying to witness to all the parties to a conflict, at least those resorting to violence.

E. The Emergence and Eclipse of Nonviolence as an Alternative

Through the civil rights and anti-war movement, broad sectors of the American public became acquainted in a first-hand way with the techniques of nonviolence. So much so that many forms of nonviolent direct action have become an accepted part of American life and the democratic process. It is difficult today to pick up a daily newspaper and not read of one or more groups using some form of nonviolent direct action, whether it is a group of police using "job action" to protest the lack of bullet-proof vests, or community groups occupying police stations to protest the lack of police protection. Nonviolence has demonstrated its availability as a technique for domestic change. It is accessible to anyone who chooses to use it.

At the same time, both the civil rights and anti-war movements experienced limits in their ability to sustain nonviolent campaigns, particularly when the issues become more subtle, such as racism in northern urban, as opposed to southern, environments or when an escalation of outrages occurs in a war that seems unstoppable – with increased cries for ever more militant responses. Still, never in US history had so many been trained in nonviolent techniques and actually undertaken experiments in their use.

Just as *Speak Truth* described a "military paradox," the sixties gave rise to a kind of "pacifist paradox." Just when nonviolence was accepted by the American mainstream as a domestic method of change with considerable demonstrated potency, the effectiveness and even the moral legitimacy of nonviolence came to be seen by many, including some who had been in the forefront in its domestic use, to be discredited, eroded, and irrelevant when addressing international issues.

The confident expectation that "nonviolence is an idea whose time has come, a key idea of our age" (*Speak Truth* draft outline, 1954) was not fulfilled. Indeed, there was a growing acceptance that violence, at least in the form of the "just revolution," might be the only alternative after all. Nonviolent actions were increasingly limited to actions by Americans against American policy.

For some believers in nonviolence, this focus on American policy was the natural outgrowth of a political perspective which saw America as the heart of the world's problems. For others, it represented a belief that efforts to assist directly indigenous nonviolent struggles abroad were futile unless there was such a movement already in place and prepared to undertake the sacrifices a nonviolent campaign required. Seeing none, or dismissing the importance of those existing in a particular instance, one must accept the fact that "the oppressed do not share our faith in nonviolence" and turn one's attention to work with nonviolent means to achieve a revolution in the American status quo, striving to bring about radical changes in attitude and radical shifts from the practice of exploitation to the pursuit of justice.

This approach was illustrated in the widely circulated AFSC booklet written in 1972 by Jim Bristol, a member of the *Speak Truth* working party, entitled *Nonviolence: Not First for Export*. In it he wrote:

"It will make it easier for the disadvantaged to succeed in their revolutionary struggle if we can remove both direct American domination and/or American support for their oppressors, and this, in turn, will serve to minimize the violence which they felt compelled to use to reach their goals....Instead of trying to devise nonviolent strategy and tactics for revolutionaries in other lands, we will bend every effort to defuse militarism in our own land and to secure the withdrawal of American economic investment in oppressive regimes in other parts of the world....It is up to the Latin Americans and the Africans to decide how they will wage their struggle for freedom. We cannot decide for them. Certainly, we dare not judge the morality of their choice." (Bristol, "Nonviolence: Not First for Export," *Gandhi Marg*, October, 1972)

This argument, with variations, became the dominant view in much of the pacifist peace movement. In the instance of Jim Bristol, it was put forward not by an enthusiast for wars of national liberation but by a veteran pacifist, a member of the *Speak Truth* working party, and an activist in efforts to strengthen the effectiveness of nonviolent defense and struggle methods in Africa. This was no facile effort to jettison nonviolence in favor of violent revolution, but a reluctant admission that the optimism of an earlier period had hit the hard realities that those in struggle appeared to find violence necessary, and that America itself was complicit in their oppression.

But was it true? Had nonviolence really "failed" or had its contributions been obscured by the rising attraction of violent paths? Had all those in struggle accepted the necessity of violence or were there continuing efforts to mount nonviolent challenges?

Gene Sharp, in an unpublished letter in response to Bristol's article, took sharp exception to the central thesis and conclusions even as he shared Bristol's view that "pompous moralizings of 'pacifists' are politically irrelevant and ethically most dubious." Nevertheless, Sharp suggested, Bristol's "honesty" in facing his lack of answers to the problems of effective struggle is combined with an abdication in the real search for answers" (Sharp letter to Bill Rose, 2). He criticized the type of pacifism that has:

"Emphasized moral commitment to nonviolence as a principal witness against evil, serious concern for human needs, and opposition to social injustices, but which has neglected really serious exploration of nonviolent struggle for use by ordinary people. This pacifism has assumed that we really know most of what we need to know in that field. Instead, I maintain that we are still largely ignorant of it.

"That ignorance results in part from the erroneous perception that ultimately the most effective power derives from violence and, in part, from the extensive neglect of the vast history of human experience with nonviolent forms of struggle separated from pacifism."

He concludes that the idea that one "cannot prescribe for others is a retreat into personal beliefs and a withdrawal from the attempt to extend the role of nonviolent struggle in politics...."

The title "Nonviolence: Not First for Export" begged the question of when, if ever, nonviolence is "second" or "third" and under what conditions. In effect nonviolence was effectively cornered – reduced into an ever smaller and tighter place.

V. THERE MAY BE A DEEPER PROBLEM: A CRISIS OF FAITH

While *Speak Truth* expressed its confidence in nonviolence in the most sweeping terms, and Sharp argues for "political audacity" in forwarding nonviolent alternatives, the clear reality is that, from the Vietnam War on, there has often been a greater sense of conviction and clarity about the relevance of political ideologies than there has been confidence that pacifism or nonviolence has anything really important to commend it to those engaged in revolutionary or social struggle.

What is the source of our collective loss of faith in nonviolence as a means of addressing oppression? Is it a "failure" of the technique to demonstrate its effectiveness, as Bristol argued, or rather our "failure" to be attentive when it is effective and our neglect of the vast history of human experience with nonviolent forms of struggle not associated with pacifism. What is to be said of us if we continue to assert the importance and even relevancy of nonviolence and simultaneously do little to realize it in our own efforts to address issues of human oppression?

Regaining confidence in nonviolence and its relevance will not occur as an act of will, if at all, but through a determination to push our understanding of its meaning and use in our own current context.

We must consciously seek to build the alternative. Ed Lazar, in an article in *Friends Journal*, observed:

"Unless people see that we are even-handed in supporting nonviolence in our own society, in the Middle East, in Southeast Asia, in South Africa, in Northern Ireland, anywhere in the world, they will rightly not be able to see the nonviolent movement as an alternative – rather, nonviolence will be seen as a temporary tool to be laid down when violence is seemingly needed on a particular issue."

A. Military Power vs. "People Power"

There may be several points of departure in this task.

There is widespread recognition, even within the military, of the limits of military power to achieve its goals given the rise of "people power."

Perhaps the most important and widely shared "lesson" of Vietnam is that large-scale infusion of troops, money, and arms cannot shore up an essentially unpopular, repressive and corrupt government. The "military quick fix" just doesn't work. War doesn't work to achieve the goals it sets for itself!

Ironically, having absorbed their own "lessons" from

Vietnam, frequently the most reluctant institutions in the world to enter into violent conflict are military! The Doctrine of Overwhelming Force has acted as a restraint on both political and military leadership. The disaster and humiliation in Somalia reinforced that lesson.

But it has been in the area of "People Power" that we have seen the most revealing developments. Following Vietnam, we first saw this played out in Iran where the Shah, with every support the US was able to provide over nearly three decades, and the most sophisticated military establishment his money and US technology could buy, couldn't prevent his overthrow by a people united against him. The US lost Iran, not because it was paralyzed by dovish lessons of Vietnam, but for the very same reasons that it lost in Vietnam. Iran teaches and reinforces the lesson of Vietnam, rather than annulling it.

Military power, whether American or Soviet or whatever, is less effective than ever before as an instrument of control over others, of thwarting the popular will of a mobilized people.

* Nuclear weapons did not prevent the taking of hostages in Iran, nor could they free them.

* Nuclear weapons, or any deployment of conventional arms (Rapid Deployment Force), could not prevent Soviet intervention in Afghanistan and were useless in securing Soviet withdrawal.

NATO arms could not prevent Soviet intervention in Poland nor could Soviet military might bring Solidarity to its knees. (The Soviet army sat threatening but still for well over a year while one of the most remarkable challenges to any government in this century took place – a movement of workers in a workers' state challenged the communist party's sole control over that country's affairs and insisted upon, and largely obtained, a role in the governance of Poland.)

In Iran and Poland, then Tien an Mein, and Latvia, the White House in Moscow, the Philippines and Indonesia, the real power of masses of people mobilized and prepared to paralyze the major institutions of their own societies has been demonstrated essentially without violence. The willingness to use counter-force was present, but was of limited value as real power slipped from the grasp of a single centralized government into the hands of people mobilized in their own organizations.

The most truly revolutionary responses to the complexity of modern society may be occurring before our eyes in these examples where organized, mobilized civilian populations – "People Power" – have successfully taken on heavily armed centralized authoritarian states.

B. Witness, Relevance and the Role of a Minority

What happens when pacifist and non-pacifist political perspectives combine in diversified coalition? The question of whether pacifist insights do, in fact, permeate the whole or are dissipated can be debated heatedly.

Discussion of that question is not new. It has a history, and Charles Chatfield, author of *For Peace and Justice, Pacifism in America, 1914-1941*, is one of the primary historians of that interaction. He has a particular interest in the pacifist dimension, while Christopher Lasch, author of *The Agony of the American Left*, and others have attempted similar reviews, with particular attention to the political dimensions.

Chatfield, in the midst of the Vietnam era, addressed the issue of pacifists "in the eye of our political storms" and argued that:

"...the political impact of pacifists depends largely upon the role they play within the antiwar movement, for this is the source of their deepest motives and the clarity of their sharpest insights.... The Caribbean hurricane is the image of this essay. Pacifists will be the voice that seems still in relation to the movement swirling about them; but in relation to the contours of political and social injustice, they will cut a broad swath into the future. It was the powerful impulse to reform or change society at all its levels that brought pacifist leadership into close association with the radical new left that emerged in the mid-'60s in SDS and in other groups which had a recent history of involvement in civil rights and poverty issues."

Accordingly, he believes the New Left used the war for its radical purposes and the war rarely has been an issue in itself for radicals.

The consequences of this have been at least two-fold. Anti-war work has been diffused by the efforts of the left wing to radicalize society; and it has been compromised by internecine debates over radical theory and strategy:

"...Too often they have been tempted to confront the liberal community with their own social theories, rather than to work with liberals in order to confront the conservative and non-committed community with the issue of war and peace. Most importantly, it tended to obscure the harsh reality of the war and the possibility of alternatives to it."

Finally, he concludes that the effectiveness of pacifists in coalition will depend upon the strength of their motives and the clarity of their insights.

Historically, this has meant the strength of their religious conviction. They will stand at the center of a diversified movement, relating radicals and liberals, militants and moderates, to harsh realities of life and death. They will apply their values to social policy and peace action alike. They will oppose the mystique of violence and focus attention upon the basic terms of social and foreign affairs. They will bring both the movement and the State "within the compass of the redemption which is the deepest motive" (to quote Geoffrey Nuttall) behind truly revolutionary pacifism. They will not be carried off by random, violent gusts of activity swirling about them but, rather, will move forward in the eye of our political storms.

VI: SPEAKING TRUTH TO POWER IN 1998 AND BEYOND: IS THERE ANOTHER WAY?

We may be in a situation now roughly analogous to that of the mid-fifties, when again we see central assumptions about the world changing and being challenged from many directions.

What is needed now is a decision to renew the effort to define a pacifist or nonviolent posture and to translate that into political action. That process would carry forward important and carefully examined new insights from the past forty-five years and would address an agenda of concerns different from those faced in 1955. If the work of peace requires what one AFSC veteran called "humble megalomania," then this effort will require "chastened boldness" if it is to break new ground.

Does the very act of self-definition by itself "set us off" from those who do not share that definition? It does, of course, though the result may not be the "pulling away" from others that is imagined, but a clearer and perhaps different basis of collaboration.

Pacifists, or those committed to nonviolent alternatives, will always be a minority within a larger peace and change movement, which is itself, now, a minority within American society. To use the analogy of bread in a pan, we can't presume to shape the loaf, but we can be an ingredient.

But which ingredient? What do we look like before we are mixed in with the other ingredients? Is there a danger that marinating in the juices of a larger movement and society, as we inevitably must, we will not only become indistinguishable from the "mix" but will ourselves lose the capacity to represent a visible alternative? The difficulty of defining ourselves "in the mix" is complicated if we do not know, before we are added, the texture, shape, and contours of our belief.

If an active and confident advocacy of nonviolence in the international arena is in "eclipse" among those who are its guardians, what would be required for it to again be seen as a viable path for the future? Several questions for examination would have to be addressed:

To what extent does the future of the human community depend upon the realization or success of nonviolence as what Bondurant calls, "an instrument of fundamental social change"? Do we regard testing the power of nonviolence as a desirable option or as an urgent necessity for human survival?

Will the recrystallization of nonviolent strategies require close engagement with those undertaking nonviolent struggle in diverse circumstances? Would we, for example, make special efforts to understand, first-hand, the largely non-military character of those engaged in "People Power"?

Carole Reilly Urner (*Friends Journal*, June 1/15, 1981) in an article entitled "Quakers, Nonviolence and Third World Christians," argues that

"Quakers in particular need to seek out our spiritual allies in these developing countries, enter into relationship with them, share in their sufferings, and actively support them with our presence and our love. This does not mean that we should cease to seek communication with those in liberation movements who use methods we cannot condone or that we should cut ourselves off from dialogue with those in oppressive governments. We have faith that there is that of God in everyone and seek it in each. But surely when we find those of kindred spirit struggling nonviolently and against great odds for social and economic justice, it is to their sides that we must fly."

I want to close with a poem by Walt Whitman that encourages us to believe the task of revitalization is achievable:

What we believe in waits latent forever through all the
    continents
Invites no one, promises nothing, sits in calmness and
    light, is positive and composed, knows no
    discouragement,
Waiting patiently, waiting its time.
Perhaps that time is now.

Stories of Quaker Peace Witness

Panel presentations

David Hartsough

Anne Morrison Welsh

July 17, 1998

Nonviolent Witness During the Vietnam War

David Hartsough

I was a Friends' lobbyist for FCNL 1966-70, working to educate Congress about the truth about the war. My work included helping organize national opposition to the war to pressure Congress to end support for the war and finally working to get Congress to cut off funds for the war.

But I came to feel that Congress was not going to stop support for the war until there was broad-based opposition to the war across the country. Thus my participation in and help in organizing nonviolent direct actions. I believe Friends played an important role of leavening the loaf – helping set the tone, getting creative actions started, strengthening the commitment to nonviolence in the demonstrations, etc. A few highlights of actions in which I was involved:

1969 – Reading the names of the war dead on the Capitol Steps in Washington. Each Wednesday at noon we stood on the Capitol steps reading the names of the war dead and were arrested. After several weeks of going to jail, I went to Congressman George Brown (D-California) and told him what we were doing and asked if there were ways he could help.

After a moment of reflection, he said, "Yes, I will join you" and he sent a letter to every Member of Congress inviting them to join him. When we were arrested the next day, the Congressmen were not arrested because they had Congressional immunity, and they continued reading the names of the war dead. This got nationwide publicity and soon there were hundreds of groups of people all across the country reading the names of the war dead in front of Federal buildings and post offices.

October 69 – the Vietnam Moratorium with the theme "Stop business as usual to help stop the war." There were teach-ins, demonstrations, candlelight vigils, demonstrations in high schools, colleges and work places, and town halls across the country – two million people were involved. Church bells rang, flags flew at half mast, and in Congress we organized an all-night debate on the war. It became difficult for the President to talk of the "Silent Majority."

The effect of our actions: During our mass demonstrations President Nixon said he was watching a football game. But he had made an ultimatum to North Vietnam in which he said that if the North Vietnamese did not give in by Nov. 3, the US would unleash unbelievable firepower against North Vietnam – including in urban areas and possibly using nuclear weapons.

But when he saw the breadth and depth of the opposition to the war all across the US, the Nixon administration realized they could not go through with their threat of massive bombing and possible use of nuclear weapons without unleashing a "war" at home. A very important victory!!

November 1969 – Vietnam Mobilization in Washington and San Francisco which included a "March Against Death" in which 45,000 participated – a beautiful, solemn and powerful action which continued for forty hours. The next day 500,000 people marched in Washington and another 150,000 in San Francisco against the war.

April 1971 – there was a large Friends Meeting for Worship in front of the White House in which we were praying for an end to the war in Vietnam. President Nixon could not allow Quakers to worship praying for peace in front of his White House. Therefore 151 Friends were arrested during that meeting for worship.

My wife Jan and our young children, Heidi and Peter, ages 7 months and 2 years, were part of that meeting for worship. But the police did not want to arrest these young children – especially not in front of the national media. The Chief of Police pled with us to leave, saying that if they arrested us, they would have to separate the children and he was worried what would happen to them in the juvenile jail.

We replied that part of our reason for being there was concern for what was happening to the children of Vietnam, and we would continue the meeting for worship even though we were now the only Friends left on the sidewalk in front of the White House. Finally when they told us we were under arrest, we agreed to walk to the waiting police car which took us to the police station where they released us. The photo of the Police Chief squatting down to plead with us not to allow our young children to be arrested was in the papers across the US. Perhaps this helped humanize the war for many people who saw this picture.

Spring of 1971 – some Friends helped organize the People's Lobby in Washington, in which 10,000 people were arrested that week. The die-in in front of Selective Service headquarters was particularly memorable. We were there all night and knelt in prayer so the next morning the workers (if they were to get into the building), would have to walk over our defenseless bodies as they were doing every day to the people of Vietnam.

Spring 1972 – The People's Blockade. We had a memorable meeting for worship at the Life Center in West Philadelphia after the intensive bombing in Hanoi and Haiphong had started and massive numbers of the civilian population were being killed. In that meeting for worship we felt the horror of what was happening to the people of Vietnam, trying to discern God's leading for us. We found a commitment to somehow attempt to put our lives and our bodies between the bombs and the people of Vietnam who were getting killed and to support one another in making that commitment.

Soon thereafter we found that ships were being loaded with bombs at Leonardo, New Jersey and being sent to Vietnam. We assembled canoes and began what we called a People's Blockade – putting our canoes and our bodies between the ships carrying the bombs and the people of Vietnam who would be killed by those bombs.

The first ship we blockaded was the USS Nitro. As we

paddled out along the pier, the military police boat came over and threatened us with charges of criminal conspiracy – with possible sentences of 20 years in prison.

Our response, as we looked at all the anti-personnel bombs and napalm and many other kinds of explosives was: "Thanks for warning us, but if these bombs reach their intended destination, the result will be even worse than 20 years in prison," and we kept paddling.

We met some of the navy sailors who were also not very happy about going with the deadly cargo of bombs to Vietnam. After six days of our sea vigil/blockade, while the ship was being loaded with bombs, the ship was ready to leave. From our 18 canoes in front of this ship, as we looked up at the bow of the ship far above us, seven sailors jumped off the ship into the ocean to join our human blockade. This was on nationwide TV and newspapers around the world. Our courage had helped give these Navy sailors courage to do what they believed was right.

Word about their resistance went around the world and helped strengthen the courage of many others in the armed forces to follow their consciences and strengthen their resistance to this horrible war. With AFSC's support, the People's Blockade soon spread to ports on both the Atlantic and Pacific coasts of the US.

It was very important for all of us to listen to and follow our consciences and to organize nonviolent resistance to the Vietnam War. The American people played a crucial role in helping end this war. I highly recommend the book by Tom Wells, *The War Within*, published by the University of California Press, in which he interviewed hundreds of top administration officials and a broad cross section of the anti-war movement. He concludes that the American people played an absolutely critical role in ending the war. All our hard work, sitting through endless meetings, years of organizing, and years in prison, were not in vain.

I want to give heartfelt thanks to all of us who lived through this horrible war and followed our consciences and acted courageously and worked so hard over many years to help end this war.

Norman Morrison: Deed of Death, Deed of Life

Anne Morrison Welsh

"The Church of the Spirit is always being built. It possesses no other kind of power and authority than the power and authority of personal lives, formed into a community by the vitality of the divine human encounter.

"Quakers seek to begin with life, not with theory or report. The life is mightier than the book that reports it. The most important thing in the world is that our faith becomes living experience and deed of life."
– Norman R. Morrison, 1965, notes from a lesson in process for an adult class at Stony Run Meeting.

In the early evening of November 2, 1965, Norman Morrison gave his life in witness against the Vietnam War, in a desperate hope of helping to end it. Through conscience *in extremis*, he immolated himself in front of the Pentagon. Over thirty years have passed, but the memory of his devastating act still lives in many hearts and lives. In this sense, the fire he lit has never gone out.

When I learned of what had happened, George Webb and Harry Scott Sr., of Stony Run Friends Meeting in Baltimore, took me to Ft. Myer, Virginia. Somehow, after I identified Norman's wallet and comb, and once again held our baby Emily in my arms, I was able to write the following statement for the waiting news media. George and Harry presented it to them on my behalf.

"Norman Morrison has given his life today to express his concern over the great loss of life and human suffering caused by the war in Vietnam. He was protesting our government's deep military involvement in this war. He felt that all citizens must speak their true convictions about our country's actions."

There is and perhaps always will be a mystery about Norman's sacrifice and about Norman himself, even for me. I knew Norman for 10 years and was married to him for eight of those years. I want to tell you what I can about him. I want to let his thoughts speak to you.

Setting the stage

Where was the peace movement in the fall of 1965? At the time, the civil rights movement was going strong, and the anti-Vietnam War movement was becoming stronger. Yet the war in Vietnam was far from being in the forefront of the national consciousness. But it was gaining momentum.

1965. In April, when 25,000 students marched against the war in Washington, there were about the same number of American soldiers in Vietnam. By the end of the year, there were 184,000 troops. We had been bombing the North Vietnamese infrastructure since the first of the year, as well as mining the Haiphong harbor. Although there was questioning of the war in Congress and the press, a great majority of Americans supported President Johnson's increasing commitment to send US combat troops to the rice paddies and jungles of Vietnam. We know now from historians that Johnson, in spite of his doubts, took a stand and intensified the war early in the year. By mid-year, US bombing and defoliation of rural Vietnam was killing and wounding the civilian population in the south, driving the peasants who survived from their homes and hamlets.

Here is how Chester L. Cooper describes 1965 in his book, "The Lost Crusade" (in Paul Hendrickson, *The Living and the Dead,* p. 181):

"By the autumn the war began to intrude seriously on the normal life of Americans. Draft calls had increased substantially,

American casualties were now beginning to be felt across the country, military funeral corteges moving across Memorial Bridge and among the trees at Arlington Cemetery were a common sight....Some McNamara-watchers claim the secretary underwent a discernible change in mood in late 1965. It was not so much a transition from "hawk" to "dove." It was rather a change from overflowing confidence to grave doubts."

On August 9, around 200 participants in the Assembly of Unrepresented People were arrested in Washington, in protest of the war. The march will be dramatically remembered as the one in which its leaders, Staughton Lynd, David Dellinger and Robert Moses, had red paint thrown on them by counter-demonstrators. Norman was eager to be part of the march, but was strongly advised by Mary Cushing Niles, his mentor at Stony Run Friends Meeting, that he had better attend the Baltimore Yearly Meeting and do his professional duty as Executive Secretary at Stony Run.

During the year preceding his death, Norman became increasingly active in opposing the developing war. He wrote to our representatives in Washington and "letters to the editor," helped plan peace vigils and conferences, and lobbied in Washington. I fully supported him in this, but as the mother of three small children, my war protest was mostly rear-guard. Often I edited his talks and letters to the editor.

On May 6, 1965, Norman again wrote to the editor of the *Baltimore Sun:*

"It is my opinion that any nation which insists that there is no choice but to fight is no longer a great power. We have not won the minds of men, in fact in the last few weeks we have been rapidly losing them by our belligerent activities....

"All of us are appalled by the human tragedy and suffering involved in Vietnam and the Dominican Republic. We like to think of ourselves as living in a peace-promoting country where no one likes war. However, the United States has over-extended itself and can only make more enemies by continuing with its present policy of intervening on the side of unpopular and unstable governments in foreign countries. We should not expect Communists to stay out of neutral or free world countries when we show such readiness to commit men and machines to far-flung battlefields.

"Ultimately countries will return to their own ways and lay aside foreign attempts at intervention and subversion. So far as I know there is no one who believes that the time is upon us when one power could or should police the whole world, or even half of it....

"Those who find they are in agreement with what has been said up to this point and are sufficiently aroused to register their protest to the government in Washington should want to join in a silent vigil at the Pentagon Building, Washington, DC, May 11th and 12th.

We will be there to convey this message:

1– To express before God and men the sincere desire of American people for a peaceful settlement in Vietnam.

2– To express concern at the escalation of the war, especially the US bombing of N. Vietnam.

3– To register our hope that the United States will continually press for a settlement through unconditional discussions involving all concerned parties.

4– To support and encourage Pres. Johnson in a program of international cooperation for human welfare and economic development in Southeast Asia.

The vigil next week is being sponsored by the Interreligious Committee on Vietnam...100 Maryland Ave. NE, Washington D.C.

In this crucial time it is necessary that faith and reason become courageous.

This is one man's opinion, what is yours?"

– Norman R. Morrison

Increasingly Norman was agonized by our military's immoral killing of Vietnamese civilians – old men, women, and children. Norman could not accept the unspeakable human toll the war was already taking on the innocent ones, as well as on our soldiers. He was convinced that if the war continued it would take a heavy toll on the conscience of America. His convictions proved to be prophetic.

He saw that our country was knowingly destroying people, villages, and an ancient culture. That was unacceptable enough, but he was also apprehensive that China or Russia eventually might enter the war on the side of North Vietnam, making a little war into World War III, a nuclear war to end the world as we knew it. Now we know that his fears were not groundless, that nuclear options were officially proposed at our highest military level. He also expressed apprehensions about the possibility of worldwide catastrophe through the collapse of the stock market.

During the latter part of 1965, Norman and I spoke almost daily of Vietnam. I shared his deep concern about the war. Both of us were moved and awed by the self-immolation of Vietnamese Buddhist monks, as well as that of Alice Herz, an elderly Quaker from Detroit, about whom little was known to us, unfortunately. After Norman's death, I learned that he had discussed a variety of dramatic protests against the war with a close friend. He kept all of that from me.

November 2, 1965, and afterwards

In his daily life, Norman relied on conscience and internal guidance, which he sometimes referred to as the Inner Light. "Without it, Anne, where would I be?" he said more than once to me.

On the day of his death, because of a cold he was home from work, preparing for a New Testament class he was planning to lead at the meeting. We were together during most of the day. Around noon I put Emily down for her nap. As I was making our lunch of French onion soup and grilled cheese, we talked about the war.

"What more can we do?" asked Norman, in a calm and grave way, sitting on a stool in the kitchen.

"I don't know," I replied, "I just know that we must not

despair." Norman kept to himself the overwhelming mission he felt called to that day "without warning." Had I known, I would have gone to any length on earth to have stopped him.

While I went to fetch our six-year-old Ben and five-year-old Tina from school, Norman took Emily, almost a year old, with him to the Pentagon. She was with her father up to the end, until he released her physically unharmed. It was reminiscent of Abraham's taking his beloved son Isaac up to the sacrificial altar in an "unreasonable, unconventional act of faith" (as Norman had once called it) before an angel intervened and saved Isaac.

Emily's proximity to danger was horrifying. Had she been injured or died it would have been unspeakable, and maybe impossible for me to have forgiven him. But in a real sense, Emily's presence became a symbol of the many precious Vietnamese children who were victims, if not targets, of the war. Now, years later, I have an intuitive sense of how important it must have been for Norman to hold onto a child he loved dearly and the family and life she represented, right up until the end.

We were shocked and devastated by the loss of our husband and father. Our lives were altered forever. It was as if a heavy curtain fell upon us, creating a Before and After in our lives. Much later, I learned how incredibly hard it was for Tina and probably Ben too, that their father left without a personal goodbye. I believe had Norman tried to do so, his impending sense of loss might well have stopped him.

The next day after his death I received a letter in the mail. The envelope was in Norman's handwriting and postmarked Washington, D.C. I opened it with shaking hands, wondering for an instant if somehow the horror of November 2 had just been a nightmare, that indeed Norman was alive.

It was his personal goodbye to me, written probably just before he left home. It included the following:

"Dearest Anne, Please don't condemn me...For weeks, even months, I have been praying only that I be shown what I must do. This morning with no warning I was shown, as clearly as I was shown that Friday night in August 1955 that you would be my wife....at least I shall not plan to go without my child, as Abraham did. Know that I love thee but must act for the children in the priest's village. Norman"

Who were the children in the priest's village? Their story was told in an article Norm evidently had been reading the morning he died and which he enclosed with his letter. The article was entitled, "A Priest Tells How Our Bombers Razed His Church and Killed His People" by Jean Larteguy, in *I.F. Stone's Weekly* (Nov. 1, 1965).

The article, which originally appeared in *Paris-Match* (Oct. 2, 1965) quotes a missionary priest named Father Currien, whom Larteguy found wounded in the St. Paul Clinic in Saigon. Fr. Currien had been pinned under the beams of his church in South Vietnam, which was wrecked from our aerial bombardment.

"I have seen my faithful burned up in napalm," said the pastor from his bed. "I have seen the bodies of women and children blown to bits. I have seen all my villages razed. By God, it's not possible!"

"Suddenly the priest burst into tears," said Larteguy. "His nerves had given way. He cursed the war and its attendant horrors and absurdities. He railed at the Americans in English, as if they were there to hear him. He finally calmed down: 'They must settle their accounts with God'"

With his newsletter, I.F. Stone rendered courageous service to the cause of peace and justice.

In his letter, Norman asked me to try to explain his action to Ben and Tina. The next morning I gathered them up and told them their Daddy had died for the sake of little children like them in a land far away, in a war they had no way to grasp. My words were a noble effort, but did not address their shocked and broken hearts. I held back my own tears in an effort to be brave and to uphold Norman's sacrificial witness. (After all, we were in the midst of a war which needed to end.) I know now that the children and I should have talked and cried our hearts out together. Because we did not, we remained in a state of frozen grief for years.

Though our family life was brightened by friends and loved ones and remarriage, we continued to suffer inwardly for years. We held so much grief and maybe even shame inside us. Ben died in 1975 at the age of 16 after a courageous, five-year battle with bone cancer. During Ben's illness, I got in touch with my grief enough to be angry with Norman for not being with us in this long battle. However, most of the time I just tried to be brave. I am so grateful that Christina and Emily and I have become better able to face our personal histories with honest sharing of our emotions. We are gradually becoming healed.

After Norman died, many individuals in America and abroad were affected by his sacrifice, and let us know. Some said they were moved to publicly oppose the war and work harder for peace. The many expressions of sympathy, encouragement and inspiration which we received gave me strength to meet the challenges I faced in the wake of Norman's death. Without the tangible support of these friends, known and unknown, I and the children could not have made it to the extent that we did.

"We grieve with you, but we also rejoice that a Friend should make so heroic a sacrifice as witness to his beliefs."

"I was moved indeed to read in today's Scotsman about Norman's very brave act. I had always realized that he was more sensitive, felt things more deeply, than most of us, and so you must be proud of him for having been a pioneer for peace."

"We don't really understand this deed. Did Norman actually expect that such an utmost sacrifice would change politics and opinions? I think he sacrificed too much; and didn't he think of his family?"

"This morning we read (about) 'Two Types of Ministry.' One type feeds people the thoughts and ideas they already have, thus ensuring a quick and enthusiastic response. It is easy and superficially rewarding but accomplishes nothing. And then Rufus Jones has this to say: 'The prophet has a very different task. He cannot give people what they want. He is under an inescapable compulsion to give them what his soul believes to be true.' This surely was what Norm was doing. And he had the courage to make the supreme sacrifice in order to accomplish his purpose. Although I am terribly saddened by this event it is good to know that Quakers of this calibre still exist."

"...Your husband was a casualty of an undeclared war for which our President bears the responsibility but for which we all bear the shame."

"Dear Anne, I have been thinking of you all day and wondering what I could possibly say that could be of any help whatsoever to you in this moment of your world turned upside down.

"I do know that we each have to go down a very private road to find our own meaning in life, our own special commitment. There is no fuller commitment than the one Norman made. As for you, you are left to pick up the pieces. It's no help to be told you are strong at a time like this, but you are. I was so proud of you – your pictures, your published statement. And my heart broke for you, too."

"He touched a great many people at a very deep level, including myself. His sensitivity and dedication will be a challenge to me the rest of my life."

In his death, Norman became a folk hero in Vietnam. The Vietnamese wrote poems and songs about him, named a street in his honor, and issued a commemorative stamp. His sacrifice communicated a love and respect for the Vietnamese people. Self-immolation, considered the strongest possible statement of one's conscience through suffering, is accepted in the Buddhist tradition.

Over the more than three decades that have passed since his

death, I have continued to learn of the impact Norman's protest had on others, including then Secretary of Defense Robert S. McNamara. The immolation took place about 40 feet from the Secretary's office at the Pentagon, but I have no idea if Norman knew of this proximity or not.

In his 1995 memoir, *In Retrospect: The Tragedy and Lessons of Vietnam,* McNamara states that Norman's "death was a tragedy not only for his family but also for me and the country. It was an outcry against the killing that was destroying the lives of so many Vietnamese and American youth." I am grateful that McNamara found the courage to re-assess the war and to publicly admit that our policy was "terribly wrong" and a tragic mistake.

In recent years, there seems to have been a renewed interest in Norman's act. On July 30, 1995, a three-page feature on Norman and our family appeared in *The Baltimore Sun.*

In the spring of 1996, James Carroll published a memoir entitled, *An American Requiem: God, My Father, and The War That Came Between Us.* The book won first prize in non-fiction at the National Book Awards. The author's father was a high official in the Pentagon at the time of Norman's death. In the memoir, James Carroll states that Norman's act was a catalyst in his own developing opposition to the war.

Later in 1996, *Washington Post* journalist Paul Hendrickson's book, *The Living and the Dead: Robert McNamara and Five Lives of a Lost War,* was published. Norman's is one of the "five lives." Hendrickson suggests Norman's witness subtly yet decisively helped erode McNamara's enthusiasm and confidence in our pursuit of the war. Hendrickson's book was one of the five finalists in non-fiction in the National Book Awards.

Yet after all this time, even with renewed attention to his witness, Norman is unknown to many, even within the Society of Friends. And for many of those who do remember, he still remains a puzzling and mysterious figure.

Who was Norman Morrison?

What kind of man was Norman Morrison? I can tell you that he was completely dedicated to a life of self-giving, yet he was fascinated with the stock market. That he was different, at times off-putting and perplexing in his manner; that he was frugal, even to the point of being a pinch-penny; that he had a natural dancing rhythm, yet couldn't carry a tune; that he had a quirky, off-handed sense of humor; he loved to wear a beret at a rakish angle and (though essentially a tee-totaller) occasionally enjoyed a rare cigar or glass of beer. He had a big green thumb.

Norman had premonitions that he couldn't easily share, even with me. He wasn't alone in this. In his personal memoir, *Memories, Dreams, Reflections* (p. 356), Carl Jung says he always experienced loneliness, that he lived in a kind of secret world:

"It is important to have a secret, a premonition of things unknown. It fills life with something impersonal, a *numinosum*. One who has never experienced that has missed something important. We must sense that we live in a world which in some respects is mysterious; that things happen and can be experienced which remain inexplicable; that not everything which happens can be anticipated. The unexpected and the incredible belong in this world. Only then is life whole. For me the world has from the beginning been infinite and ungraspable."

When I came across this reflection by Jung, I immediately thought of Norman. Like Jung, Norman was a loner. He had secrets and premonitions, held views which were different from his fellows. It was often hard for him to communicate with others things that were important to him. For Norman, the world was essentially spiritual, numinous, surpassing comprehension. He loved the unexpected. And in the end he did a totally unexpected, absurd, mysterious and ungraspable act. Yet I believe, although his act took his life and tore ours in two, paradoxically, it made his life more whole, of a piece.

Norman was born in Erie, Pennsylvania, but grew up in nearby Chautauqua Institution, New York, a place which was influential in his religious and intellectual development. A Presbyterian, he graduated in history and education from The College of Wooster, Ohio in 1956 and earned a B.D. degree at Western Theological Seminary in Pittsburgh in 1959.

A pacifist by persuasion, Norman began his association with the Society of Friends while at Wooster. At about the same time, while a student at Duke University and a restless Methodist, I found a spiritual home among Durham Friends. We met at Chautauqua in the summer of 1955 and were married two years later in the new Durham meetinghouse. After a honeymoon year of study at the University of Edinburgh and travel among Friends on the continent, we returned to Pittsburgh, where Norman finished up his theological degree and we joined the Friends Meeting. From 1959-61, we worked with a group of Friends in Charlotte, N.C., to establish a Meeting and outreach program. At the time of his death at the age of 31, Norman was executive secretary of the Stony Run Friends Meeting in Baltimore, Md., a position he had held since 1962.

Norman and I had a loving and purposeful marriage; we felt like two mules hitched together to a wagon of work and destiny. But like most unions, ours was not without its difficulties and challenges. We should have shared our hearts and souls more, and been more honest with each other. But, in retrospect, neither of us knew how to be truly open. I am so grateful that our last year together was the best and closest one for us.

Concerns and Beliefs

What were Norman's concerns? What did he believe in? Norman left answers not only in his death but also in lecture notes, articles, letters to the editor, diaries, and sermons while a seminarian as well as messages to both Charlotte and Stony Run Friends Meetings. Norman was a radical Christian and radical Quaker. In his words:

"We serve the Christ of the New Covenant. Because of our concern for men in every walk of life there will be many times when it will be necessary to lay aside temporal laws and prohibitions in order to reach real need. Our strength and assurance is the result of the indwelling spirit of Christ which we would recognize in every individual soul.

"If we would know God we need also to know our neighbor. To know our neighbor we need to sacrifice something on his behalf. It is the father and Creator of us all that can help us to sufficiently rise above the fears and apprehensions resulting from self-centered living so that we might make necessary sacrifices. In this way we would become a creative means in bringing life and comfort to mankind."

As his writings and life revealed, Norman was willing to live a selfless life. In the end, he gave it away.

For Norman, life was not an end in itself, nor death the end of individual existence. He firmly believed in an afterlife in eternity with God and Christ. Death was not something to be feared. "When men have conquered the fear of death, they can face anything that life may have in store for them," he said.

He believed in a whole, organic universe. We are all part of it and one another; one humanity. His loyalty was to the world community, even more than to his own family.

Earlier in 1965, a well-known and loved member of Stony Run Friends Meeting took his own life, an event that shook Norman and the meeting. Norman admired Dr. Jack Neustadt greatly. In his remarks at his memorial service Norman said:

"[Jack Neustadt's] many skills are treasures which we believe in God's enormous universe will be preserved. In life and in death he exercised the freedom of choice which is the very essence of living in this world. Yet we gather here in the wake of a tragedy of complex meanings. The impulse to take command of one's own life is part of any religion which seeks to nurture the individual. Basically, men long to relate to meaning in life; some long with greater intensity than others. Out of basic human need springs man's capacity boldly to seek to understand death which awaits him, and at the same time to experience all the exuberance which life brings him."

A serious boy, Norman was raised in the Presbyterian Church of the Covenant in Erie. In his early teens, at around the time of his father's untimely and unexpected death from ulcers, Norman began to diligently read the Bible, considering it the source of spiritual knowledge, direction, and inspiration. It wasn't long before he made the decision to become a Christian minister.

One might say Norman was schooled in Christ, who eventually became for him the Quaker's Inner Light or Inward Christ. For Norman, a commitment to Christ, the Inner Light, and unconditional love was primary. Though steeped in Presbyterian religious education, he came to believe that essential religious knowledge and action result not from knowing scriptures and ordinances but from experiencing God's love and reality first-hand. For him, this was best achieved in worship on the basis of silence in the manner of Friends.

To this radical Quaker, the individual was ultimately accountable only to God; loyalty to one's state or government was secondary. Of greatest importance was to be obedient to one's internal authority as informed by God and the Inward Light or Inward Christ.

"Jesus' concern was to do the will of the Father. Doing God's will by bringing love and truth into the world for mankind will always end in crucifixion when it is done as thoroughly and completely as Christ did it. This then is the way of the gospel of which Christ spoke. Sharing Christ's concern, doing God's will today involves real human suffering."
– (NRM, undated Communion sermon, '58-'59)

"In our sophisticated age we are particularly disposed to separating feeling from action. But to speculate with truth and not obey it is deadening. For long ages a spirit has been moving man to feel compassion for humanity. And feeling is the mainspring of the hands that create history. Yet if we arise from feeling without

passing into duty we become living falsehoods....Without obedience further truth is withheld."
— (NRM, Stony Run Newsletter 3/1/63)

Our life in Baltimore was challenging. The 60's were a turbulent time for our country and for our family as well. Things didn't come easy for Norm at Stony Run. He admitted his lack of social graces and diplomacy. In his writings, he was often preaching to himself as much as to others.

"Yes, all things do work together for good but I haven't seen much evidence of it on an individual basis and from [a] selfish standpoint. It is only when we lose ourselves in love that we gain any measure for ourselves."
— (NRM, undated notes, probably '63-'65)

Norman wrestled with a sense of inadequacy, professionally and personally. I suspect this had its roots in his childhood, in relation to a perfectionist father whom he could never please.

"...When we do discover that there is value in us and great decisions to be made then we can begin to make worthy decisions about others. In a real sense then we must come to value our own lives before we can place real value on the lives of others."
— (NRM, Charlotte sermon, 10/60)

He felt the important thing is sowing a seed in faith and not knowing what will happen. The spiritual challenge of the Christian faith is being willing to "pay the price" for our faith and spiritual gifts in joy and humility, and without anxiety for self.

"I have refined thee, but not with silver; I have chosen thee in the furnace of affliction." — Isaiah
— (NRM, Easter sermon, Charlotte, '60)

To Stony Run Friends in 1963, Norman urgently defined

what he felt to be the important distinction between faith and reason, and what the times required. His words now seem prophetic in light of his action at the Pentagon two years later.

"Mankind is rapidly finding it more necessary to meet universal challenges...To meet the ever growing problems of a unifying world we need more vitality than the strictly reasonable approach can offer. The religious life depends not only upon the individual thought processes, but brings to focus on human problems the combined resources of the universe. One might call this the balancing of reason with faith. In the Quaker experience this is essential and has permitted us to enter upon right and creative endeavors when no amount of human reason would have provided enough energy. Without the inspired act no generation resumes the search for love, the source and end of existence."
 – (NRM, Stony Run Meeting Newsletter (9/1/63)

Some personal reflections on sacrifice and self-immolation

Self-sacrifice may be the most extreme form of suffering. When it is freely given for the sake of others, it may be the ultimate form of *caritas*, or love. The Buddha regarded the world of human experience as essentially one of suffering. I believe that suffering (to allow, make room) and sacrifice are at the heart of the universe. They are ways we nurture and preserve one another, bear one another's burdens, tenderly hold each other and our tears. Each time we lovingly give of ourselves for the sake of the world, we sacrifice a little bit. The mystery and wonder is that this can bring joy; that suffering and joy are linked together. Indeed, suffering and sorrow often awaken us to life.

Sacrifice by self-immolation is a strange thing. It is hard for us to comprehend it. It is not part of our culture, but it was part of the culture of Vietnam. In a letter to Dr. Martin Luther King, Jr., in June, 1965, Thich Nhat Hanh, the well known activist Vietnamese Buddhist monk, explained it this way:

"The self-burning of Vietnamese Buddhist Monks in 1963 is somehow difficult for the Western Christian conscience to understand. The press spoke then of suicide, but in essence, it is not. It is not even a protest. What the monks said in the letters they left before burning themselves aimed only at alarming, at moving the heart of the oppressors and at calling the attention of the world to the suffering endured then by the Vietnamese. To burn oneself by fire is to prove that what one is saying is of the utmost importance. There is nothing more painful than burning oneself. To say something while experiencing this kind of pain is to say it with the utmost of courage, frankness, determination and sincerity....

"The importance is not to take one's life, but to burn. What he really aims at is the expression of his will and determination, not death....

"The monk who burns himself has lost neither courage nor hope; nor does he desire non-existence. On the contrary, he is very courageous and hopeful and aspires for something good in the future. He does not think that he is destroying himself; he believes in the good fruition of his act of self-sacrifice for the sake of others. Like the Buddha in one of his former lives – as told in a story of Jataka – who gave himself to a hungry lion which was about to devour her own cubs, the monk believes he is practicing the doctrine of highest compassion by sacrificing himself in order to call the attention of, and to seek help from, the people of the world.

"I believe with all my heart that the monks who burned themselves did not aim at the death of the oppressors but only at a change in their policy. Their enemies are not man. They are intolerance, fanaticism, dictatorship, cupidity, hatred and discrimination which lie within the heart of man."

(Note: this letter was published in France in June, 1965, then in *Liberation* magazine in December of the same year.)

Self-immolation occurs in Christian tradition in the Apostle Paul's famous treatise on caritas-love-charity in his First Letter to the Corinthians, Chapter 13, v. 1-4:

"Though I speak with the tongues of men and of angels and

have not charity, I am become as a sounding brass, or a tinkling cymbal.

"And though I have the gift of prophecy and understand all mysteries, and all knowledge, and though I have all faith, so that I could remove mountains, and have not charity, I am nothing.

"And though I bestow all my goods to feed the poor, and though I give my body to be burned, and have not charity, it profiteth me nothing."

In my Christmas letter of 1965 I shared a passage from T. S. Eliot's *Murder in the Cathedral*, the famous statement of Thomas à Becket shortly before his death:

Thomas:
>You think me reckless, desperate and mad.
>You argue by results, as this world does,
>To settle if an act be good or bad.
>You defer to the fact. For every life and every act
>Consequence of good and evil can be shown.
>And as in time results of many deeds are blended
>So good and evil in the end become confounded.
>It is not in time that my death shall be known;
>It is out of time that my decision is taken
>If you call that decision
>To which my whole being gives entire consent.
>I give my life
>To the Law of God above the Law of Man.
>Those who do not the same
>How should they know what I do?...
>We are not here to triumph by fighting, by
>>stratagem, or by resistance,
>Not to fight with beasts as men. We have fought
>>the beast
>And have conquered. We have only to conquer
>Now, by suffering."

In response to my letter, the former Dean of the Duke Chapel at Duke University wrote to me:

"The other night an advanced class in Preaching was studying T.S. Eliot's *Murder in the Cathedral* for sermonic purposes. I read them the passage which you quoted in your letter to your friends. It brought the play into contemporary life for them as nothing else had done. Moreover, it helped them to understand your husband's action. You and your children are often in my thoughts. I wish there was some specific way in which I could help you. Yet I have the feeling that, if we sat down together, you would help me....God bless you."

In the spring of 1997, I had a memorable experience at Pendle Hill. While on a writing retreat, I was invited to share with the community about Norman and the book I am writing. On Sunday afternoon, some of us met in the library, where I spread on a large table some of the newspaper clippings, articles, letters I received, books, poems and Norm's writings.

I knew I was going to cry during my presentation, but I didn't know how much. Several of us cried, off and on, throughout our time together. These friends encouraged me to tell our story. I began by saying, "I have been frozen with grief for 30 years, and now I am thawing."

Throughout the presentation I noticed a young Vietnamese man, Dat Dutinth, whose wife works at Pendle Hill, holding their beautiful six month old baby boy in his arms on the edge of things, so the baby wouldn't bother us. When the discussion was over Dat came up and told me that he was South Vietnamese, and had been in Saigon when Norman died. He had older brothers in the South Vietnamese Army and he barely escaped the draft before emigrating here in 1969. He had friends who died in the war.

Picking up a copy of the poem, "Emily, My Child," by the Vietnamese poet To Huu, which I had on the table, Dat said, "I once knew this poem. Everyone did. People in South Vietnam were also moved by Norman Morrison's death, not just those in the north. All we knew about America was bombers and bombs and helicopters and soldiers. Then came Norman Morrison, this voice of conscience."

It was a powerful and healing moment for me. The next day, a young Friend present gave me a little note which said:

"I was in college from 1969-1972 and appalled at the Vietnam War. It was a definitive influence on my growing up. But I never knew what to do about it. Your family did for me what I didn't know how to do. Thank you."

Several years ago, I received a loving note from a Friend whom I had met at a Friends Conference on Religion and Psychology. She wrote:

"We hope that all is going well with you. You are with us always, as is Norman...whenever there is the quietness, the staring out the window, the wonder."

Yes, we are together, with the wonder and the mystery. And with acceptance and gratitude.

Now, I am planning to go to Vietnam. Soon after Norman died, I received an official invitation to visit North Vietnam. It was not the right thing for me to go at that time. Over the weeks and months that followed, I received letters and gifts from officials and people in Vietnam, some with invitations to come for a visit. Still, I was not led to go.

Twenty years after the war ended, I had another opportunity to go to Vietnam, in connection with the dedication of a Peace Park, a project supported by a veterans group and the Madison, Wisconsin, Friends Meeting. That was around the time of McNamara's book on Vietnam. I was drawn into national involvement with it and into an emotional upheaval. Although I was tempted to go with Betty Boardman on the Peace Park dedication trip, I was afraid that if I went, I would get sick or cry most the time, so I chose not to go.

Earlier this year, I had another invitation to go to Vietnam, accompanying a World Team Sports bike trek involving disabled Vietnamese and American veterans biking the Ho Chi Minh trail. Although it was a great idea, it didn't feel like the way I should visit Vietnam.

However, it set me to thinking again about the possibility of a trip. I was surprised that I felt as ready as I did about it. I found myself buying a tourist guide to Vietnam. I made some enquiries through the American Friends Service Committee. I talked with my daughters, Emily and Christina, and found they were quite open to a trip.

We decided to wait for Way to open. It did, on Saturday, March 14, 1998, in the mail, in a long white envelope with a return address which read:

> The United States of America
> Official Business, US Embassy
> 7 Lang Ha, Hanoi

Even though I did not know the contents of the letter, I was excited to receive it. With a little smile, I stared at it a while before slitting it open with a knife. Inside was a welcoming letter from Pete Peterson, our US Ambassador to Vietnam, adding his "encouragement to any plan you and your family may have to visit Vietnam."

Peterson was responding to a letter from Rev. Robert Hull of Cleveland, Ohio, a former classmate of Norm's at the College of Wooster, suggesting such a visit. A strong interpreter of Norman's final witness, Hull had taken the initiative on his own to write Peterson during the summer of 1997 suggesting the Embassy invite me to Vietnam. I thought nothing would come of it.

In his letter, Peterson said, "I would look forward to meeting you if you came to Hanoi. As you know, Vietnam and US-Vietnam relations are in a period of tremendous evolution. Daily, we here in the Embassy have the privilege and pleasure of witnessing and facilitating acts of reconciliation, big and small. I hope you will notify me if a visit develops so a meeting could be arranged."

I cannot find the words to describe how happy this letter made me feel. To be welcomed by the United States Ambassador in Vietnam. I felt like cheering and crying at the same time. I put it back in its envelope and kissed it on the return address. Somehow I could feel Norman's presence nearby, smiling.

Why did that letter mean so much? What did it symbolize? Only 33 years of my life. After Norman's death, letters from officials and citizens in North Vietnam were always sent through intermediaries, often Quakers abroad. Because of this need for secrecy and protection, the letters felt somewhat clandestine and contraband. I was afraid to speak of them publicly.

I never received an official letter from my own government after Norman died. Until now. Now that I have received a letter from the top American official in Hanoi, it struck me for the first time, and in a palpable way, that the American Embassy is located in Hanoi, not Saigon! And that the war is really over.

At last, I am ready to go to Vietnam. Now, with the assistance of the American Friends Service Committee's Asian staff, I can go to Vietnam on a mission of personal healing and friendship, not in secret but in the open. To be greeted by the American Ambassador and to meet the Vietnamese people. I want to bow to them in respect and love.

Now I can go. Now I can finish the book on Norman that I have been working on for several years. No doubt, the trip to Vietnam will be the final chapter.

Now I can reclaim my life.

Praise God.

A few years ago in London, I saw the play "Mother Courage and her Children" by Berthold Brecht. Through the hardened, cynical eyes of Mother Courage the underbelly of war is revealed – the greed and corruption that so often lie beneath the honor, glory and idealism of war. If Mother Courage is courageous, it is mainly just by surviving the Thirty Years War – a needless war. Although she survives, the war takes her three children one by one, and she is worn down and finally silenced.

To me, the real heroine of the play is her childlike, mute daughter, Katrin, who climbs on a rooftop and beats a drum to warn a village of the oncoming army. Katrin knows she will be killed by this bold act, but she has a great heart. Her heart – her compassion – was her gift, and she gave it away for the sake of a village.

Like Katrin, like Jesus, some are called to the ultimate sacrifice of their life so that others may live. Parents sometimes do this; soldiers often do this, too.

Norman Morrison gave his life to try to stop the war in Vietnam. He was answering what he considered a divine call, and he was following his conscience.

We are not all called to make the ultimate sacrifice. But we are all called to live sacrificially so as to share our gift of life with others. The question remains, and is always, what will we do with our gift? Where will we stand with our lives? What will we stand for? Who will we stand with?

As peacemakers, we each find our own places to stand. However we do this, I hope we know that we are never standing alone. Others, seen and unseen, are standing with us whenever we are standing for the basic goodness of humankind, which, in the words of the poet Gerard Manley Hopkins is – in spite of everything to the contrary – immortal diamond.

Plenary Presentation:
On Being Conformed to This World:
The Impact of the Vietnam War on
The Religious Society of Friends

Gordon Browne, July 18, 1998

My title refers to a favorite verse of scripture: Romans 12, verse 2, which says in the King James Version, "and be not conformed to this world but be ye transformed by the renewing of your mind, that ye may prove what is that good and acceptable, and perfect, will of God." We Quakers like to comfort, yes, congratulate ourselves with that verse when our tradition or our inspiration causes us to go cross-grain with the ordinary practice in our world. It is my belief, however, that cultural influence is much stronger among us than we realize, and I want us to be aware of that.

Let me illustrate. In 1982, Friends World Committee for Consultation held its Triennial in Kaimosi, Kenya. A young Midwestern Friend, a graduate student whose concern for issues of poverty had led him to make poverty the subject of his studies, persuaded his yearly meeting to send him as a representative to the Triennial. He told me he had never seen Third World poverty and wanted to get some sense of that, too. Six months after our return, I met him and asked him his reaction to Kenya. He said, "Surprise! I had bought into American materialism so completely and so unconsciously that it had never occurred to me that desperately poor people could build communities filled with love and joy."

Again. Friends take pride in their early rejection of slavery and in the stories of the Underground Railroad, where we tend to present as heroes the brave Quaker conductors, rather than the fleeing slaves who were risking everything for freedom. In 1954, the US Supreme Court banned racial segregation in the public schools. At that time, most Quaker schools and some Quaker colleges did not enroll people of color. We are part of American culture. Even peace activists can be shaped by the world around them. Hence my title.

I also wish to say something obvious but important. I am not of the Vietnam generation. I am of the generation that lived through the Depression, through World War II, and that *planned* the Vietnam War. I cannot imagine a sharper break between generations than that between the WWII generation and the Vietnam generation. There was a peculiar, specious kind of logic for us ordinary American WWII folk arriving at Vietnam. With the kind of broad, historical generalization which is always vulnerable to challenge, let me try to explain.

World War II was our "good" war. Except for the lunatic fringe of anarchists, communists, socialists, and pacifists, it united us as a nation as nothing had since World War I. Even the First World War was regarded with distaste. We had to go and save Europe's bacon at the cost of thousands of good men. The parents of my generation spoke of the arms dealers as "merchants of death." US military forces totaled only 200,000 men when, in 1940, faced with the possibility of our involvement in WWII, Congress approved the first peace time draft in our history. But so reluctant was Congress to appropriate any money for the military that the first draftees had to train with wooden rifles because there weren't enough real ones....I am not making this up.

But we were attacked at Pearl Harbor, and in Europe, incredibly, the Nazis were bombing civilians and strafing fleeing refugees and invading peaceful nations with ruthless violence. No civilized people would do such things! We were called to face raw evil in the name of good. Women who had never considered the possibility before, whole communities of Southern black Americans moved into the factories of the North to produce weapons. We all went without meat and sugar and coffee and nylons so that "our boys," as they were always called, would not lack. The nylon was for parachutes, by the way.

I doubt if many who attended the Pendle Hill reunion of WWII pacifists and CPS men fully appreciated how heroic those men had been to stand for conscience's sake against a flood tide of patriotism and war spirit. In Germany, many of the small number of men who refused service for reasons of conscience were put to death. Here, without that threat, CO's felt they had to contribute to human good and the good of the country. They fought forest fires and cared for the mentally ill and took mortal risks in dangerous medical experiments. Alternative service was aptly named.

When the war ended, service men and women were heroes. They went to college under the G.I. Bill, and they came out prepared literally to rebuild the shattered world and, incidentally, to become prosperous doing it. As a people, we Americans were filled with the certainty that human beings could and must learn to live together without war, and we warmly supported the creation of the United Nations, which would repel any future aggression and would provide a vehicle for all nations to cooperate for peace and justice.

The wounded world looked to America, and we confidently accepted the responsibilities of leadership and, when it was challenged, as it soon was by the Soviet Union, the responsibilities of power. It was our responsibility to make the world over in our democratic, capitalist image, and, as we had learned from Hitler, who said we must imitate him to defeat him, we accepted that there might be some ugly, nasty work that had to be done, but we would do it.

We didn't know what was happening to us. Never before a world power, we did not know how addictive and insidiously corrupting the exercise of power and the accumulation of wealth could be. It was a long time before most Americans were able to question the behavior of the nation of which they were so proud. The police action in Korea, in which 33,327 Americans and thousands more Koreans and Chinese and Australians and others died, taught us almost nothing. Twisted idealism, in the form of anti-communism and neo-imperialism, led us and the multi-national force we demanded into Vietnam. Most Americans still believed in our national righteousness. For most of my generation, opposition to the Vietnam War was unpatriotic.

During the Vietnam years, I was teaching at Cape Cod Community College in Massachusetts. I had my first Vietnam veteran as a student while the President of the United States was still saying we had no combat troops in Vietnam. My student had come to college after six months in a military hospital, where he had had a silver plate put in his skull and had another to replace one knee cap. He had been wounded in an exchange of mortar fire with the Viet Cong.

Somehow he heard that I was a Quaker and active in the anti-war movement as a draft counselor and organizer of anti-war activities on our campus. He came to my office to talk about the war. He described going into a village which had been looted and burned by the Viet Cong and finding, trussed to a tree, a young woman, still alive, who had been tortured in hideous ways which he described in detail that I will not repeat here.

He exploded, "When you see something like that, all you want to do is kill the bastards who did it!"

There was a silence filled with pain. Then, incredulously, I heard myself say, "Yes. That's how we deny we are capable of the same cruelty."

I could not believe I had said that. My student turned white. He half rose, and I thought he was going to attack me. Then, he sank back, trembling.

"Oh, God!" he groaned. "No one ever said that to me before. But it's true, isn't it?"

George Fox spoke of the ocean of darkness, of God's requiring him through temptations to come to understand all conditions of men that he might also know the infinite love of God, the ocean of love that covered that darkness. The journals of early Friends are full of their suffering as the Light showed them the darkness in themselves. Other Friends upheld them while they struggled in tears and in prayers till at last, miraculously, the same Light revealed the path out of darkness.

I taught scores of veterans over the years that followed.

With rare exceptions, they were wounded men, struggling with nightmares and alcohol and drugs. They knew the darkness. It is heartening that increasing numbers are returning to Vietnam in various services of expiation and, in time, reconciliation. The first time they came home, peaceniks spat on them and called them baby-killers. Not Friends, I hope, though we were not immune to cruel self-righteousness.

But isn't it remarkable and sad how confidently we divide the world into "us" and "them," even when our own deepest religious insights show us that in the eyes of God there is no "them," only a large, diverse "us"? I am not aware of any Quaker effort to assist the healing of Vietnam veterans, though, thank God, many Friends and Quaker organizations have worked for the healing of their Vietnamese victims.

Like most teachers, I carry many of my students with me all the time: the ones who thrilled me with their accomplishments, the ones who challenged me to be what I claimed to be, the ones who fed me hope as I saw apparently blighted lives made productive by their courageous efforts. I pray for the many Vietnam veterans I knew that they have found peace and redemption from what my generation in its ignorant hubris made them do.

But I am meant to talk about the effect of Vietnam on Friends. Others present have already spoken or soon will speak of many of those effects: the voyages of the *Phoenix*, Quaker service at Quang Ngai, the sacrifice of Norman Morrison, Quaker draft counseling, and many other expressions of our hunger for peace. I don't need to duplicate that.

I find it impossible, however, to be confident about a great number of cause-effect relationships between the Vietnam War and developments in our Religious Society. I believe, for example, that the Faith and Life Movement, initiated in 1970 by Evangelical Friends to see if there were any religious principles on which all Friends could unite, was a very important, influential Quaker event. A number of fine booklets on basic religious themes came out of it. Two national gatherings and a number of regional conferences brought together Quakers of all traditions to explore their faith. The

New Call to Peacemaking, which has linked Friends, Brethren, and Mennonites on peace issues, grew out of it. I cannot see, however, that it was shaped by or related to Vietnam.

Yet, as I have been saying, we are shaped not only by our faith but also in part and mostly unconsciously by the world around us. Those influences are difficult to identify, but we are all subject to them. I am going to use some historical bookends, therefore, two Quaker events, and try to discern changes and developments between them.

In 1967, Friends World Committee for Consultation held the Fourth World Conference of Friends at Guilford College in Greensboro, NC, USA. Nearly 1,000 official representatives from 35 nations were present. The three representatives named by the Friends Meetings in East Germany were not present, having been denied visas by the United States government. Another 1,000 or more Friends who were not official representatives gathered at the so-called "Greensboro Gathering" off campus for their own programs and joined the World Conference at the large, public events.

Clyde A. Milner, President of Guilford College, had carried invitations from North Carolina Yearly Meeting and the Trustees of Guilford College to the FWCC Triennial meeting held in Kaimosi, Kenya in August, 1961, inviting FWCC to bring the World Conference to Greensboro.

The invitations were not well received. European Friends made clear they would not attend a Quaker conference held in a Quaker institution which had been racially segregated since it first opened in 1837. Thomas Lung'aho, however, a leader at the Kenyan Quaker Mission and, later, first Superintendent of East Africa Yearly Meeting, suggested that accepting an invitation might strengthen those in the United States who were committed to racial equality. Helpfully, if somewhat ambiguously, FWCC accepted the invitation, "if way should open."

Clyde Milner carried the message back, and at its October 1961 meeting, the Guilford Board of Trustees, after many hours of painful discussion, set aside local tradition and personal feelings any of them might have had and announced their intention to begin the integration of the College at once. Between then and the Conference, FWCC sent Clyde Milner and his wife on a year-long visit to Friends all around the world to offer in person the invitation to come to North Carolina.

During the Conference, a Friend from India was refused service in a Greensboro barber shop. As might be expected, a number of Friends wanted to confront that issue with a public demonstration. Carolina Friends pleaded with them to allow them, who would have to continue to live in the community after we all had left, to deal with it. In 1960, the first lunch counter sit-ins had taken place in Greensboro and brought the KKK marching through their streets. Quakers should not invite such trouble again.

There was one other concession to local sensibilities. There was a powerful wish at the Conference to have some sort of public witness for peace in Vietnam. Local Friends feared public reaction to a demonstration in the streets and persuaded the organizers to hold their demonstration on campus. So for one day, the walks of the Guilford College campus were lined with Friends in silent meditation. Quakers were respectable, and most US Friends valued that respectability.

U Thant, the Burmese Secretary-General of the United Nations, had been invited to speak at a meeting open to the public. He came, and in that place made his first public denunciation of the Vietnam War. In deep worship sessions, the huge body of Friends was moved to call for those of us in the affluent North to tax ourselves 1 percent of our total incomes for development in the impoverished nations of the world, hoping by our example to move our governments to more generous response to the needs of others. This was the birth of the Right Sharing of World Resources Program and of Partnership for Productivity, a program devised by David Scull of Baltimore Yearly Meeting to provide training and guidance in self-help programs in the developing nations.

The latter program was so successful that it soon spread from Kenya, where David started it, all over Africa and elsewhere. Its success brought US AID money, which funded it growth. Later, when Congress legislated that all private programs using AID funds must have at least 20 percent of their income from private sources, there were not enough Quaker contributions to keep the program alive.

Out of the many special interest groups at the World Conference, some concerns made their way to the plenary sessions. The Conference adopted a number of powerful minutes. A long one on the Peace Testimony and Peace Making said, "Our peace testimony is under Divine compulsion," and listed ways both to say "NO" to war and to say "YES" to peace. In saying "NO", Friends were encouraged to engage in nonviolent ways of correcting injustice, whether political, racial, or economic. Further, Friends were to consider "the implications of our employment, our investments, our standards of living, our payment of taxes, as they relate to war-making." They were urged to refuse participation in armed forces and, where there was conscription, to be conscientious objectors or to refuse to register. Civil disobedience in work for peace was identified as part of the Quaker tradition. The section on saying "YES" to peace was longer than the one on saying "NO" to war and emphasized building a community of nations and strengthening the rule of law in international affairs. It called for universal and complete disarmament and international efforts to meet human needs. It said, "...political solutions must be consistent with moral and spiritual truth."

This was not a report from a tiny workshop. This was a minute adopted in plenary session by the representatives of Friends from all over the world. It was the Religious Society of Friends speaking strongly out of its understandings of the Christian faith. For that was another reality of that World Conference. Friends were a Christian body, and there was no doubt of it. Today's boring arguments between universalist and Christian Quakers were still ahead in our individualistic future. Divided as we were even then into liberal, orthodox, and evangelical yearly meetings with various manifestations of each and quarrels between us, we were yet a Christian denomination.

For me, as for many others, the Fourth World Conference

of Friends was a life-changing experience. I heard Betty Boardman describe the voyage of the *Phoenix*. When I learned they were recruiting crew for further voyages, I immediately volunteered but was not chosen to go.

I had a conversation with two French Friends that haunts me yet. They had been helping escaping Jews. The local Gestapo chief had been fed by Quakers after WWI and gratefully sought out local Friends and tried to befriend them. On the day the order came to round up all Jews, he led a squad house to house, searching every room. At the Friends' house where there were at that time Jews in transit, he said to his squad, "We don't have to search here. These are Quakers. They don't lie." Then, turning to the Friends, he said, "Are there any Jews in your house?"

Breathlessly, I said, "What did you say?"

They looked astonished. "We said 'no,' of course." Then seeing my expression, they said, "We felt a clear conscience was a luxury we could not afford at that time."

I, never tested as they had been, dared not speak, but the slippery slope of expediency and relativism stretched before me. Their terrible dilemma has remained with me ever since.

The press had been invited to cover all sessions of the conference, including our large meetings for worship. Let me read part of a story written by John Knox of the *Greensboro Daily News* which appeared on Sunday, August 6 – Hiroshima Day – 1967.

> It was so simple, so overwhelmingly powerful, anyone who heard will never forget. Surely it is marked for memory as long as anyone on earth cares about fellow creatures.
>
> It happened during a silent worship of Quakers who had come to Greensboro from four corners of the world to talk to each other. A few more than 1,000 of them were in the resplendent Dana Auditorium.
>
> They had just finished singing a stately hymn, 'Breathe on Me, Breath of God,' and the hall was silent.
>
> It was a Quaker silence, quite unlike any I had ever known in a church. For all the vast gathering of people, there

was no sound – a quiet of unbelievable quietness.

The Quakers were at worship in their traditional manner. I can't remember how long it lasted. It may have been for a moment. It could have been ten times that long.

Then the silence was consumed by a voice from somewhere among the thousand, powerful, charged with emotion, praying:

"I am a Negro in a ghetto.
I cannot hear you!
I am a burned child in Vietnam.
I cannot hear you!
I am a mother in a South American slum.
I cannot hear you!
I am a soldier in Vietnam under orders to kill.
I just don't hear you!"

For all the millions of words the Quakers exchanged during their conference and the tens of thousands they put to paper none told so well what they were talking about than these few.

Just who did they think they were, anyway, this handful of presumptuous people, assuming responsibility for sufferers of all the calculated cruelties people inflict on people?

Why, there are more Baptists in North Carolina alone than Quakers in all the world!

During days I met with them to report a very few of their doings, I came to see them as a small band of conspirators, sensitive, well-informed, articulate, extraordinarily intelligent, tough-minded, opinionated, fussing among themselves to live their preachments, needling the conscience of the world to be about the business of the Sermon on the Mount.

Most astonishing of all, they were being heard and attended to from humblest home to highest council of state. What they say is historically so profoundly respected that, among religions, perhaps only the Pope commands as much respect.

One small measure of their worldwide prestige was the appearance here of U Thant. Effectively, this Burmese Buddhist, whose United Nations voice is never unattended, was only an extension of their own voice crying out for goodwill and peace on earth.

They invited him. He accepted. Could Baptists, Presbyterians, Methodists or whoever have gotten him to Greensboro? Would they have thought to ask? Would they have wanted him?

* * * * *

A fundamental Quaker preachment is that the way one lives must reflect the Christian way in all things. "Let your lives speak." That's a tough one to abide, and perhaps accounts, in part, for their small numbers.

In our day, it just won't do, loving a neighbour as you love yourself, especially if the neighbour is ignorant, black and needs a bath, or even if he is educated, black and sponges off now and then.

It occurred that these Quakers must be dreadfully embarrassing to Christians.

They must also be embarrassing to governments who surely wish they would just hush up and go away.

One wonders how many Quakers would be in jail for giving aid and comfort to the enemy (in an amazing variety of ways) if the United States would declare an official "war" against North Vietnam.

This police action we're in gives the Quakers a license of sorts to do and say what they want to. At least not many of them have gone to jail yet.

Thus they say the jungle war has solved and will solve nothing, an idea many an American is buying in sober agonizing silence, and thus he is asked to break silence and demand the government bring an end to the war. Just stop fighting.

John Knox did not report, perhaps did not know, of the few, ugly things that happened in Greensboro. The representatives from Central America Yearly Meeting based in Chiquimula, Guatemala, attending their first international gathering of Quakers, were told by some patronizing, liberal Friend that they were, of course, not real Quakers because they had pastors and their only Yearly Meeting programs were evangelism and discipleship training. It was another ten years before Guatemalan Friends attended an international Quaker gathering again and thirty years before they chose to affiliate with FWCC. In 1984, when I visited in Chiquimula with one of their representatives to Greensboro, I heard still of her hurt and anger.

My other bookend is the World Gathering of Young Friends in 1985. But first, I must look at some developments between them. For example, we've heard about humanitarian aid to North Vietnam being sent through Canada. In New England Yearly Meeting in 1967, the Peace and Social Concerns Committee proposed that the Yearly Meeting send $150.00 to Canadian Friends for such aid. The Yearly Meeting program was put on hold while this issue was debated for ten hours in business sessions. At the end of that time, the minute said we were unable to unite on the Committee's recommendation, but individual Friends were encouraged to consider what they might be led to do.

Basic to Quaker understanding of God is that there is neither place nor ritual nor formula needed for us human beings to meet the Divine. When we build a church or meetinghouse, we do not expect that place to be especially sanctified, even though many of us find our worship in a familiar place and fellowship richer than elsewhere.

Vietnam, however, reminded some Friends of the ancient religious tradition that treated houses of worship as places of sanctuary. The Old Testament makes provision for cities of sanctuary where persons guilty of blood crimes may be safe from revenge. In medieval days, similar protection was traditionally provided within a church. In Vietnam days a number of meetings took refugees from the military into their buildings, offering not protection from arrest but a community of support through the trials they would face. And Friends were led into experiences they hardly anticipated. The entire social revolution of the period, in dress, in sexual behavior, in drug use, in music, in rhetoric, in attitude was suddenly at their doors.

In Atlanta Meeting several soldiers appealed for "sanctuary." Atlanta Monthly Meeting offered them "hospitality and moral support" and set nonviolence and no secrecy as conditions of their offer. In Pasadena, California, three members of the armed forces who wished to "resign" sought sanctuary. Orange Grove Monthly Meeting wrote to the Marine Corps commandant: "In no sense is the Meeting attempting to interfere with due process of law...or concealing fugitives from justice."

The Meeting offered hospitality. Food was brought in. The three men and their supporters took over the meetinghouse. People slept – and made love – on the Meeting benches. The meetinghouse rang with their music.

But the Meeting valiantly affirmed, "Beyond discussions, beyond the bongos and rock music, beyond the problems of life style, there has emerged a strange and beautiful community, a community of the concerned. Young people who had rejected the church and religion have found a new dynamic in the silent worship; they have discovered Quakerism."

One of the men, Timothy Springer, asked to be married under the care of the Meeting. He was arrested and put in the stockade before that could happen. Friends attended his court-martial. When the court adjourned for the day, Friends gathered in the open air outside for worship. During the worship, attended by military guards, the couple was married. The prosecuting officer was present and wished them happiness. The next day, Timothy Springer was found guilty of desertion and given a dishonorable discharge.

The most prolonged and, in some ways, the most interesting of these events occurred in Cambridge Meeting in Massachusetts. The meetinghouse is located in Longfellow Park, across the street from the famous poet's home, a short walk from Harvard

Square, and shares the park with some fine homes and a Mormon church. Frederick Rutan, called Eric, AWOL from the Army for two months because he could not in conscience obey his orders to report for shipment to Vietnam, asked for help from New England Resistance, a group committed to "moral opposition with physical obstruction." Somewhat surprisingly, the Resistance brought Eric to Cambridge Friends.

The expectation was that once Eric came out of hiding he would be arrested immediately. Cambridge Friends invited him, his mother, and his girlfriend Janet to join them in Sunday morning worship. Resistance members attended, too. They had wanted to chain themselves to Eric, but the Quakers didn't want that in their meetinghouse. Friends did not intend to interfere with Eric's arrest. At the normal hour for closing meeting, the Clerk rose and announced Eric's presence and the expectation of his arrest. Worship would continue uninterrupted till that arrest occurred. Eric made a brief, grateful statement.

Word spread throughout Harvard Square of what was happening, and Longfellow Park soon swarmed with bare feet, long hair, guitars, etc. A few Friends went around the park explaining to worried neighbors what was going on. Others picked up the trash already accumulating. The worship continued all afternoon. Ministry asked whether Friends could really help Eric and the seeking young people gathering there.

The police did not come. Worshipers came and went as their schedules demanded. Food was brought in, and that night Eric was bedded down on a cot in the AFSC clothing room in the basement of the meetinghouse. Shifts of Friends sat at the end of the driveway to greet the police when they came. Worship continued all night.

Morning newspaper stories brought people from all over. Ministers, nuns, rabbis, people of no religion filled the meetinghouse benches. Of that time, Daisy Newman wrote, "The passionate longing for peace that hung over the country had found a focus." Strangers brought in heaps of food. Hungry people showed up at mealtime and were fed. Parents brought their children to experience deep worship. The police did not come.

On the tenth morning, the Soviet invasion of Czechoslovakia was reported, adding a further dimension to the event. More than protest was needed to overcome evil.

By the third week, there were fewer hands to do the work, more mouths to feed, yet mealtimes were rich with joyful community. Once, the meeting for worship got down to a single person, a Unitarian woman whose son was applying for CO status.

At 11:00 a.m. on August 29th, the 18th day, the Friend waiting at the end of the driveway saw an unmarked car drive up. It had to be the police, but he had prepared nothing to say to them.

The officers asked if Frederick Rutan were there.

He said, "Yes."

They showed him a warrant for Eric's arrest.

The Friend said, "He's in the meetinghouse. I'll take you in. But we've been holding a meeting for worship for the past eighteen days and nights. Won't you allow us five minutes to finish it up?" At the door, he said, "Won't you come in and join us?"

The officers sat in the back row. Eric was once more on the facing bench, Janet on one side of him, a Friend on the other. After a moment, the Executive Secretary of the meeting rose and spoke of Friends' willingness to suffer rather than to kill anyone, since to kill a person was to kill a part of God in his Creation.

At length, the officers walked forward and handed Eric the warrant. He stood and walked out with them. The worship continued for another fifteen minutes. Then the Friends shook hands.

Eric was sentenced to six months in the stockade. He had applied for CO status, which was not granted. With the completion of his sentence, however, he was assigned to non-combatant duty. On a weekend pass, he and Janet were married.

I am convinced that in these witnesses to the claims of common humanity was born the concept of the Sanctuary movement, which later cared for Latin American refugees. I can't prove that. I do know, however, that Canadian Friends, having learned to greet with compassion and care the wandering US refugees from the Vietnam War, deserters and draft dodgers, far from home and families, readily transferred those lessons in caring to the refugees from brutal Latin American regimes and brutal US policy there. So did Friends in Mexico City. And many a Latin American Sanctuary resident was, in fact, en route from caring Mexicans to caring Canadians, by way of caring Friends Meetings in the US.

The Quaker acceptance of the troubled young people resisting the war had other far-reaching effects. Some asked to join Friends, thinking Quakerism was some kind of peace movement, and Friends welcomed them without ever letting them know who we are and what our traditions and religious experiences have been. Individualistic youth set out to make their meetings over in their own images, and some Friends, in the name of tolerance, let it happen. Neither Friends nor their new members were fulfilled by that experience, where meeting discipline and accountability to a community disappeared. Others, however, had glimpsed something they desperately wanted in their insecure world. Membership statistics for the late sixties and seventies show the largest increase in membership in decades, especially in the unprogrammed meetings where the young had more room to find their ways at their own pace.

It was not just "their own ways" these new members wanted. They hungered for more, for God's way, and struggled to find it. In 1985, A World Gathering of Young Friends took place, once again in Greensboro. Liberal Friends, conservative Friends, evangelical Friends – British, European, Latin American, African, Australian, Asian Friends – all were there. They labored with one another and shocked one another and suffered with one another and fought with one another. And some were humbled by what they discovered about themselves and their pale Quakerism, and were opened to new growth. Others were ratified in their devotion to Truth and in their hunger to grow in it. And an incredible community of faith was formed. Out of that Gathering came an epistle which is surely one of the most remarkable and profound documents of modern Quakerism. Let me quote:

"We have often wondered whether there is anything Quakers today can say as one. After much struggle we have

discovered that we can proclaim this: There is a living God at the center of all, who is available to each of us as a present teacher at the very heart of our lives. We seek as people of God to be worthy vessels to deliver the Lord's transforming word, to be prophets of joy who know from experience and can testify to the world as George Fox did, 'that the Lord is at work in this thick night.' Our priority is to be receptive and responsible to the life-giving Word of God...which is available to each of us who seek the Truth. This can be made easier if we face the truth within ourselves, embrace the pain, and lay down our differences before God for the Holy Spirit to forgive, thus transforming us into instruments of healing."
Amen!

As I near the end of this exploration, it appears to me that my title, which was given to me out of prayer last winter, was given to me to warn against the attractive temptation of self-righteousness which so often afflicts religious people. There were plenty of examples during the Vietnam era. Perhaps one of the ugliest was the action of some Eastern Friends in writing to East Whittier Friends Church, where Richard Nixon's name remained on the membership list, demanding he be disowned, as if that Meeting were unable to conduct its own responsibility to its members without their advice.

My title was also to warn us against being conformed to the world without our knowing it. The telephone tax, assessed specifically to pay for the Vietnam War, prompted many Friends to refuse it and led a number to become military tax refusers of their income taxes as well. When their funds were seized and interest and penalties added, some of them decided to return to paying their taxes, since the government was going to get their money anyway. They were, perhaps, conformed to the values of this world. Military tax refusal is not about money. It is about witness.

World War II CO's had withstood overwhelming popular pressure to take a lonely stance which God seemed to require of them. It seemed inevitable to many, then, that they could not return to ordinary, selfish pursuits when the war ended. They continued to feel the Divine prod to be healers of human suffering, to seek new ways to justice, peace, and Truth. They became leaders in Quaker service and Quaker witness. In ministry and mission, they called all Friends, all the world, to the pursuit of God's Truth and the fullness of life it promises.

What of the Vietnam generation of CO's, of birthright Quakers and new Friends, of rebels and individualists, of Baez fans and Deadheads? Can the world, can the Religious Society of Friends, look to them for leadership in these harsh times?

Some have already accepted such responsibility. Others are ready, awaiting it. But where will they lead? My crystal ball is as murky as ever. I dare not predict. But I am struck by their rising calls for community, for their demands for accountability to that community. I see them exploring deeply the practices and the truths of the past and experimenting hopefully with new avenues to spiritual understanding and guidance. I believe they are being faithful to the promise they made to themselves a dozen years ago at the World Gathering of Young Friends when they said in their epistle:

"Our five invited speakers presented vivid pictures of economic, ecological, and military crisis in this world today. We acknowledge that these crises are in fact a reflection of the great spiritual crisis which underlies them all. Our peace testimony inspires us, yet we must move beyond it to challenge our world with the call for justice. We are called to be peacemakers, not protesters.

"It is our desire to work cooperatively on unifying these points. The challenges of this time are almost too great to be faced, but we must let our lives mirror what is written on our hearts – to be so full of God's love that we can do no other than to live our corporate testimonies to the world of honesty, simplicity, equality, and peace, whatever the consequence."

Amen, amen, amen!

Plenary Presentation:
From Protest to Resistance – The Quaker Peace Testimony
During the Vietnam War

Jeremy Mott

July 18, 1998

I'm going to start out with two quotations that I hope we will keep in mind during this speech.

First, "We are not for names nor men, nor titles of Government, nor are we for this party nor against the other...but we are for justice and mercy and truth and peace and true freedom that these may be exalted in our nation, and that goodness, righteousness, meekness, temperance, peace and unity with God, and with one another, that these things may abound."

Who wrote that? Of course it was a Friend – Edward Burrough, in 1659, when this Puritan stalwart was changing by necessity from a highly political revolutionary to a more spiritual, but still highly political, revolutionary – a Friend in today's sense.

I took the quotation from the letterhead of Quaker House of Fayetteville, NC, which – quite fittingly, I think – is the only soldier's coffeehouse project of the Vietnam era to survive until the present day. It makes a difference to have a peace testimony. Even if that testimony does change sometimes.

Second – and I hope you'll recite this with me:

"The Lord is my shepherd, I shall not want;
He makes me lie down in green pastures.
He leads me beside still waters, he restores my soul.

He leads me in paths of righteousness for his name's sake.
Even though I walk through the valley of the shadow of death,
I fear no evil; for Thou art with me;
thy rod and thy staff, they comfort me.
Thou preparest a table before me in the presence of my enemies;
Thou anointest my head with oil, my cup overflows.
Surely goodness and mercy shall follow me all the days of my life;
and I shall dwell in the house of the Lord forever."

When I first heard the great civil rights leader Bob Moses introduce a talk with the 23rd Psalm, a year ago in New York City, the audience was mostly non-religious pacifists from the War Resisters League, and few could recite the psalm. I'm glad that Quakers can do a little better.

But all joking aside, please keep these two passages in mind. Partisanship, and fear – both surely of the very essence of war – played central roles in the making of the Quaker Peace Testimony and in its remaking during the Vietnam War. Even though I rarely refer to these matters, I always have them in mind.

Are Friends ready for a leap of faith? Maybe the Quaker Peace Testimony can best be described as God's method, or a collection of methods, given to Friends for countering partisanship and fear. Because these are God's methods, they work if used for their intended purpose. We can and must spread this knowledge.

Yet we can't spread knowledge about the Quaker Peace Testimony if we don't know it ourselves. As we unknowingly approached the Vietnam War, way back in the fifties and early sixties, what was the Quaker Peace Testimony?

It was a collection of ideas and attitudes that often seemed not to fit together very well. It still is a miscellany of this kind. In the marvelous description that Chel Avery, the organizer of this conference, provided in 1995 at the first Quaker Peace Roundtable, the Quaker Peace Testimony was described as a "Questing Beast."

(Her essay is found in the collection *A Continuing Journey,* edited by Chuck Fager and published by Pendle Hill, 1996.) The original Questing Beast, in the King Arthur legends, has "the head of a serpent, the body of a lizard, the haunches of a lion, and the feet of a deer" as well as the bark of sixty hounds. A very improbable creature. A strange mess.

When I first read about this Questing Beast in Chel's 1995 paper, I laughed aloud. Finally someone had properly described our peace testimony. Quakerism has many theological messes, but the peace testimony may be the biggest mess of all.

Right from its beginning (or "crystallization") in 1660-61, the Quaker Peace Testimony consisted of at least five major parts, some of them hardly compatible with others.

First, and most urgently needed in the early Restoration days, the Quaker Peace Testimony was a statement of Quaker non-participation in, and opposition to, violent revolution or secret "subversive" activity of any kind. In the slightly abridged version of the long original peace testimony in the Nickalls edition of George Fox's *Journal*, at least three-quarters of the material is repetitive statements of our non-complicity in violent revolution.

Of course! Other Puritan revolutionary groups that still existed in the early reign of Charles II were plotting and revolting against the monarchy, and Quakers had to clear themselves from any involvement (and any suspicion of involvement) in this activity if they were to survive the consequent repression. George Fox, Margaret Fell, and Richard Hubberthorne, along with other leading Friends, saw this clearly and wrote this testimony. Even our Friend Edward Burrough was compelled by good sense to go along with the peace testimony statement of January 1661, despite his radical Puritan sympathies, though he didn't sign it. There were other Friends like him.

All this poses an obvious question: why didn't the original Quaker Peace Testimony simply oppose violent revolution, and say nothing else? Certainly some Friends would have chosen this course.

This leads us to the second of the major purposes of the

first Quaker Peace Testimony. Friends were then engaged in one of the greatest – maybe the greatest – campaigns of nonviolent civil disobedience which we have ever engaged in. This was the struggle for religious freedom in Massachusetts, which had already cost the lives of four Friends and had (and would) subject countless Friends to imprisonment, whippings, and tortures and punishments of many kinds.

(I know of nothing more similar to this campaign than the great campaigns of the civil rights movement of the 1950's and the 1960's, in which many Friends were engaged. In each case there were hometown agitators and outside agitators, and there were distant safe bases where supplies and money could be gathered, newcomer agitators trained, and sufferers helped to recover. Rhode Island, with freedom of religion already established and a large Quaker population, was the major distant base for the Quaker campaign against Massachusetts.)

To their everlasting credit, the Quaker leaders who wrote and published the first Quaker Peace Testimony put their support for nonviolent civil disobedience right into the document, where it is quite prominent. So we have the second original part of our Quaker Peace Testimony: nonviolent civil disobedience for religious liberty or against intolerable injustice of any kind. One can hardly conceive of a Quaker Peace Testimony without nonviolent civil disobedience, any more than a Gandhian pacifism without it.

The third major element of our original peace testimony is harder to find, though it's very strong, beneath the surface. The Quaker Peace Testimony was issued only a year after the Restoration of Charles II to the throne. The years from 1640 to 1660 had been filled with civil wars, plots and counter-plots, changes in Parliament, the execution of King Charles I, changes in the established church – the Church of England was Presbyterian for a time – and the rise and fall of various radical sects – Quakers being one of these. All sorts of religious and political groups had tried to establish their version of the Kingdom of Heaven by force of arms, and none had succeeded in establishing anything but chaos, destruction, and suffering. Quakers, in the England of 1661, partly by God's

Providence, partly by the wisdom of George Fox, were the one religious group not implicated in the years of savage warfare.

Yet English Quakers, like practically all English men and women in 1661, must have been terribly disillusioned, disheartened and even cynical about war and the zealotry associated with war. General disgust with war remains an extremely important part of our peace testimony to this day, and connects us with sensible and humane people of all politics and all religions. Imagine how important their disgust with war must have been to the English Quakers of the 1660's. This disgust may have enabled Quakers to survive and grow among a people who had turned their backs on Puritanism of all other forms.

Now, everyone here knows, or should know, what the fourth – and certainly most important – element of our original peace testimony is. Christ forbids violence and war. The Christ of history says this repeatedly, especially in the Sermon on the Mount and, by example, in his crucifixion. The resurrected Christ, the Spirit of Christ, Christ Within (if you prefer a Quaker phrase) says no to violence and war whenever anyone (or any group) will sit still and listen to Him. And for those who do not know the Spirit of Christ by name, or do not believe in Him, God will still send a powerful message of love and nonviolence, if they will only listen for it.

I note that Christian and religious pacifism of this sort is not and cannot be entirely rational. Whenever we try to think rationally about violence and war, though we know that these are great evils, we come up with exceptional cases where violence and war seem to be rational and justified. Loving one's enemies does not seem always to be possible for a rational person. The Voice of the Inward Light, saying we must love enemies and never go to war, is truly supernatural or at least spiritual, as early Friends said. It is the Voice of God and the Spirit of Christ, our best window on God.

This all-important Christian pacifism in our peace testimony, present from its beginning, unites the Society of Friends with those other Christian churches that actually follow, or attempt to follow, the teachings of Christ concerning war: The Catholic Church before the Emperor Constantine, the Mennonites and Hutterites, the Church of the Brethren, the Jehovah's Witnesses and Christadelphians. It also unites us with many millions of Christians of all denominations who believe in pacifism although their denominations do not. It is positive proof that the Society of Friends is a Christian church, even though some of our more liberal meetings admit non-Christians into membership.

Paradoxically, our pacifism also unites us with all the other Inner Light religions of the world, for most of these also believe in nonviolence (or something close to it): Taoism, many kinds of Buddhism, several forms of Hinduism and Islam, and doubtless other Inner Light faiths I have never heard of.

Most important, because we know our peace testimony is not really ours, but an assignment from God, we have the strength to live out its difficult demands. George Fox had a prison term extended for half a year in 1650, simply because he wouldn't be a soldier. Conscientious objection's recorded history in North America probably begins with Quakers in Maryland about 1658. The first conscientious objector law in North America – probably the first such law in the English speaking world – thus the granddaddy of all conscientious objector laws in the world today – was enacted in 1673 by a Rhode Island Quaker government at war, for the benefit of Quaker and other conscientious objectors. Quakers in America pioneered war tax refusal during the Revolutionary War, and a few years earlier Pennsylvania Quakers ran their province successfully without an army for more than 70 years. A few years ago, six Friends in Burundi were martyred for offering refuge to both Hutus and Tutsis.

"Ordinary" – I'll put that word in quotation marks – prophetic protest against war, as well as conscientious objection, has also kept Friends busy since our early days. One should note that the larger society requires a sense of the meeting for one activity: war. If a nation tries to conduct a war for any significant length of time without consensus among its own citizens, trouble, big trouble, lies ahead. This happened during the Vietnam War.

Yet I am getting ahead of myself now. For most of our history, like true prophets, Friends have spoken the truth in war protest, as God gave it to them, without worrying too much about effectiveness.

It's easy to see how these four elements of the Quaker Peace Testimony sometimes work against each other. For example, it's hard psychologically to be completely opposed to violent revolution and also support nonviolent revolution. Though I've described the Questing Beast quite differently from the way Chel Avery describes it – maybe one must expect different people to describe a Questing Beast quite differently – I've certainly described a Questing Beast. Yet the strangest element is still to come.

The Quaker Peace Testimony is the one thing in Quakerism that, we are told, will never change. Read the original document: "That the spirit of Christ, by which we are guided, is not changeable, so as once to command us from a thing as evil and again to move unto it; and we do certainly know, and so testify to the world, that the spirit of Christ, which leads us into all Truth, will *never* (my emphasis) move us to fight and war against any man with outward weapons, neither for the Kingdom of Christ, nor for the Kingdoms of the world." (That's from the Nickalls edition of Fox's *Journal*.)

Because of this statement, the peace testimony is the most permanent part of our ever-changing Spirit-guided religion. Yearly meetings – most of them – have abandoned silent worship. Several yearly meetings have explicitly downplayed the Inward Light, almost to the point of denying it. Yet we read that no yearly meeting, even if virtually none of its members are pacifists, has ever repudiated the Quaker Peace Testimony. To do so would be to write oneself out of Quakerism, to disown oneself – all because this would contradict a declaration made by a handful of Friends in 1660.

Of course, supposedly unchangeable human creations have a way of changing. Within thirteen years of 1660, the Quaker Peace Testimony had grown a new limb, as it were: Friends would endeavor to prevent wars by bringing about the settlement of disputes by peaceful diplomatic methods. In 1673, Nicholas Easton – the same Quaker governor of Rhode Island who approved the first conscientious objector legislation in North America – made desperate last-ditch attempts to prevent King Philip's war by initiating negotiations between colonists and American Indians.

More successfully, in 1682 William Penn and other Friends who settled Pennsylvania with him negotiated the Treaty of Shackamaxon with the Pennsylvania Indians. William Penn and John Bellers made early proposals for leagues of nations, and countless out-of-power Quakers have quietly lobbied against war and militarism with their own governments.

I call this new part of the still-young Quaker Peace Testimony the "upper-crust peace testimony" or, less invidiously, the "closed-door peace witness." It seems a slight addition to the original, but surely adds an emphasis on effectiveness largely absent from the original Quaker Peace Testimony.

In the late 1700's and 1800's Quakers gradually created one of the largest and most important parts of our Peace Testimony: the testimony of service. Some Friends believe that our testimony of service is or should be separated from our peace testimony. However in history and in the hearts and minds of Friends and friends of Friends and the world at large, the service testimony is intimately joined to the peace testimony, and this is how I will treat it. It is noteworthy that the testimony of service, like several other parts of the Quaker Peace Testimony, is little-mentioned in Faith and Practice books. Don't you think these books might be made current as of 1790 or 1870?

One reads that large-scale Quaker service, involving relief to the general population (not just other Friends), began in Boston during the Revolutionary War. I believe that large-scale volunteer relief and rescue became the Quaker norm – or at least the North American Quaker norm – during the time of the Underground Railroad (which is said to have been operated mainly by Quakers and free African Americans.) During the Civil War and Reconstruction, Northern Friends mounted an enormous relief campaign among the newly freed slaves in the South. (One can read about this in Linda Selleck's wonderful book, *Gentle Invaders*.) British Friends did extensive relief work during the Boer War and earlier.

One may say, without fear of contradiction, that war relief work, sometimes extended into other volunteer service to sufferers, was an integral part of the Quaker Peace Testimony by the turn of the 20th century.

Our Peace Testimony had one additional noteworthy change in the mid-1800's: we subtracted the previous expectation that every Friend would be a conscientious objector if called for military service or required to perform certain other war duties (such as loyalty oaths). In the Civil War, a young male Friend could obey the conscription law and serve in the Union army without much fear of being disowned, and half of them did so (it is said), making only perfunctory acknowledgment in many cases. It is difficult to see how either Quakerism or the Quaker Peace Testimony could have survived any continued attempt to compel young Friends to live by the Quaker Peace Testimony.

The domain of the Questing Beast deserves a brief description. The Quaker Peace Testimony is the peace testimony of the entire Quaker movement and, almost without change, of pacifists in the "mainline" Protestant churches. In other words, our peace testimony is also the peace testimony of pacifist Episcopalians and Presbyterians and Methodists. Furthermore, Jewish pacifists generally adopt the Quaker Peace Testimony with only slight changes.

Of course, Mennonites have a peace testimony that is distinctly their own, as do Jehovah's Witnesses. Roman Catholic pacifists, still few in number as the Vietnam War approached, have a peace testimony slightly more radical than Friends'. Gandhians and Buddhists, also not numerous in the US as the Vietnam War approached, have still another peace testimony, also highly influenced by Friends. The Muslim peace testimony was as yet unknown outside Muslim communities.

The oldest and most influential of these peace testimonies, at least of those attempting to influence the affairs of state and war and peace, is the Quaker Peace Testimony.

What happened to our peace testimony during America's longest war?

This question is as difficult as any in Quaker history that I know of. Few written sources exist outside archives, which I have not explored. There were fierce struggles among Friends, making memory even more suspect than usual. Nevertheless, I must and do rely on my own memory, the memories of a few other Friends, and a few memoirs. You will find errors here. Please correct them in writing if possible, as soon as you can.

First, let me state a few facts, and assumptions which I treat as facts:

(1) The American war in Vietnam lasted from 1961 to 1975. This war was enormous from 1965 to 1973 – eight dreadful years.

(2) Draft calls, which had been very small from 1953 to 1965, increased greatly in 1965 and did not diminish greatly until 1970, finally being ended in 1973.

(3) In Vietnam, nationalism and communism merged and the result was a nation of fighters who could hardly be beaten, short of extermination.

(4) A US anti-war movement emerged in a major way in 1965 and nearly vanished only in 1973.

(5) Quakers and other pacifists were among the leaders of the anti-war movement from beginning to end.

(6) Assorted left-wingers were also among the leaders of the anti-war movement from beginning to end.

(7) In the post-McCarthy era, US left-wingers, including pacifist and Quaker left-wingers, were angry at and afraid of their country and their government.

(8) Not until the McGovern campaign of 1972 were anti-war forces finally brought into conventional politics.

(9) The US government and military officials who planned and promoted the Vietnam War were extraordinarily ignorant about Vietnam and the war. Even now, their ignorance boggles the mind.

(10) At various points between 1965 and 1968, almost every high US government and military official involved in the war learned enough to lose faith in the war.

(11) Yet the US continued to fight the war until 1973. Half the American military deaths during the Vietnam War took place after Richard Nixon was first inaugurated. The Vietnam War from 1969 onwards, led by a Quaker president, was the greatest exercise in cynicism ever conducted by Americans.

(12) To say these things fills the eyes with tears and the heart with fury. One wishes to take our government's leaders then and tear them to pieces, limb from limb.

(13) The Vietnam War was not an auspicious time for the Quaker Peace Testimony.

Let's take a look, part by part, at the Quaker Peace Testimony during the war.

During the war, more than a few Friends and other pacifists came to give qualified support to violent revolution in Vietnam and other Two-Thirds World Countries. American military defeat in Vietnam was welcomed, not only as the quickest method of ending the war, but also as a good way of ushering in a better society there. A very few Friends went so far as to advocate violent revolution even in the United States. It is difficult to think of a period since 1660 when so many Friends supported violent revolution.

A war spirit also weakened Quaker support of nonviolent revolution and nonviolent radical activism. As the war ground on, Friends and AFSC staff who persisted in nonviolent civil rights activism found themselves more and more isolated. Perhaps more to the point, Friends who engaged in illegal shipment of medical supplies to all parts of Vietnam, in tax resistance, and in draft resistance, found their support from the Society of Friends and AFSC was spotty, to say the least.

One should not complain too much. Quaker nonviolent action flourished during the Vietnam War as it had at no time since the Revolutionary War, with the possible exception of the period from 1948 to 1965. In cities like Chicago, where the entire Quaker community supported nonviolent war resistance, draft resisters' trials became great celebrations of the power of nonviolence and truth.

There can be little doubt about Quaker cynicism about war:

it flourished during the Vietnam period, eventually being extended to nonviolent radicalism as well in many cases.

Before we consider Quaker conscientious objection during the Vietnam War, we should consider two related matters: the *Seeger* decision and draft counseling.

Fortuitously, the Supreme Court decided *US v. Seeger* in the spring of 1965, just as the greatest escalation of the Vietnam War was occurring. In this case, the Court defined "Supreme Being" so that the phrase meant nothing; accordingly, Congress eliminated the Supreme Being clause from the draft law two years later. Also, the Court defined "religious training and belief" for conscientious objectors very liberally, so that even agnostics and members of no religious society could be recognized as conscientious objectors.

The *Seeger* decision received enormous publicity, informed many people about legal CO recognition who had never known that the CO exemption existed, and informed even greater numbers that they too might be eligible for CO exemption that they had wrongly thought was available only to Quakers and Mennonites. In fact, only one conscientious objector was released from prison because of the *Seeger* decision: Fred Etcheverry, a Quaker who, Selective Service and the courts had decided, lacked religious training and belief even though he was clearly a Christian!

Unfortunately, Friends did not mount a major political campaign to ensure enforcement of the *Seeger* decision, and the US Immigration and Naturalization Service does not abide by it today. However, the *Seeger* case brought a flood of men to see the fast-expanding group of mostly volunteer professionals known as draft counselors. Some draft counselors worked for or volunteered for AFSC or CCCO. Other draft counselors volunteered for local peace groups and Friends meetings. Men of all ages were draft counselors, and by 1967 they were joined by many women counselors.

Those counselors who were "public" – not counseling only the members of their own church or students in their own college, etc. – overwhelmingly were Friends, or closely associated with Friends. (I say this with authority, since from 1969 to 1973 I was the Editor of CCCO's *Draft Counselor's Newsletter*, which had about 5000 subscribers.) Draft counseling, from John Woolman's day to the present, is identified with Friends. During the Vietnam War it was one of three major antiwar witnesses dominated by Friends, along with tax resistance and medical aid for all parts of Vietnam, which were much smaller activities.

Draft counseling helped millions of men gain CO exemption and other exemptions and deferments. It helped speed the demise of an active draft. It inspired military counseling and (in Canada) immigration counseling. Perhaps most important, draft counseling went far to re-create a sense of community for young men who felt themselves abandoned by peers, schools, families and government. Young men sometimes broke down in tears as they realized that counselors – often the unheard-of Quakers – cared for them and would try to help.

Quaker conscientious objection during the Vietnam War is complicated. As the war approached, a combination of factors made the "testimony of deferments until age 26" the preferred course for most draft-age Friends. However, reduced availability of deferments during the war, plus increased guilt about taking deferments and exemptions in wartime, as well as better availability of draft counseling and wide knowledge of the Seeger decision, all made the various conscientious objector choices (other than I-A-O) something that many young Friends considered and used.

Quaker prisoners for conscience's sake were almost all non- co-operators or draft resisters. If one meets a Friend now who sought CO exemption and was imprisoned after not receiving it, that Friend almost certainly joined Friends after imprisonment. The same situation prevailed for Mennonite, Brethren, and Jehovah's Witness prisoners. Jehovah's Witnesses made up the great majority of CO's in federal prisons throughout the war.

Quakers who did alternative service usually did it the normal way: a low-wage job for a hospital or other nonprofit agency, alone or with one or two other CO's; such jobs were mostly chosen by the CO; often there was no pastoral care and no connection whatever to other Friends. (In Chicago, the draft resister community provided some camaraderie for the CO's working alone in mental hospitals around town.) Many of these CO's were lost to Friends and to organized pacifism.

Very few Quakers chose the other type of alternate service, done by so many Brethren and Mennonites: volunteering for assignments chosen by a church service agency; no pay other than subsistence; orientation and other programs, usually in large groups; many women and others not doing alternative service participating; some assigned overseas (usually for three years, not two.) AFSC had made a principled decision not to have this sort of program in 1948, at the start of the peacetime draft. As a Friend who served in Brethren Volunteer Service (until I decided draft resistance was an even better witness and I could handle it), I am a member of a privileged few. CO's who served in BVS and similar programs usually remain members of the peace churches and strong pacifists to this day. Some are radical Christians.

Though the AFSC decision not to have a long-term volunteer service program like BVS was principled, it must be the worst mistake AFSC ever made. There is no doubt in my mind that such a long-term volunteer program would have become a powerful witness for peace *and* a powerful engine of draft resistance during the Vietnam War.

By the time of the Vietnam War, few Quaker men served in the military as noncombatants. The war created a new CO option: emigration, especially to Canada. Many Friends did this, especially early in the war.

As for ending the war by encouraging diplomacy and negotiations, that hardly seemed possible, at least during the early years. Nevertheless, one intrepid Friend, Staughton Lynd, did travel to North Vietnam as early as 1965 in a private diplomatic venture to end the war. Many AFSC people followed his example. At home, American Friends continued to press a great, little-known lobbying effort throughout the war.

No part of the Quaker Peace Testimony was more worn down by the long war than our testimony of service. During the 1960's AFSC started eliminating its famed short-term work camps and its peace institutes, so that few were left by the beginning of the Vietnam War and almost none were left at the end. One must admit that programs like this were almost impossible to manage during the late 1960's. Youth rebelled against all authority on all matters. Yet why weren't programs continued for other age groups? Or resumed when things calmed down?

However, the Quaker service record during the Vietnam War also includes the AFSC prosthetics work at Quang Ngai – one of the finest Quaker service programs ever undertaken. I note that this was long-term volunteer service, even if not so labeled.

Wasn't there more to the Quaker Peace Testimony during the Vietnam War than this dreary record of worn-down witness? Of course there was, much more, and it may be summed up in the popular Movement phrase, "from Protest to Resistance." For the first time – at least the first time for American Quakers and pacifists – Friends were determined not just to protest war or to witness against a war but to end a war by any and every nonviolent means available.

The Questing Beast grew a new limb, which remains to this day and seems permanent: concerted nonviolent resistance against war.

This new part of the Quaker Peace Testimony is unique in that it is a combination of two older parts, both refashioned to serve in a new way. One of the older parts now taken over is the campaign of nonviolent resistance, often involving extensive civil disobedience, against injustice. Friends had used this part of our heritage in leading the great nonviolent campaigns against nuclear weapons in the late 1950's and early 1960's. Now we were to wage nonviolent war – spiritual warfare, if you will – against a war itself. A little consideration will show that nonviolent war resistance is far more complicated and difficult than most other nonviolent social activism, even when extensive civil disobedience is involved.

The other part of the Quaker Peace Testimony now taken over – subverted, some might say – is conscientious objection, of both legal and illegal varieties. Once mass draft resistance began in 1966 and 1967, with draft card turn-ins and draft card burnings, sometimes involving hundreds of men, non-cooperation with the draft was as much an act of nonviolent war against the US government as it was an act of witness to one's Quaker or pacifist beliefs. Even the filing of a legal CO claim was sometimes meant as an act of nonviolent war against the military system.

Acts and campaigns – note the martial language – of draft resistance and tax resistance were intended to deny manpower and money to the government *and* to overburden the courts *and* to catch the attention of uninvolved citizens and get them involved in opposing the war. Acts and campaigns of shipping medical aid to all parts of Vietnam were also meant to overburden the courts and to catch the attention of uninvolved citizens and involve them. Acts of legal, nonviolent protest generally had only the latter purpose. Any idea of convincing government officials by one's witness was usually discarded as impractical. The US government and military, war resisters agreed, responded only to force – hopefully nonviolent force.

Yes, yes, you might say, but these nonviolent war resistance campaigns involved hundreds of thousands of people, very few of them Friends. I can't argue with that. But many of these campaigns were thought up by Friends and many were led by Friends. A Quaker Action Group is the prototype, and the largest, of those informal groups of Friends who came together to resist the Vietnam War. The most remarkable "official" Quaker body that acted with this purpose was the Peace and Social Action Program of New York Yearly Meeting, led by Larry Apsey and Ross Flanagan. And one of the nation's major draft resistance groups – which engaged in other types of war resistance as well – was CADRE, Chicago Area Draft Resisters, which was led mainly by Friends, and friends of Friends.

What can one say about this Quaker- and pacifist-led campaign of all-out nonviolent resistance against the Vietnam War?

First, it certainly did much to reduce the American ground war in Vietnam, and ultimately to end it. Conscription was almost destroyed.

Second, military resistance – the refusal of American

troops to fight – was surely even more important than civilian resistance in ending the ground war. Yet the civilian resistance stimulated military resistance, and helped military resisters with counseling, coffeehouses and the like. Maybe we should thank the civilian resistance for the amazing nonviolence of the military resistance.

Third, in 1968 and 1972 war resistance cracked open a closed American politics, and allowed a new diversity of views to be heard.

Fourth, war resistance brought everyone back to old knowledge: wars are not conducted by majority vote but by Quaker-like consensus. Someone said that war resisters demonstrated dissent by putting on the "biggest temper tantrum in history." We did, to good effect.

Fifth, AFSC and many other Quaker groups adopted nonviolent war resistance, and many of the programs connected with it. What is more, the resistance idea spread widely, and was even used to *prevent* a war earlier this year.

Yet much must be said which is not so positive:

First, a war-spirit developed that made many Friends and pacifists provide nonviolent support – often ideological and emotional support – to violent revolutions worldwide, and to socialist and communist revolutions in particular. This divided Friends and helped no one.

Second, the same war spirit sometimes prevented Friends from being friends with those with whom they had political disagreements.

Third, some identified a particular political order with the Kingdom of Heaven, and were blind to great failures in that order. This happened most notably in the case of Cambodia.

Fourth, soldiers in the antiwar were subject to emotional and spiritual pressures like regular soldiers. Some burned out, or became cynics, or both. Many left Friends and left nonviolence.

Fifth, continual experiences of pain and loss, coming

during many years of antiwar work, have left many Vietnam War opponents suffering from what can only be described as a type of Post-Traumatic-Stress Syndrome. Other Friends, and the victims themselves, have sometimes dealt with this PTSS by denial.

Sixth, the anger characteristic of war and PTSS has destroyed the mental stability, marriages, and families of many anti-war Friends and friends.

Seventh, the denial characteristic of PTSS has given some of us a poor grip on reality. Alcohol and drug use to assuage pain has not helped some Friends' sense of reality either.

Eighth, the collapse of sexual morality typical of a long war affected anti-war people as much as anyone. In a profound sense, the antiwar became part of the war.

Ninth, thousands, probably tens of thousands, of members and attenders felt so dissatisfied with the Society of Friends that they left it.

How many *Faith and Practice* books mention this new part of our Quaker Peace Testimony – a nonviolent resistance campaign against a war – and the problems it can bring? How many Quaker historians, sociologists, psychologists and religious leaders are trying to understand all this? Why do no Quaker schools other than Pendle Hill show any interest in this subject?

Nonviolent war resistance – very costly but sometimes extremely effective – is now, after the Vietnam War, the eighth major part of the Quaker peace testimony. Yet it is not the newest part. I can see three even newer parts, at least two of them growing directly out of the Vietnam War experience.

1) The Quaker Peace Testimony now includes a tremendously expanded and strengthened practical testimony against personal violence of any kind. We've always opposed capital punishment. Now we are learning how to prevent and treat child sexual abuse, and teaching prisoners how not to be raped, and teaching schoolchildren and prisoners how to prevent fights. There must be dozens of Quaker and Quaker-founded organizations, from the Alternatives to Violence Program, to Stop Prisoner Rape, working on personal violence. This new ninth major part of the

Quaker Peace Testimony proves how vital and innovative our testimony is.

2) Don't we have a new tenth part of the Quaker Peace Testimony called "unity with nature" or "nonviolence to all living beings (including the Earth)"?

3) And as an alternative to massive costly war resistance campaigns – or maybe something to go with that – now we have "accompaniment," an eleventh part of the Quaker Peace Testimony. There are experts on accompaniment at this conference, so I won't say anything more about this topic.

The Vietnam War was an unparalleled catastrophe for everyone involved, including the Society of Friends. Yet good things sometimes come from catastrophes. If we Friends could only admit and reconcile ourselves to our losses, then maybe we could teach the world how a massive war resistance campaign should be waged – before the war, not during it, of course!

I suggest that we think for a moment about Alice Herz and Norman Morrison, the two Friends who publicly immolated themselves in protest of the Vietnam war. We might think of Rick Thompson, killed in AFSC service in Vietnam. And who knows how many Quakers' names are listed on that long black wall in Washington?

Let us pray: Our Father, who art in heaven, Hallowed be thy name. Thy Kingdom come, thy will be done on earth as it is in heaven. Give us this day our daily bread. Forgive us our trespasses as we forgive those who trespass against us. Lead us not into temptation but deliver us from evil. For thine is the kingdom, the power and the glory forever. Amen.

Acknowledgments:

Thank you to Peter Brock, friend of Friends and author, whose books include *The Quaker Peace Testimony, 1660-1914,* the standard work in the field.

Thank you to Alice and Staughton Lynd, the best friends a writer could have, who made suggestions and corrections for this speech on two or three days' notice. Their own books include *We Won't Go*; *The Resistance;* and *The Other Side.*

An enormous thank you to the pacifist communities I have been part of: The family of John and Kathryn Mott; Ridgewood Friends Meeting; New York Yearly Meeting of Friends; Brethren Volunteer Service (BVS); Chicago Area Draft Resisters (CADRE); Midwest Committee for Draft Counseling (MCDC = the CCCO office in Chicago), and many others.

Plenary Presentation:
Canadian Friends –
Trying to Serve God in the Spirit of Christ

Kathleen Hertzberg

I would like to begin my reflections on the period in Quaker life in Canada from about 1955 to the end of the Vietnam /Indo-China War in 1975 as it refers to the work of the Canadian Friends Service Committee – a period which we are attempting to revisit at this conference. We are not writing history *per se*. I want to keep my reflections in the context of the Quaker faith and, in particular, the Society of Friends in Canada during that period.

The three branches united in 1955 to become Canadian Yearly Meeting. It was Quakers from the British North American colonies who brought Quakerism to Canada at the time of the American War of Independence.

The total membership of the unified Yearly Meeting in 1955 was just over 500. Membership has grown to a constant 1,200 across Canada, a number which keeps pace with deaths and new members. There are 26 meetings across Canada and a larger number of worship groups.

New strength came from immigrant Friends from Europe after the Second World War. They came from England and Ireland and from small Yearly Meetings on the continent (Germany and Holland). Their experience of Quakerism had been in yearly meetings which had not separated in the 19th century, notwithstanding a century of theological differences in London Yearly Meeting and the fact that some Friends from England had been influential in triggering the Separations in North America.

The postwar immigrant Friends from Britain had gone through the traumatic experience of being Quakers during a World War. They had been conscientious objectors and had participated in Quaker Service during and after the war. Those from the continent of Europe had lived under the Nazi regime. Their experiences had been even more challenging to their Quaker faith. They had idealistic expectations of life and work in and through the Society of Friends in Canada. They received a warm welcome and assistance from Friends in settling into their new country.

The Canadian Friends Service Committee was founded in 1931 by members from the three Canada Yearly Meetings, with impetus from Young Friends and, after the war, Young Friends who had served abroad in the Friends Ambulance Unit in China were a source of strength towards unity.

In 1955 when the three branches united to become Canadian Yearly Meeting, the Canadian Friends Service Committee became a committee of Canadian Yearly Meeting (not an independent Quaker service corporation like the American Friends Service Committee). CFSC is subject to the guidance of Canadian Yearly Meeting. Interaction between the Service Committee and Yearly Meeting in witness and service is essential.

At the time of the Vietnam War most of the Friends appointed to CFSC came from Central Canada. Toronto Meeting, the largest in Canada at the time, was active in CFSC. The offices of the Yearly Meeting and CFSC were in Friends House in Toronto.

The work of the CFSC attracted not only Friends from traditional Quaker meetings, but also recent members and attenders. There will be four points on which I want to elaborate:
  – Peace Education Program and Grindstone Island
  – Medical Aid Program
  – A Quaker Action Group
  – Draft Resisters and Deserters in Canada.

The main efforts of CFSC in the fifties were directed towards the Doukhobors in Western Canada, abolition of capital punishment, disarmament and peace (with the Peace Churches), atomic weapons, refugees and displaced persons in Europe and the

"Cold War," as well as the plight of Canada's native people.

New members were attracted by the Quaker Peace Testimony and the reputation of Friends in service and relief.

Thus began the unfolding of Canadian Friends' concern and service in response to the tragedy of the American War in Vietnam and the tremendous impact of that war.

In 1964 I became chairman (clerk) of the Canadian Friends Service Committee. I had done ten years of Quaker Service prewar, during the Second World War and after the war, in devastated Europe. I had been a conscientious objector when women were called up in 1942. The religious basis of Quaker witness and service had been important to me as a Young Friend who felt called to give Quaker service.

Peace Education Program

I had just been appointed when CFSC felt led to establish a Peace Education Program. A timely offer of service was received from Murray Thomson, a well-qualified and experienced social worker who had participated in the Quaker South-East Asian Seminars. He was a member of Toronto Meeting. Almost simultaneously a Canadian, Diana Wright, offered her island, Grindstone Island, in the Rideau Lake, near Ottawa, to the CFSC as a Peace Education Centre. CFSC accepted.

CFSC held programs on the island for ten years. Grindstone became a centre to experiment and to learn in a way which did not seem to be done anywhere else. There were encounters which would not have taken place otherwise. Distinguished resource people, Canadian, American and Vietnamese, participated in the programs. The programs centered on peace, training in nonviolence, Peace Research, French-English Canadian Dialogues, Inter-Faith Dialogue, the famous socio-drama "Thirty-One Hours" as well as Conferences for Diplomats intended to move people from the position they held. Participation from the United States was quite substantial.

The peace agenda and the antiwar agenda were not always

identical. The programs were not only about ending the Vietnam War. The programs were organized by Murray Thomson with the help of the Peace Committee chaired by Ursula Franklin. Murray did seven years of fruitful peace education during the Vietnam War. However, the war in Vietnam hung over the work of peace educaion as a real war which affected us all. It was the ever-present challenge for the understanding and application of the Quaker Peace Testimony and the longing to "stop the war now." Of course, people from the US were attracted to Grindstone Island. It was an important experience in training in nonviolence for young people. Between 1965 and 1969 over 1600 adults and 300 children participated.

When CFSC Programs on Grindstone Island were laid down, the Canadian Peace Research Institute (now the Dundas Peace Research Institute), under the directorship of Alan and Hanna Newcombe, continued their groundwork for peace. Later a peace co-op ran the island.

Vietnam Medical Aid Program

Concern for the suffering of the people of Vietnam on all sides of the conflict arose in the early 60's amongst Canadian Friends and others in Canada. It was the first time that TV had brought war into the homes of people everywhere. Canada had outstanding reporters. Their reports moved many – the bombing, the napalm, the use of defoliation chemicals, the destruction of villages, the wounding, maiming and death, were all brought home to us. The Canadian Government would have liked to have been neutral. The Canadian public was almost as divided in its opinions about the threat of Communism and the justification for the war in Vietnam as was the American public. The "protest movement" was the atmosphere in which the CFSC Medical Aid Program had to function.

People from the New Left applauded CFSC's action, not only our medical relief to all parts of Vietnam, but also our statements to government.

The "Teach-Ins" were a useful means of public education. Young people were enthusiastic about the music of the Beatles and Joan Baez – some of it moving and expressive of the longings of youth. We experienced it with our own children. The use of drugs was a concern to parents. On one occasion a visiting US professor, lecturing at Grindstone, promoted the use of LSD.

It was popular in some circles to be a "Peacenik" – the public did not always differentiate! Quakers sometimes seemed to the public to be part of the "fashionable groundswell"!

The Medical Aid Program was a labor of love embarked upon with dedication, careful planning and execution. This proved to be difficult in the prevailing atmosphere. Also in the knowledge that our efforts could only meet a very small part of the great and continuing need. It was not to be a token band-aid, however, but an expression of Quaker witness against war, care for the victims of the war, and a desire to bring an end to the war.

Friends and other Canadians who supported the work just wanted to do good relief work in the Quaker tradition.

Already in 1964, a Meeting for Worship was called by the Toronto Meeting Peace Committee which gave the first spiritual impulse but asked Friends to be clear on the issues. The concern was presented to Yearly Meeting in 1964. Friends made a strong statement of sympathy with the people of Vietnam and pointed to the dangers of escalation of the war to other parts of Southeast Asia. It was sent to the Canadian government. This statement said: "We believe it to be the moral duty of the Canadian government towards the United States to strongly oppose this policy in Vietnam. To do so would be an act of friendship, fulfilling also our duty to the people of Vietnam and to the world."

In 1965, CFSC organized a conference on Vietnam at Carleton University, Ottawa. The conference called upon Canada to be a reconciler and to send aid to the victims on all sides of the conflict, to organize local groups across Canada to seek public support and donations, and the support of church groups, labour and others. Over the period of the Medical Aid Program, CFSC benefited greatly both morally and financially from the support and contributions of people in all walks of life.

The Conference also sent Dr. Vo Tranh Minh and two Canadians on a Peace Mission to Vietnam.

As CFSC gathered strength for the organization of a Medical Aid Program, 15 Canadian Friends attended the 1967 Friends World Conference in Greensboro, North Carolina. The Conference heard movingly from U Thant. A statement was issued on the Vietnam War which greatly moved and inspired Friends present and confirmed CFSC in its endeavors to send impartial medical aid. The statement also encouraged Friends everywhere to help stop the war but to keep the spiritual and religious leading and inspiration.

CFSC made efforts to establish the need in all parts of Vietnam, through consultations with the Canadian Red Cross, who in turn enquired through the International Red Cross to the Russian Red Cross about how to get relief supplies to all parts of Vietnam.

After prayerful deliberation and with the sincere desire to express the religious basis of Quaker relief work as an expression of Christian compassion, witness against war and the positive motivation of the Peace Testimony, the first brochure was published in September 1966 with the following Statement of Purpose:

"We, members of the Religious Society of Friends (Quakers) in Canada, feel moved to send medical aid to the non-combatant sufferers in the present tragic war in Vietnam.

"We believe all wars are contrary to the Will and Spirit of God as against the sacred purpose of man's existence on earth. We are moved by Christian love to act now by sending a practical contribution of medical aid for the healing of the wounds of innocent fellow men in all parts of Vietnam, regardless of political, religious or ideological barriers.

"We appeal to all men of goodwill, wherever they may be, to assist us in this work of mercy, which, with God's help, may bring the spirit of reconciliation and peace into the hearts of men."

This statement was a modification of the Statement of Purpose issued by London Yearly Meeting for their aid program to people on all sides of the conflict in the Franco-Prussian War (1870-71), the time when the Quaker Star was born! The brochure was used for fundraising.

Through the good offices of the Canadian/International Red Cross, permission was received to ship our first deliveries of medical supplies aboard the Russian vessel "Alexander Pushkin" which docked regularly in Montreal.

Three large consignments of carefully chosen medical supplies were prepared – all labeled with the Quaker Star. Members of CFSC, Montreal Meeting and US Friends met the Alexander Pushkin in the docks in Montreal with two of the packages: one addressed to the Red Cross of North Vietnam and the other to the Red Cross of the National Liberation Front (PRG); the third parcel was mailed at the main Post Office in Montreal addressed to the Red Cross of South Vietnam. The supplies on the Alexander Pushkin traveled via Moscow to Hanoi and were acknowledged by Mme. Tran Thi Dich of the North Vietnamese Red Cross. In time we received photos showing the supplies being unpacked.

A press release was issued prior to the distribution of packages and it was made clear that we were sending impartial aid to suffering people on all sides of the conflict. Following the deliveries, a Meeting for Worship was held in the Montreal meeting house. The message arising out of the worship was that no matter how dedicated the efforts of human beings may be, the blessing can come from God alone.

Examples of drugs and medical supplies requested by the North Vietnamese Red Cross included penicillin, streptomycin, surgical instruments, maternity kits, medical textbooks in French and later school supplies.

The medical supplies and drugs were often manufactured in Canada by Canadian subsidiaries of American pharmaceutical companies, who soon informed us that they could not fill our orders because of restrictions under the US Trading with the Enemy regulations. We appealed to Canadian pharmaceutical companies, to drug stores, hospitals and Canadian physicians to donate drugs.

We shared a Medical Aid Distribution Centre for a while

with the United Church of Canada. Frank Dingman, who went twice to Hanoi to consult with the North Vietnamese Red Cross, was appointed director of the Centre. Friends and Young Friends worked at the Centre, sorting and packing.

The program soon benefited from the frustration which some American Friends and pacifists and other concerned people felt when the US Government prohibited the sending of aid to the "enemy" and refused export permits for the transfer of money and supplies to CFSC.

The eagerness of some American Friends and others to circumvent the US regulations resulted in some moving and strange experiences. When parcels and cheques addressed to CFSC were stopped by the US post office and by both US and Canadian banks, some US Friends sent parcels and cheques to me personally and to other Friends.

By 1969, CFSC had ceased to collect, purchase or ship supplies from Canada. Arrangements were made instead to use the facilities of Quaker Peace & Service in London, England, and for transportation through a shipping company in London under the care of the British Committee for Aid to Vietnam. Canadian funds were sent to London which included, on one occasion, a large grant from Oxfam Canada. The London Quaker Conference on Aid to Vietnam agreed that all Quaker supplies from wherever they originated would be labeled "QUAKER SERVICE – VIETNAM" in English and French. This arrangement continued until the end of the war.

Photos were received from the North Vietnamese Red Cross showing the unpacking of CFSC supplies.

CFSC also sent funds to the Vietnamese Overseas Buddhist Association in Paris, France for the Buddhist School of Social Service, which trained young Vietnamese for social work.

CFSC asked the Canadian Government to intervene for the release of imprisoned Buddhist leaders in Saigon, in particular the Ven. Thic Thien Minh.

When the program wound down, and the American army withdrew from Vietnam, we estimated that medical supplies of various kinds had been sent to the value of approximately $300,000.

In this total were many sacrificial gifts from individual Canadian and American Friends, especially through A Quaker Action Group, and also from AFSC.

Canadian Friends welcomed the encouragement and practical help which came to us through A Quaker Action Group and other American Friends. CFSC accepted funds in support of the Medical Aid Program and offered friendship and solidarity to them in their pacifist stand against the war. CFSC said: "We are not encouraging US citizens to contribute but we are willing to accept donations from wherever they may come."

In a statement at the 1969 London International Friends Conference on Vietnam, Ross Flanagan said:

"We wish to send supplies from people of goodwill in the United States to the victims of the war in all parts of Vietnam. The voyage of the *Phoenix* is a public witness and an act of civil disobedience."

He asked:

"Should AFSC commit civil disobedience to aid suffering people in all parts of Vietnam? Has AFSC's image at home suffered because it has not done so?

"AQAG fulfills the concern of Young Friends of North America – they want an international Quaker organization under which they can serve."

On one occasion Murray Thomson and I were interviewed by a reporter from the Soviet daily newspaper *Pravda* in the breakfast room of the Royal York Hotel in Toronto. He wanted to know about the Medical Aid Program to help victims of the war on all sides of the conflict. He found it surprising that people could have religious motivation for what seemed to him to be a political act. He asked us: "Who do you think you are – Don Quixote?" In explaining the religious basis of Quaker work we referred to Quaker work in Russia during the famine in the twenties.

It was not the intention of CFSC to make the Vietnam Medical Aid Program the main service of CFSC. In 1968 a Minute of the 37th Annual Meeting said: "Relief is not a solution but a way in which Canadian Friends can demonstrate their concern for the suffering people in all parts of Vietnam." Some outside the Society considered the CFSC Medical Aid Program to be facile and unendurably idealistic. There was a danger that the religious message would get lost and that our work as a religious society would "get off track." No doubt this is an ever-present danger whenever Friends feel led to act in the world.

It was difficult to make it clear that the Program was not civil disobedience for Friends. It brought CFSC tremendous publicity and brought us into the national limelight – we had to "bite our way through" – endeavouring to make our witness and work clear. And there was not much point in Canadians saying "It couldn't happen here!" The Quebec Crisis in 1970, when the War Measures Act was introduced by the Liberal Government, showed that we had problems in Canada though they were not as immediate, grave or polarised as in the United States.

A 1970 Survey of Interests of Canadian Friends in relation to service work and concerns revealed that relief and medical aid were well down on the list and it was self-evident that support of the Friends Rural Centre in India, to which Canadian Friends had been committed for many years, along with FSC, London, would continue. Peace and reconciliation headed the list, followed by Canadian Indians and Eskimo, young people, community development, mental health, civil liberties, work camps and, finally, relief and medical aid and immigration.

After the Medical Aid Program was laid down by CFSC, concern about the aftermath of the war did not end. With the help of CFSC, Nancy Pocock, who died in March 1998, went four times to Vietnam, and CFSC continued to send some aid. A small clinic on the Mekong Delta is named the "Nancy Pocock Clinic."

During all these years Canadian Friends were thankful for the dedicated and efficient service rendered by a series of well-qualified Friends who served as General Secretaries.

Transnational Quaker Service

Arising from the Friends World Conference in Greensboro in 1967, Canadian Friends were attracted by the hope expressed for the development of a Transnational Quaker Service and saw the Vietnam Medical Aid Program in that light – as an opportunity for Friends around the world to work for a unified Quaker effort to help the people of Vietnam. To some extent this did in fact come about at the London conference, at which representatives were present from Quaker Peace and Service, AFSC, A Quaker Action Group, Australian Friends and CFSC.

CFSC saw the service which each national Quaker organization was able to render to the suffering people of Vietnam, within the circumstances in which each national Quaker service body could operate, as a component of the international community of Friends' witness and service to fellow human beings. We were thankful to be able to participate in that service and welcomed the Mission and Service Conferences which took place later.

Throughout the period under review, and of course since, the Service Committees exchanged information, made plans to send Quaker delegations to Hanoi and engaged in efforts to mediate an end to the war.

Draft Resisters and Deserters

This section will deal with the general impact of US draft resisters and deserters and how some of them have related to the Society of Friends in Canada.

Canada had no military draft. Canada became synonymous with "freedom" for thousands of draft resisters and deserters. There was a steady stream through to the late 1960's. There was no Extradition Treaty between Canada and the US for draft resisters and deserters. They could be admitted to Canada as immigrants. There was a points system. The draft resisters were English speaking, mostly college educated and had little difficulty in meeting the points required.

Deserters were more difficult. Most were from the working class and scored much lower in the points system. Up to 1967 they could cross the border as visitors and apply for landed immigrant status from within Canada but after 1972 tighter immigration regulations were introduced by the Trudeau government which made it impossible to apply for landed immigrant status from within Canada. This practically closed Canada as a haven for draft resisters and deserters.

Numbers differ about immigration because the Canadian Immigration Statistics did not distinguish the reasons why US citizens emigrated to Canada. It is estimated that 18,000-25,000 draft resisters and 10-12,000 deserters entered the country. When partial amnesty was introduced by President Carter, many who had come to Canada as draft resisters or deserters returned to the United States. The Toronto Anti-Draft Program's "Manual for Draft-Age Immigrants to Canada" went through six editions and sold 25,000 copies.

Canadian Friends assisted in the Aid & Advisory Centres established by the draft resisters themselves. As part of the supportive network Quaker families took young men into their homes, counseling them and helping them to adjust to their new country. Part of this network was the Toronto Ecumenical Counseling Service, on which the CFSC Peace Education Secretary served.

In the Second World War British war resisters faced a moral dilemma about the evil of the Nazi regime and the wrongfulness of war, whereas in the Vietnam War it was clear to conscientious objectors that both the cause and the violence of war were wrong.

US draft resisters and deserters were fortunate that there was somewhere to which they could escape. German pacifists had nowhere but death to escape the draft during the Nazi regime.

In our discussions with Quaker peace workers from the US who came to Canada to investigate the situation, we often found that it was not only conscientious objection to war and violence and their rejection of the cause for which the United States was supposed to be waging the war in Vietnam which motivated them, but also their disappointment because the war in Vietnam offended their understanding of the "American Dream."

A few Young Friends were amongst those who came to Canada as draft resisters. It is assumed that the number was low because it was less difficult for members of the Society of Friends to get CO status. Some who came to Canada participated in Friends meetings. A few other young people became members of the Society of Friends later. A recent attempt to identify those who are still active members of the Society of Friends in Canada today has proved more difficult. Only a rough count could be made with the result that there are probably about 60 in various meetings across Canada years later. Some are active and dedicated and helpful in the life of their meeting and in Canadian Yearly Meeting. A friend commented: the fact that so few joined is a sobering thought!

None of us would want to label them "Americans" now. Friends who came from the United Kingdom tend to be more "conservative" than those from the United States.

However, an 18-year old draft resister who came to Canada thirty years ago will have matured, made a career and have raised a family in Canada but will still have strong connections with the United States, having family there. This would also apply, of course, to the millions of immigrants from many other countries who have entered Canada in the past thirty years. During that time the population has greatly increased from 24 million to 31 million. Canada has become a multi-ethnic country and nowhere is that more visible than in Toronto or Vancouver.

Our meetings are also a reflection of this ethnic diversity and an enrichment to us. Through integration we may become a harmonious community of Friends, not always without friction because people do have different backgrounds, understandings and experiences, but we recognize that the teaching ministry is essential to our growth in faith beyond our diversity.

In a Quaker Meeting we are working towards, perhaps longing for, a fellowship of shared faith and witness in a world in which the challenge seems to be the impact of the global economy and in which the rich seem to get richer and the poor poorer. We are all apprehensive about what is being done to the environment in which we live. Therefore we should not emphasize our different backgrounds or origins, but recognize what it is that unites us in our common Quaker-Christian Faith, careful not to point fingers at differences which, by fate, have brought us into the Quaker community. Time passes and national backgrounds and country of origin blend into the new community. Cultural traditions can be an enrichment.

I had dinner a few weeks ago with a Vietnamese young woman who came to Canada as a Vietnamese boat person. In our sharing about CFSC's Medical Aid Program she said: "It is important to me to know that somebody cared."

Some Literature

CFSC Minutes and Reports – 1960 - 1974.

CFSC Reports to Canadian Yearly Meeting – 1960 - 1974.

Grindstone Island Reports for 8 years – 1966 - 1974.

CFSC Brochures–
> Friends Rural Centre, Rasulia, India.
> Grindstone Island Peace Education Centre.
> CFSC Medical Aid Program to Suffering People on All Sides of the Conflict in Vietnam.

Canadian Indians: "Right to a Future" – John Melling. 1967.

Canadian Yearly Meeting – Organization and Procedure – Recent Developments. 1990. Introduction.

Canadian Friends Historical Association *Journal*, No. 61. Fall 1997. "50 Years of Peace Pursuits – Unfinished Business: The Legacy of Grindstone Island" – Murray Thomson.

"Crossing Borders" – Carl Stieren. Canadian Quaker Pamphlet Series No. 47. 1998.

US Draft Resisters & Deserters:

The New Exiles: American War Resisters in Canada. Roger Neville Williams. Liveright Publishers, New York, 1971.

War Resisters Canada:

The World of the American Military-Political Refugees. Kenneth Fred Emerick. Knox, Pennsylvania Free Press, Knox, Pa, 1972.

Corporate Efforts: More "War Stories"

A Panel

Liz Yeats (Draft Counseling)

Ken Maher (Underground Railroad)

David Finke (Military Counseling)

Bill Eagles (Quaker House, NC)

My Work as a Draft Counselor

Liz Yeats

About a year ago the young people in my Friends meeting did a survey and organized a session in which they joined with 30 or so adults to compare answers to a series of biographical questions including, "What is one way you have put your Quaker testimonies into practice?" I was surprised to learn that more than five of us answered that question citing participation as draft and military counselors during the Vietnam War years.

I was one of those Friends. A young woman in my early 20's in the late 1960's, I found draft and military counseling made good use of my gifts. During the War years I counseled many young men facing these life-transforming decisions. From the spring of 1968 into the early seventies I did draft and military counseling and trained counselors under the auspices of the American Friends Service Committee in three regions, and as a released Friend for New York Yearly and Monthly Meetings.

For most Friends and their meetings, interest in providing draft counseling began when an increased number of young men in the meeting began to ask for help preparing CO applications. Many Friends became more involved as young men in the community sought similar help. These men needed assistance in understanding the growing complexities and vagaries of draft law, as well as the inconsistencies of local draft boards and the US government in applying draft law. As the Vietnam War progressed, Friends were involved in draft and military counseling all over the United States, in Canada, and occasionally in other parts of the world. Many Friends became organizers of local interfaith draft counseling teams, while in metropolitan areas AFSC and other Quaker groups served as coordinating bodies for counseling.

Counseling centers sponsored by Friends served hundreds of men each month, exposing them to Quaker individuals and views. Quakers influenced many young men through their counseling. Simultaneously, draft and military counseling, in which Friends of all ages and genders participated, had a significant effect on the Religious Society of Friends.

Friends, with their long history of conscientious objection to war in all forms, were natural leaders in the draft counseling movement. Many of the first counselors were men who had resisted conscription during World War II, serving instead in Civilian Public Service or going to prison. Friends saw counseling as a way to serve the growing community of young men who, for many reasons, opposed the war in Vietnam enough to want to avoid participation. Not many Friends believed that draft counseling could paralyze the draft system as well as it ultimately did or bring an end to the war. Their participation grew out of an impetus to answer the call to "hospitality toward others" and offer information about CO status and draft law to anyone in the community who contacted them.

I began draft counseling when I became the secretarial support staff for the AFSC Area Office in Madison, Wisconsin in the spring of 1968. The Peace Intern in that office had recently decided to be a complete resister to the draft and left a few weeks after I was hired because he expected imminent arrest. Before he left he trained me in the rudiments of draft law and introduced me to others, including several members of Madison Monthly Meeting who were involved with this work.

For me, draft counseling soon became more than just giving out accurate legal information. Coming from an inner city background, I recognized early that the constituency to whom draft counseling was accessible remained the white, educated, upper middle class, but these young men often came seeking counseling in great pain. In their late teens and early twenties, they were being asked by their government to make life and death decisions, not only to put themselves at risk of injury and death but also to face maiming and killing others, including civilians, in a country halfway across the world.

For some few of the men who came for counseling, the draft and service in Vietnam just appeared to present a disturbing disruption in their career and personal plans. But for most of the men I counseled, involvement in the war in Vietnam went against what they had been taught about the United States as a peace-loving protector of democracy. John Kennedy had told us, "Ask not what your country can do for you. Ask what you can do for your country." But military service in Vietnam appeared antithetical to being a good citizen and a good human being.

The decision about what to do about the draft involved a deep examination of values and, often, religious convictions. For many young men this caused a change in the direction of their lives. Sometimes their decisions had to be made without the support of family, religious leaders and friends. Many recognized that the decision to become CO's or leave the country, for instance, would divide them both physically and emotionally from family and other loved ones. They sought help in making such painful and difficult decisions.

As a draft counselor I defined my role and the role of those I trained as presenting all the options and offering an impartial listening ear to sort through those choices. During my time coordinating the counseling service at AFSC in New York City, many men expressed great loneliness during this decision process. They cited their draft counselor as the only one who would listen. This made it a heavy responsibility to be a draft counselor. These young men were in a very vulnerable position, forced to make decisions the implications of which they would have to live with the rest of their lives. It was necessary to present accurate and timely information in a balanced way. Many counselors became very good at this.

However, the counselor was powerless to influence the often arbitrary application of the law by local draft boards or the behavior of the family and friends. For example, it was difficult to watch men who sincerely embraced the peace testimony lose their bid for CO because they were raised Jewish or atheist and lose the support of their families and community in the process.

I did my draft and military counseling in the context of Quaker institutions. Friends had and have some very special gifts to bring to this kind of work. Foremost is Friends' conviction that each of us can know God as an Inner Teacher and that discerning God's will is a corporate responsibility. As draft and military counselors, Friends guided young men to honor that Inner Teacher, to discern truth and to act on their leadings.

I did not use these words to articulate the role of counselors back then. But as I look back, such words reflect accurately my experience. Quaker counselors helped men through a kind of clearness process, encouraging them when possible to consult broadly with others. If no friends or family were available, counselors provided that listening ear, keeping their opinions to themselves. Though there were draft and military counselors who saw their role differently and pushed certain options, few found that type of advocacy a comfortable stance within Friends' institutions.

During 1970-1971, I was released by New York Yearly and Monthly Meetings to counsel men in the military. As a released Friend I counseled mostly men of color who came from the inner city or men from rural areas. Most had been drafted or joined the military because they were unable to find employment. They had not had access to counseling and, often, had not had a chance to examine the implications of participation in the military. Many of the men I saw had already served in Vietnam and sustained injuries. Yet, they were being sent back.

They wanted out. There were few legal avenues for men to gain discharge from the military, even if their experience in combat led them to become sincere conscientious objectors. I only had one successful CO case during that year. Most of my counseling involved presenting the options of leaving the country, going underground or returning to the military to serve again in Vietnam. Helping men discern the most appropriate option between such choices was best done by men who also had served recently in the military. After presenting the options, I often referred men to veterans for the discernment part of the process. Once they had made their decision how to proceed, I could help them again through a network of support services and contacts, many provided by Quakers.

During this period I also trained draft counselors to work in rural areas, where the climate ran against anti-war sentiment and men had little access to counseling. It was encouraging to train Friends and others in upstate New York and Vermont, so that they could provide counseling to men like those I was seeing in military counseling. For some of those Friends and their meetings, providing counseling involved some risk. Some Friends were harassed at work or in public for their participation in anti-war activities. Regardless, most of the meetings in New York Yearly Meeting were providing counseling by the end of that year. I suspect that was true of most Friends meetings in the US by 1971, regardless of the branch of Friends to which they belonged.

Draft counseling brought some of the core elements of Friends' faith and practice out from under the bushel. It met a need and exposed the public to Quaker beliefs. Friends practiced a particular kind of counseling, striving to accurately inform others about their options, to lead them to their Inner Teacher and to assist them in discerning and carrying out the appropriate action. Friends worked together to serve communities beyond their own, seeking to apply the same core elements to counseling men in the military. Meetings were strengthened by acting corporately to support counseling centers, develop networks of support services and support the Friends who did the work. All of this had a positive effect on the Religious Society of Friends.

Some of those I counseled explored the Religious Society of Friends further and became members. Some of those who were trained and worked as counselors also joined the Society, including me. Did this influx of seekers from other faiths and no faith weaken the Society, polluting the faith and practice of Quakers in the United States?

It is still too early to tell. But as 21st century historians examine the Religious Society of Friends in the late 20th century, I believe they will find that draft and military counseling during the Vietnam War was one of the most visible public manifestations of a small but vital religious movement. They will discover that those people exposed to Quakerism through draft and military counseling, who subsequently joined that movement, helped revitalize it, becoming some of its strongest leaders later in the century. Though the rapid growth of the Society through many new, small, geographically dispersed meetings during the 1990's has challenged the limited number of seasoned Friends to share their experience, the Vietnam-convinced Friends can play an important role in responding to this need.

Friends who served as military counselors have valuable experience with people of color, different ethnic backgrounds, cultures and classes. Ultimately, I believe that participation in draft and military counseling will be seen as a source of growth and revitalization for the Quaker movement in the late 20th century.

The Vietnam Era Underground Railroad:
A Conductor's Story

Ken Maher

18 July 1998

In the late 1960s, I underwent what might be described as a born-again experience. At meeting for worship every First Day and at many other times during the week, I found myself thinking such remarkable sentiments as "Jesus saves" and "Jesus is the answer" and "Give it to Jesus."

I did not often verbalize these thoughts, because Jesus was my little secret. Another member of the Buffalo Meeting had given me Jesus as a gift. He told me that, in case I happened to know anyone involved in the new Underground Railroad, we might want to call this serendipitous, fly-by-night network of Quaker meetinghouses and other more or less subversive waystations by the acronym JESUS.

That is, "Just Escape from Servitude in the United States."

During the Vietnam War, the meetinghouse in Buffalo, New York, served as headquarters for the Western New York Draft Counseling Center, which operated probably 50-80 hours a week during the height of the war. Upstairs, the meetinghouse resident couple opened their home as a commune to assorted bohemian types, myself among them. Soon after moving into the meetinghouse in the fall of 1968, I was asked to take responsibility for the increasing numbers of young men who showed up at the meetinghouse door looking for a friendly face.

These were not the young men looking for draft counseling.

I was to take care of the growing numbers who came unsolicited seeking help to emigrate to Canada. Although many of the draft counselors and many of the members of Buffalo Meeting were sympathetic to these young men who wanted to leave the States, working with them in the Draft Counseling Center could have seriously jeopardized both the Draft Counseling Center itself and the Buffalo Friends Meeting that housed its endeavors.

So I was given a list of people in the Buffalo area who had offered to help young men escape the draft. And that was the beginning of the Underground Railroad station that operated unofficially in the Buffalo Friends meetinghouse at 72 North Parade Avenue.

Our station was directly affiliated with the Toronto Anti-Draft Programme (TADP), run by Bill Spira and Naomi Wall. And we soon became incredibly well organized for an operation such as ours, that was run by a bunch of

"commsymphippiepinkofaggotfreaks."

The Canadian government had a very clear and detailed immigration policy at that time, based on a point system. Anyone who wished to emigrate to Canada had to achieve a certain minimum number of points based on education, profession, family members living in Canada, and other criteria.

In addition to providing food, temporary housing, and often substitute parenting for our guests, my job was to make sure that we sent to the border only those young men who had enough points to guarantee their admission. To this end, we offered quite a makeover service. We provided haircuts for the long-haired hippie types, straight-looking clothes, and a packed suitcase for those who showed up with no luggage.

We had a $500 revolving cash fund, which Canadian Immigration considered enough to live on while resettling in Canada. This money was returned to the driver after passing the Immigration interview and was then available for the next emigrant. Through the Toronto Friends Meeting and the TADP, we arranged for a job offer, worth ten points (or ten percent) of required Immigration Department points, for almost every emigrant. Our most vigorous supporters in the Toronto Meeting were the late John and Nancy Pocock.

We had personal letters of reference sent to the meetinghouse from sympathetic clergy, teachers, and employers associated with our guests. And all of these documents, along with the money and the revolving clothes closet, were gathered in the suitcase that we handed over with each young man to the volunteer driver. Our drivers were nuns and priests and other clergy and ordinary citizens who looked as straight as the most prominent Quaker of the day, Richard Nixon.

The Toronto Anti-Draft Programme helped us keep track of the changing Immigration Department shifts at the four US-Canada bridges in the Buffalo area. TADP kept records of Immigration officers who gave our young men a hard time, and we avoided using those bridges on their shifts, especially for those young men with only a marginal number of points who would thus need to rely on the discretionary ten points that the Immigration officer personally controlled.

How did those heading for Canada know to come to the meetinghouse door? Well, a number of young men were sent to us from Toronto, because it was necessary to apply for landed immigrant status at a border or at a point of disembarkation. But instead of being told to follow the drinking gourd, most of those who arrived at the Buffalo meetinghouse said that they had been told by someone in the peace movement something to the effect that they could find Friends in the telephone book of any big city. And once they had found Friends in one city, they were referred to other Friends along their route north. So I heard stories of men moving from one meetinghouse to another to get to Buffalo. Unlike the Underground Railroad of slavery days, however, the stations along the Vietnam era railroad were much more loosely connected, largely because of the very real threat of infiltration and prosecution.

When I obtained my FBI file after the Freedom of Information Act, all my fears were confirmed and in fact multiplied. Almost all of my antiwar activity was documented with a lot of hearsay records that could only have been provided by agents who had actually known me personally. We were rather sure at the time that all the phone lines into the meetinghouse were tapped, and the later evidence confirmed those fears.

Who were these young men going to Canada? At first when Canada was accepting only those avoiding the draft, they were largely college-educated, middle class whites with great futures if they could stay away from Vietnam. Then Canada decided to open its borders as well to military men who were absent without leave, and the whole picture changed. We were suddenly flooded with younger men, some of whom were not white, most of whom had barely a high school education and were much harder to place because of their general lack of education and needed job skills. I remember one of them, a young farm boy from Kansas, who actually told me that all he ever wanted was 40 acres and a mule, and he was sorry that he would have to go to Canada to get it.

In the late summer of 1969, we had a report from TADP that one of the young men we had helped and who had stayed with us in Buffalo for about a week reported a very suspicious incident when he arrived in Toronto. When he came out of the Canadian Immigration Office after his interview, he recognized a car and its driver sitting outside the office. He told TADP that he had seen the same car and driver over a week earlier outside the Syracuse Peace Center and again outside the safe house he had stayed at in Syracuse, New York, over 100 miles from Buffalo.

Somehow, the unidentified driver of that car from Syracuse had known where and when the young man was crossing into Canada.

That was the end of my being a conductor in Buffalo. I handed over my contact list of drivers and safe houses, the suitcase, and the money to one of my most supportive drivers, a suburban homemaker, and left town for a few months.

Later that fall, TADP sent me to Detroit to set up another Underground Railroad station there. Both of these stations continued operating to some degree until supply and demand allowed them to be laid down. And that is the story of how I worked for Jesus during the Vietnam War.

Military Counseling: Comments to Saturday Afternoon Panel

David Finke

We're looking at the variety of responses Friends and their institutions made to the war. I'm asked to address "Military Counseling" – perhaps because for a decade or so I chaired the "Midwest Committee for Military Counseling," an outgrowth of the Midwest Central Committee for Conscientious Objectors (CCCO). But I'd also like to pay tribute to something broader, what we might call "the GI Movement," which was both amorphous and special. What I experienced touches on what each of these other panelists is addressing, and I look forward to our discussion in hearing how indistinct were the boundaries between our work with civilians and those in the military.

The first point I want to make has to do with image *vs.* reality. I want to raise a strong challenge to the popular and press-induced view of the Vietnam antiwar movement as hostile to the soldiers who fought in it. I don't doubt for a minute that there was a "lost generation" who came home feeling rejected and unappreciated – part of the motivation for the outpouring of support during the Gulf War, from a country still feeling guilty about Vietnam, I suspect.

But the too often repeated imagery of antiwar protesters spitting on GIs is, I believe, a well-nourished myth, part of the agenda of counteracting the so-called "Vietnam Syndrome." In my decade of work against that war, I can say unreservedly that I never saw such a spectacle – though I've met plenty of demoralized Vietnam GIs and vets. In fact, one such – a personal friend, Clem Henderson – became a "mass murderer" on the streets of Chicago:

his flashback led to 5 deaths in a matter of minutes, including his own. I think of Clem when I need to remember the human cost of what America did to, and expected of, ordinary young men.

My point, though, is that the response I saw in the antiwar movement was one of solidarity with, and not rejection of GIs. More specifically, the response of Quakers I was around was one which was consistent with our testimony of equality: rather than seeing GIs as monsters or "baby-killers," GIs were treated with elemental dignity and respect as fellow children-of-God. They were another class of the victims of the institution of war. We were against war, not the warriors. I believe that Friends in their GI work – I'm speaking both of the individuals and the corporate response – brought a strong degree of humanity and compassion into a situation that was rife with dehumanization and exploitation.

We got to "military counseling" through a route that began with what we first called "CO counseling," and I was part of that early network, usually made up of a few Friends and friends-of-Friends who had been through the CO process themselves, and in understanding were several steps ahead of even high-priced lawyers. Word that such people existed somehow "got around," and as the war escalated we became inundated with cases far exceeding our personal experiences. I hope our discussion might illuminate how a new concept – draft counseling – emerged early on in the Vietnam period.

Draft and military counseling were two aspects of the same reality, though dealing with different bodies of law and regulation. Both were – and indeed are – attempts to help persons faced by arbitrary power to discern what are their core values with regard to militarism, and then to help empower them to act on their choices – with the most complete, accurate, and responsible set of facts by which to make informed choices. It may also involve following through with those individuals as they act out the drama of their lives.

A difference that soon became apparent between draft and military counseling, however, is that we as counselors were now facing a different set of class realities. Although good, successful draft counseling got out into working-class communities – beyond the campuses where maintaining student deferments might be the dominant reality – military counseling put us much more squarely into the lives of poor and working folks who may have been completely unaware that they had choices. New sensitivities and vocabularies had to be learned, and I believe that the horizons of many counselors were broadened (or to use the cliché, "radicalized.")

I suspect that in the ordinary course of my life, I would not have seen the inside of Ft. Leavenworth, or dealt with psychiatrists and chaplains and "JAG" [military legal] officers who were processing some of the human debris of the war in southeast Asia. But I am a wiser person for it, whether the young men I was working with and for were in or out of uniform. It was, in the grand scope of things, an accident of fate whether a Vietnam-era American male youth had "taken the step forward" in the induction process or not. But regardless of their jurisdictional or legal status, we tried to "be there" to assist them.

In the day-to-day work of a peace program within AFSC, and indeed in the life of my Friends Meeting at 57th Street, there was no hard and fast line between "draft" and "military" counseling, except that some folks had technical specialty in one more than another. To me it is significant that, in 1967 when there were only perhaps six people in the Chicago AFSC network who were able to do this kind of counseling work, one was Peter Caplan from 57th Street. He had applied for and been discharged as a CO, from within the military. His perspective, his experience, was a very valuable asset for the rest of us – not just for the GIs who were sent his way. It showed, in principle, from the start that there were people within – and not just facing – military life who were seeking some way out, some way to resolve the agonies and conflicts of conscience caused by the war and the warmaking machine.

It's important that we remember that GIs might, or might not, have their best chance of getting out by applying for recognition as a conscientious objector. That was true for the run-of-the-mill draft counselee as well. I think we as counselors assumed everyone was, as a matter of conscience, objecting to something about the military. It possibly could fit into the ever-changing legal criteria of eligibility (which fundamentally altered after Dan Seeger's witness was vindicated by the Supreme Court).

But counselors, as a matter of principle, were obligated to examine all the possible and probable recourses which could help give a counselee's life back to him or her. Thus, we had to be aware of medical, hardship, and family circumstances which might be grounds for discharge, even as good draft counselors were doing in examining all possible grounds for deferment or exemption. Our own life-choices were not the criteria to impose on our counselees: basic concepts of what it means ethically to be a counselor, as distinct from an advocate or organizer, were part of what we were trying to convey to our volunteer counselors.

What military counseling we initially did out of the AFSC office paralleled the emergence of a draft-counseling network. At first, it was the well-intentioned but often improvised work of a staff person such as myself. We soon became "paralegals," with crash courses from the few capable lawyers (and former JAG officers) who were available, and traveling seminars from staffers of CCCO. But to preserve sanity and efficiency, we soon had to train more volunteers to handle the burgeoning caseload, and set up networks of referral and accountability.

The next step was to relate to – and sometimes help set up – new organizations that were emerging, and hope to affect the ethics and tone of what went on there. (This leads to a much larger discussion of varying approaches to "coalitions" during the Vietnam era.)

In Chicago, it meant that we had working relations with Vets for Peace and Vietnam Veterans Against the War. Particularly via our intimate connection with CADRE (Chicago Area Draft Resisters), we had contact with people in the seminal national newspaper, *Vietnam GI*, and also the coffeehouse movement. (Chicago had its own "Alice's Restaurant" in the northside "hippie ghetto" toward which GIs on leave gravitated, whether authorized or not.) For years, I stayed in touch with people in CAMP, the

"Chicago Area Military Project," which did what they simply called "GI organizing."

The connections between the Chicago anti-draft and in-service GI-resistance movement were there from the beginning. In the first well-publicized burning or turning in of draft cards (Sheep's Meadow, Central Park, NYC, spring 1967) one of the best known participants from Chicago was Gary Rader, a fully-uniformed Green Beret reservist. The camaraderie and sense of common struggle was there from the outset, in the Chicago antiwar movement.

As I again discovered the newsletters and flyers from that '67-'68 period (some of which I have with me), it is manifestly apparent that involvement of and outreach to GIs was a fundamental part of resisting the war in Vietnam. We must not let the popular historians forget that, in the face of the myths I noted at the outset.

I've mentioned that we soon outgrew the ability of the lone Peace Education Secretary to deal with the AWOL fellow who showed up on the doorstep – though I kept a hand in it throughout my tenure at AFSC. I must pay tribute, in passing, to the effective network of AFSC secretaries who managed to help each other in visiting, or arranging visits, at stockades, securing local lawyers, advising on shelter and sanctuary, getting the involvement of Friends Meetings and churches. I was amazed, again, to see in my files how much work was done by Ed Sanders in southern California, near both to Marine bases and to Friends Meetings, and giving selflessly of his compassion and time.

But of necessity, we had to train and use a core of volunteers, whether "laypeople" or those with specialties in law, psychiatry, and other medicine. Those networks exist to this day, and during the last 25 years or so of no active draft (though registrations have never ceased!), it has been vital to maintain and nourish those networks.

I have in the past several years been very active in trying to revive and explicate a "culture of Quaker voluntary service," something different from the professionalized approach to service, or advocacy of social change, that we seem to have drifted into. In another setting (or as you run into me), I'll gladly help interpret what recently brought together over 100 of us, from 26 Friends organizations from 19 Yearly Meetings, to examine the current state of "Quaker Volunteer Service, Training, and Witness."

But for here, suffice it to say that in draft and military counseling we had an excellent avenue for concerned people to get involved, under Quaker auspices, in giving direct assistance as volunteers to those who were hurting, victims of the scourge of war. We must never let that tradition weaken, or take it for granted, or rest on the laurels of past generations of Quaker volunteers.

My final observation, which might well have been my first, is that our experience in working with GIs, in doing "military counseling" and resistance support work, was highly reminiscent of what might have been the experience of Quakers 120 years or so previously. I'm thinking of the analogy of the "Underground Railroad."

Although there were 19th-century Friends who were highly visible in public activity of organized abolition work, sometimes joining with non-Friends in "coalition" advocacy for the end of slavery, what we're generally remembered for was something different. It came down to how Quaker families would respond when they heard that knock on the door in the night, and they had the choice of helping those who were, in terror, fleeing oppressions, running for their lives.

I have increasingly come to believe in what I call the "No Big Deal" principle of the workings of the Kingdom of God. In other words, when people are acting in faithfulness to the will of the Divine, they just *do* it – not calling attention to themselves, and often thinking "this is no big deal, I'm just doing what I ought to, being who I am, trusting in God's help."

My testimony is that during the Vietnam War I saw Friends doing the work of the Kingdom in opening their hearts and homes to escaping GIs, taking the risk that they would indeed sometimes be "ripped off," which can happen anywhere/anytime, but bringing a human, compassionate presence into a scene of turmoil, anxiety, and sometimes terror.

As we continue to share this weekend, I hope we'll tell more of these stories, giving recognition to what Allie Walton called "Quaker saints and other ordinary people," as they simply did what needed to be done, acting as Friends.

Responding to Leadings of the Spirit:
The Origins of Quaker House of Fayetteville, NC

William A. Eagles

He was young.

The Unitarian from Omaha in the photograph, Dean Holland, was so young – like we all were. The picture could be from your high school yearbook or mine. And, like many of us, he was thoughtful and middle class and bright, a National Merit Scholar.

Dean Holland enlisted in the Army in 1968, studied Vietnamese in California, but was reassigned to the medical corps and sent to Fort Bragg in Fayetteville, North Carolina, when he expressed concern to his commanding officer about the morality of war.

He soon decided to seek recognition as a conscientious objector and appealed to local Unitarians for help in developing his application. He needed help. No one at Fort Bragg had ever been recognized as a conscientious objector.

The Unitarians in Fayetteville included members of the military, retirees from the military, and supporters of the military. They were not able to provide the help Dean sought. However, Bruce Pulliam, a Quaker college professor who was worshiping with the Unitarians, suggested that Dean seek assistance from the Quakers at the Chapel Hill Meeting.

So, one Thursday night in the summer of 1969, Dean hitchhiked 60 miles to attend meeting for business in Chapel Hill to ask for help – for himself and for others at Fort Bragg.

A few weeks later, with help from the Raleigh Meeting, the Durham Meeting, and Piedmont Friends Fellowship, Quaker House opened in Fayetteville, in a very modest rental house with enough money for meager staff salaries. Quakers were in Fayetteville and their work began.

Several months later, Dean Holland became the first at Fort Bragg to be recognized by the Army as a conscientious objector, was discharged, and became director of Quaker House. But on December 31, 1969, he and assistant director Kaye Lindsey were killed in an automobile wreck. But, Quakers were in Fayetteville and their work continued.

On May 16, 1970, Quaker House cooperated with the Vietnam Veterans Against the War in holding the largest antiwar demonstration Fayetteville had ever seen.

Four days later, Quaker House burned to the ground, in a still unsolved arson case. Zoning regulations barred rebuilding, but Quakers were in Fayetteville and their work continued.

From May to October, the Board of Overseers and the newly formed worship group met out-of-doors among the ashes of the burned building and under the watchful eye of military intelligence parked across the street. But, Quakers were in Fayetteville and their work continued.

In November, Quaker House got a new home – with help from the GI Bill. An ex-soldier at Fort Bragg, Bill Carothers, purchased a home with a VA loan and sold it to Quaker House, which assumed the mortgage.

Dean Holland, this young Unitarian, had challenged Friends. He thought Quakers should be in Fayetteville and said so – clearly, directly, and firmly. Fort Bragg is one of the largest instruments of war and death ever devised by the human mind. It is the home of the Special Forces. Pope Air Force Base is in Fayetteville and Camp Lejuene Marine Base is in nearby Jacksonville.

Dean Holland was right; in those turbulent times, Quakers belonged in Fayetteville.

North Carolina's Yearly Meeting (FUM), however, declined support, as did some monthly meetings affiliated with FUM and FGC. It was just too radical; Friends did not feel clear. But clearness came and Quaker House has been sustained by Friends of every affiliation for 29 years.

Quakers are in Fayetteville and their work continues.

Through 1972, it focused on the antiwar movement, then on military counseling. In the last decade, it has also included anti-recruitment, community building, and mediation.

So, this is a story of Dean Holland. But it is also a story of North Carolina Quakers with the gifts of discernment and recognizing leadings and with a ministry of steadfastness. Friends in Chapel Hill, Raleigh, and Durham, of a generation different from mine were open to God's leading through the young Unitarian. They were willing to wait upon the Spirit – but with an openness, so as not to wait too long.

We do not know in what form the next leading may come. We do not know what ministry will be required. The issue may be one that has been before Friends for years or it may walk in the door in the form of a young seeker, or even one who knows.

But, if we wait upon the Spirit, if we learn to be steadfast, then generations of people in need, people whom society is just not prepared to deal with, will be told – as recently a gay Fort Bragg solder was told by an unsympathetic, dismissive chaplain: "Go see the Quakers; they'll help anybody."

Note: Some of the information included in this paper was formerly published in Lamme, "Fayetteville's Quaker House: In an Ocean of Darkness," 40 *Friends Journal*, No. 10, at 12 (Oct. '94).

"But What Canst Thou Say?"

Personal Reflections of Three Generations
Of Quaker Peace Activists

Panel Discussion Among:

Bronson Clark (World War II resister)

Max Carter (Vietnam CO)

Garrett Colgan-Snyder (1990's CO)

Chuck Fager, Moderator

July 19, 1998

Generations Panel: "But What Canst Thou Say?"

Max Carter, Bronson Clark, Garrett Colgan-Snyder
Chuck Fager, Moderator

Dan Seeger: Good morning, everyone. You'll remember that having spent the first day of our conference talking about conscientious objection, the second day talking about our witness against the war and our efforts to produce social change and change policies and ending the war, the third day we've talked about the impact of that period on our Religious Society of Friends. Today we're going to talk about what the experience of the Vietnam War period means for the past, the present and the future. We're going to take a look at this experience through the lens of time. This morning's panel discussion will be a chance for us to hear from people from three different generations. Then very importantly, right after lunch we will also hear from Peter Goldberger about the road ahead before we turn to the open mike session. So this is the day when our lens or our focus will be on looking ahead and looking back.

  Chuck Fager has kindly consented to serve as our facilitator this morning. I think many of you know Chuck. Chuck is a member of State College Meeting in Pennsylvania, which gives its members a choice to be either part of Baltimore Yearly Meeting or Philadelphia Yearly Meeting. Chuck has tried to be a member of both Yearly Meetings; we'll see if that works. Chuck is a Friend who has worked for many years as a mailhandler in the post office, which is a profession I think not shared by many Friends. So he has an unusual experience in that regard. But also through all that time he has served as a kind of independent writer, editor and publisher. Many of us know *A Friendly Letter*, which he edited for a period of about 10 years. It was a publication which sought to provide Friends with needed information which wasn't available in other places. It was a publication which was held in high esteem by many Friends and one's appreciation for it tended to be inversely proportional to the number of times one was mentioned in it. Whatever that may mean.

Chuck has also written and edited some very serious books on topics of concern to us. I remember one of the early ones was *White Reflections on Black Power*, but he's published a number of books since that time. Most recently he's edited a book entitled *The Best of Friends, Vol. 1,* which is a collection of recent Quaker writings. Chuck served on the Pendle Hill staff for about three years, when he was director of our Issues Program. So I'm very glad to turn this morning's session over to Chuck, who will present you with the panel.

Chuck Fager: Thank you, Dan. Dan was right that I did work for the Postal Service for about seven and a half years. So please treat me gently. At the moment I'm pretty gruntled, but you never know when a postal worker is going to get disgruntled. And that can be hazardous.

We have a panel this morning of three Friends who each has his own experience of conscientious objection, or I should say responses to the draft, because conscientious objection is not the only response. We're going to go down the generations.

Immediately to my right and your left is Bronson Clark, retired from the American Friends Service Committee, whose experience with conscription was in World War II. He's going to tell us about that in a few moments. Next to him is Max Carter. Max is currently at Guilford College, where he directs a wonderful operation called the Quaker Leadership Scholars Program. And then we have Garrett Colgan-Snyder, a student at Colgate University, who is currently on the maintenance staff at Pendle Hill.

Now the format is going to be my best imitation of Terry

Gross and Larry King and, who knows, perhaps Jerry Springer before we're done. I'm going to ask these Friends questions and we're going to move from one to the other and back and forth for a while, and then at a certain point we'll entertain questions from our "callers around the country," so if you're interested in asking a question we'll have time to do that pretty soon.

I want to begin with Bronson. Bronson, will you tell us a little bit about where you're from and where you grew up and how you came to confrontation with the matter of conscription?

Bronson Clark: Right. I was born in the Buckeye state (Ohio). I went to Antioch, which changed my life. I met a professor named M. N. Chatterjee, who was a Gandhian. I came out a Gandhian, from Antioch. A group of us went to a place we called Ahimsa Farm, which was to be a study to see what nonviolent direct action might do and so forth. We had people out there like James Farmer, who came and talked to us and so forth.

The thing I'm proudest of is in 1941, working with five Blacks from the NAACP. We went to Garfield Park and we quietly bought tickets for the Blacks; they were not around at the moment, but we got their tickets. And then we entered the pool and we had of course a lot of people that were supporters that we brought into the pool. The strategy was we would not resist being thrown out of there. We would wait until the police showed up, and then that would be the end of it. Now, this was '41, so that was pretty good – anyway, so the Whites went through and the Blacks just ignored the gatekeeper and into the pool they went. So some Whites stepped up and said "Out of the pool, out of the pool, out of the pool!" A young lady said, "I don't object. There's no problem with them there." Of course this was a public facility and we had some guys that were getting threatening and so forth. But the sirens started to ring and, well, to make a long story short, we retreated. But we came back another week, and we did that again.

But let's jump to World War II. I visited some CPS [Civilian Public Service] camps. As a Gandhian, I admired what they were trying to do there, but as a Gandhian I wrote my draft board and asked for permission to join Gandhi's nonviolent army to defend India. Well, they got the language right. They wrote back and said permission to go join Gandhi's nonviolent army is hereby denied. Well, Judge Fried on the Cleveland public square – I had a nice lawyer, guy named Thomas, standing beside me, and Fried was going "five years, five years, five years, five years."

But when I stood up and this lawyer stood up, he glanced up, "three years." Now that's important, because if you get three years and you're a felon, you've got a chance for parole in one year. I didn't mind going to prison, but I didn't necessarily want to stay there. I sort of was naive; I thought, you go to prison, you get to sit down and relax. Oh, no way, no way, no way. In Ashland we had a guy known as Barefoot Stanley, a vegetarian.

Chuck Fager: Hang on a minute, Bronson. I want to stop you at the prison gate, leave these folks hanging for a minute and move on to Max. And then we'll come back. So we're leaving Bronson here at the gate of Ashland Federal, what is it, Correctional Institution or Penitentiary, in Ashland, Ohio. OK. And then we move west to the Hoosier state and ahead a generation to the little town of Russiaville. I want to ask Max Carter about his background and when and how he came to encounter with conscription.

Max Carter: I grew up in Indiana, and just to give some clarification on the town of Russiaville [pronounced Rooshaville], if any of you know its spelling; it's R-u-s-s-I-a. Our high school name was the Cossacks. It was named after a French Indian by the name of Rush-AH-ville, whose name the Tar Heels who came up and settled that part of the world pronounced Roosher-ville. And then when they spelled it, R-u-s-s-I-a. So just to clarify that. We were not a bunch of Russian immigrants.

I don't know what kind of animal a Himsa is, but I grew up on a Holstein farm, and as befits a rural area and dairy farmers, I grew up in pastoral Quakerism in Western Yearly Meeting. My family had been Quaker back to the 1600's on both sides. So I grew up in a deeply Quaker culture, but also one deeply affected by the

Wesleyan revivals that came in after the Civil War. So my understandings of how I ought to live in the world were affected both by Quaker stories and a culture that was deeply affected by the world. When I was facing turning 18 and began thinking about what my response would be to the draft, this was in the mid-sixties – I turned 18 in 1966, the same year I marched off to Ball State University in Muncie, Indiana – I had debated what stance I should take, both operating with the stories my uncles had told me about CO work during World War II, serving with the ambulance units in Europe, and with the popular notion of my peers and other family influences that one ought to serve one's country. At that time the war was still popular, up until the mid-sixties.

I had just about determined to join the Coast Guard in order to balance both my desire not to be in the military shooting people, but also fulfilling my duties to my country and patrol the Mississippi against U-boats or something like that, when in the summer of '64 an American Friends Service Committee peace caravan came through our area. And at New London Friends Meeting, I heard a young Japanese woman give articulate and very simple testimony to what it was like waking up the day the bomb dropped, playing with her little brother outside, being grateful for hearing only one airplane overhead rather than the fleets of bombers that had been raking that area for weeks, and then the blinding flash and her whole world disappearing.

And I knew at that moment I couldn't be a part of that system, and determined to apply for CO status, which was granted when I turned 18.

Chuck Fager: Max, before we move on, I wonder if you could say a little more about what it was like to be growing up in Western Yearly Meeting, in Indiana Quakerism, in relation to the war and sort of military stuff generally, because am I not correct that there are a good many meetings there where one may find an American flag in the part of the building that some might call the sanctuary? And wasn't there also considerable discussion and reaction to the voyage of the *Phoenix*? I think that's something that we've heard about here previously, and it may be worth getting an Indiana slant on that.

Max Carter: It's a mixed bag in the Midwest, in Indiana. You've got both very evangelical towards fundamentalist Quakerism and you have unprogrammed Friends, the results of Hicksite, Orthodox, Wilburite, Gurneyite and other sorts of separations. I grew up in what I later came to know was a Gurneyite Orthodox meeting, but all of my pastors growing up were out of the Wesleyan Holiness or Nazarene churches. My meeting never had an American flag in it until, oddly enough, the Gulf War. Of all the wars one would think they would choose to really rally around the flag, that was the one. But there were many others who did.

I'll tell a story at the prompting of Chuck, of a good friend of mine. Some of you may know Ray Stewart, who was one of the wonderful lights of Indiana Quakerism, came out of World War II out of the Nazarene Church, who became convinced that war was wrong, became a Quaker, an active member of Dublin Friends Meeting, one of the most popular Quaker heretics in Indiana. In the early 1950's he was attending the Dublin Friends Meeting, which was deeply under the control of the American Legion, and continued to protest their slant on things during the Korean War.

The final straw was during the opening exercises of Sunday school or something, I don't quite have my story straight, they marched in with the flag and all the pomp and circumstance of the military. And that was it for Ray. He stood up, took his shoes off, clapped them together and said "I shake the very dust of this place off my sandals" and marched out of that meeting with other protesters and founded the Hopewell Meeting, which still continues.

My own meeting leaned in that direction; we didn't have many active participants in the war. There were several World War II veterans, but it was a little lower key than that. But, my grandfather did quite literally sit each of us grandchildren on his knee when we were old enough to know better and told us, there are two things you've got to know in this life, son: one, marry a Quaker, or if you don't, turn them into a Quaker, and the second is, and here I quote him directly, "You can't be a good Democrat and a good Quaker at the same time." Indiana Quakers were 99 percent Republican. That was because the Republican party was the party of Lincoln. It was the liberal party. Culturally we kind of grew along with where the Republican party went. So those were some of the instances.

But the *Phoenix*, real quick like: Burl Nelson, Margery Nelson, Earl Nelson, grew up just 12 miles away from me in Kokomo, Indiana, and when Burl Nelson came back from his voyage on the *Phoenix*, and he was interviewed by the Indianapolis Star, the newspaper owned by the Quayle family [CF: Dan Quayle] and was asked basically, what were you thinking? And his response was, I was only trying to carry out the lessons I'd learned in Sunday school at Courtland Avenue Friends Church – which is the most evangelical Friends Church in Western Yearly Meeting.

Well of course, when that hit the papers, there was a letter immediately from Courtland Avenue saying, we do not teach treason in our Sunday school classes. And immediately following on that was a letter from the Greenfield Friends Meeting in Indiana Yearly Meeting saying, Greenfield supports the Johnson administration and our country and our boys in Vietnam, and [they] pushed Indiana Yearly Meeting that year to come that close to approving a minute giving Indiana Yearly Meeting's support for the administration's prosecution of the war, until someone stood up on the floor of the Yearly Meeting – I wouldn't be surprised if it was Ray Stewart – saying, our *Faith and Practice* is fairly clear on this. And they didn't approve the minute, but that was the sympathy.

Chuck Fager: Thank you, Max. Now again, moving ahead another generation to Garrett. Same question: Tell us about your background and how you came to engagement or confrontation with the matter of conscription or registration.

Garrett Colgan-Snyder: My name is Garrett Colgan-Snyder. I was born in Wilmington, Delaware, and grew up in Newton, Massachusetts, which is about four miles from the center of Boston. I'm a senior at Colgate University. I'm majoring in Peace Studies. I hope some people here have heard of Peace Studies majors across the country; there are 300. I've only talked to about three people, even within academic circles, that have heard of such a thing. I gather that's the reason I'm here, because that's my affiliation with this kind of panel.

I turned eighteen in 1995, and the conflict that I would have been associated with would have been the civil war in the former Yugoslavia and Bosnia-Herzegovina. I was surprised when I got my registration card from the post office because what I had been brought up to believe was that there was no way that I was going to be – my mom made this very clear to me – I was not going to be able to live in the house when I turned eighteen through the summers in college if I was

a) a Republican or

b) didn't sign up as a conscientious objector.

This is a combination of liberal Massachusetts society and her Quaker upbringing coming through here. So, I was surprised when I picked up my form that there wasn't a box that said conscientious objector, even in the lower right hand corner, on the back or something, somewhere where you have to find it, but it wasn't there.

So I wrote my draft board a letter that said I was disgruntled that I didn't find the box on the registration card and I was hoping that they would change that. And they wrote a letter back that said, well, it doesn't really matter because there isn't a draft, and they'll keep it in mind that I am a Quaker and I would be a conscientious objector, but as of now, they don't care. Thanks. So they didn't appreciate that.

I'm excited that I don't have to worry about being drafted at the present time – I'm not saying that it will not be reinstated; I'm not saying that my younger brother who just turned eighteen will not be drafted in the next three or four years; I'm not saying that the United States isn't going to get into another major war, but I am excited about the direction it seems we are going in.

I hold people like Bronson and Max in the highest regard

for the work that they did to prepare the ground for Peace Studies majors across the country. We have twelve at Colgate University and we study people like these two guys sitting next to me, and you all in the audience. I really appreciate that and I am excited that I don't have to worry about it at the present time, but I still have a copy of that letter on disk and if I ever have to send it again I might send a little extension on the end that says, "Well, you really should have a box there at the bottom." I think that's it, my biography.

Chuck Fager: Thank you. So now you have the three of them here. And I think we'll go back, rewind the tape a bit. We're going to go back to Bronson. Remember, we left him at the gate of the Ashland Federal Penitentiary, and this was, what year was this, Bronson?

Bronson Clark: What year was it...probably around '43.

Chuck Fager: '43. All right. And you were sentenced to three years for refusing...

Bronson Clark: For refusing to report to Big Flats CPS camp.

Chuck Fager: So you were ordered to report to a CPS camp.

Bronson Clark: Yes, I was.

Chuck Fager: And you refused to do that.

Bronson Clark: Refused to do that.

Chuck Fager: All right, well, pick it up from there.

Bronson Clark: Well, I thought prison, now we can sit back and relax. No way. There was a sandy-haired young man who I was manacled to, who had just a sublime look on his face, but he was a vegetarian. So the minute he got into that prison he took off his shoes. The psychiatrist said he's nuts, and put him in the hole. Now a group of us said hey, we've got to do something about that. Now here, I don't like to throw my good time away right the first week I'm in there, but this strained me. So Charles Butcher, three others and myself, we said well, if he's crazy, we're crazy too. So we took off our shoes. Now you can imagine the sensation in prison with padding down the corridor and entering the dining room. "There's a barefoot boy – there's another one – there's another one." We had five of us there.

Well, anyway, we kept that up, and we had an enlightened warden, and he called me and he said, "Look, you've got to take the pressure off, because I've got to think of my guards here. You take the pressure off and we know what to do." We said obviously he needs tennis shoes. Well, he did eventually get tennis shoes but it took a while, because the warden had to distance himself from that demonstration. They don't like demonstrations.

In that prison was also Meredith Dallas, who objected to censorship of the mail. So he says I'm going to starve myself to death. And he stopped eating. He did take water, he did drink water, but nothing else. Well we watched him just go pale and drawn and terrible. There were also strikes on this subject in Danbury, in other prisons, but after a long time this warden, Hagerman, declared no censorship of the mail, you can write out anything you want to say, you can criticize the institution. Completely changed. Dallas really completely changed what we were able to send and receive in Ashland.

Bayard Rustin was there. Bayard, being a musical man, he put on a musical about a penal institution, which we gave a different name, but you could tell right away it was Ashland, you see. We had chorus and singers. And we had a lot of Afro-Americans, and man they were on the kettle drums or whatever, they were banging away. So it was a pretty thing and it was going along fine and it kind of went on and on and on, and finally the head warden came over and shut the whole thing down. But it was a blessing to be in prison with Bayard Rustin.

Chuck Fager: Bronson, I gather that you were married, were you not, just before or not long before you went into prison, is that right?

Bronson Clark: Right, right. Well, I'd been married for some time, but eight months, three months and about three weeks later, I found I had a baby daughter. So that was interesting. My wife went to her doctor and said, "I think I got a tumor." The doctor says, "Since when does a tumor have a heart beat?"

It was kind of liberating, I felt like the gates had gone open. I didn't have to wait to get out to have a family. Somebody said, Bronson, you must've said, "Marshall, wait, can I go back and get my hat?"

Chuck Fager: Thank you. All right, let's leave you there again in prison, and go back to Max, who had filed for CO after deciding that the Coast Guard didn't cut it. And Max, you're still there in Indiana, at Ball State.

Max Carter: I had dabbled a bit with the notion of resistance, had read a lot of the material, was aware of resisters to the draft, and decided against it. This is probably my own rationalization, but we had a fairly friendly draft board in Howard County, Indiana. The county was chock full of Brethren, Mennonites, Amish, Quakers, and when we marched through, they said, "Oh, another one of them," and just stamped it CO and off we went. But, very many people in my meeting and young people my age were not considering the CO option. They were also being tugged and pulled by the dominant culture that said you gotta support your country, and the way to do that is to serve in the military.

My reasoning was, if I made waves, if I caused embarrassment to my draft board by being the first resister, it might make it even tougher for those coming after me. That was my rationalization.

But I went ahead and when I turned eighteen, my freshman year at Ball State, I marched down to the draft board, filled out my form 100, requesting SS form 150, got that in the mail, filled out my six questions, the first three of which were, do you believe in God? Why do you believe in God? And, How does believing in God affect the way you live?

This was pre-1970. I sent that off, and it was accepted. And I was granted my CO status, had a student deferment, but knew that, and this was before the lottery anyway, but I knew that I was going to volunteer for service. I felt I owed my country something. Others were serving, I ought to as well. I wanted to be of service.

By my sophomore year I was already talking with Friends United Meeting and Harold Smuck, who was the head at that time of the Wider Ministries Commission, asking him if there were areas of service that would be acceptable to my draft board for alternative service that would make use of what I was training to do at Ball State, be a teacher.

He said sure, here are these options. The one that struck my fancy was teaching at the Ramallah Friends Schools [in the West Bank]. I'd grown up hearing stories of my Aunt Annis Carter teaching there, and it also met another criterion I had, and that was it was in a war zone. If others were going off to Vietnam and putting themselves in danger, I wanted to be in a place where I was taking a risk as well, where I could work for peace, actually be a peacemaker. By that time I had figured out there was a difference between being a pacifist and a passivist, and chose to go to Ramallah.

My lottery number came up 79, which meant I was going to go anyway. I'd volunteered ahead of time. I was put in the odd position of when I graduated, I went off to my draft board, my contract with the Ramallah Friends Schools in hand, in the spring of 1970, said, "OK, now what do I do to go over to start my teaching." They said, "Son, you can't go." I said, "Why not?" They said, "There's been a recent Supreme Court decision opening the gates wide to anyone who has opposition to the war, whether it's religious or not. And we don't know how that's going to shake itself out. We've gotta figure this out. We've frozen all CO cases."

And for three months I was beating on their doors wanting

to serve and they weren't letting me. So finally August comes and I ship out to Ramallah, sent them a postcard saying, "I'm here, what do you want me to do now." And they sent me a card back, "Well, in that case, report to Kokomo for active duty in September," and I thought, well forget it....Well, two years later I told them I was done, and I was out.

Chuck Fager: Garrett, since you haven't actually done alternative service or gone to prison yet, I was wondering if you might talk a little bit about being a Peace Studies major. What is it that a Peace Studies major does that might distinguish you from, say, agronomy, or the MBA folks?

Garrett Colgan-Snyder: Well, I think the most important thing a Peace Studies major does is focus on the history of conflict. You look at different cultures and the way they interact and the way that they clash, so that we can avoid the necessity for future drafts. And I think that what I was saying before about there not being a draft is what is exciting because we are able now with the emergence of such Peace Studies programs – they're about 25 years old now, it was the early seventies when the first Peace Studies programs started popping up – we're able to study places where there used to be conflict such as the former Yugoslavia.

If that had been studied from a Peace Studies perspective, or even from an intelligent political science perspective, an informed international relations perspective or even a noninformed mathematics perspective, it would have been quite obvious that there was going to be conflict there again. The history of Bosnia-Herzegovina was such that there had been so much conflictual history, so much killing, so many massacres. Just even in this century, Croatians in World War II being the predominant members of the SS guard who massacred Serbians, for example, in the concentration camps. It was painfully obvious, it is painfully obvious, for those of us who have studied that conflict, World War II conflict, and the conflict in the former Yugoslavia, that that was going to happen.

And I think that is the most important thing that – well, one of the most important things, I would say there are two most important things, that come out of Peace Studies. One is the study of the history of conflict, so we can avoid the necessity for future wars. I don't even like to say that, avoid the necessity for future wars. Because there isn't [such a necessity]. A war is never necessary.

It is hard, this was one of the hardest things for me, when I was writing that letter to the draft board, was thinking about Bosnia-Herzegovina, and the things that I had heard. At that time, not everything that was going on had come out yet, so the systematic rape of Bosnian women was not known to be a tactic of the Serbian government. That's still up in the air, I don't mean to offend anybody, but from what I've read and from what I've been taught, it seems pretty obvious to me. And it was used on both sides. Instances of such atrocities, not that war is not an atrocity, but such atrocities were not completely known.

I think that Bronson can speak to this, having to do with World War II. That was one of the things that was hardest for me, was, well, if there is such thing as intervening militarily, if there is such a thing as a just war, isn't this the case? And that was one of the hardest things for me. It was not a conflict between me and my draft board, a conflict between me and my meeting or a conflict between me and my friends. It was a conflict that was in myself, realizing that there was a question here, there were intelligent arguments on each side.

The second most important thing that Peace Studies brings to the table is nonviolent conflict resolution, the mediation process, which is a constant process. It is not a save-all when conflict breaks out. It needs to be happening over time to sort of quiet things down. It does work when things do get explosive, but there has to be considerable effort on each side

This is the thing that Peace Studies brings to the table for conflicts, this kind of dialogue. This kind of dialogue that has been going on in the north of Ireland that has led to numerous accords, numerous temporary peaces and hopefully ultimate peace in the north of Ireland. That, combined with the history, studying the history, will lead us to an alternative to war, an alternative to police action, an alternative to the US being the strong arm in the international system. And that, to me, is the reason I got into Peace Studies.

Beyond that conflict I had about deciding whether or not this was a just war, whether or not in Bosnia-Herzegovina there was a reason for the US to get involved there, and risk countless more lives, it made me happy to find out there were alternatives to that as well. And to discover Peace Studies, for myself, my sophomore year at Colgate – I myself went from a math major to a Peace Studies major – was quite a change.

Chuck Fager: Thank you. Now once again I want to go back to Bronson. We left him with a new family but still in prison. Bronson, I'd like you to go a little more into your prison experiences, but then I gather that you did get out of prison. You immediately enrolled in what might be called the AFSC Future National Executive Secretary Preparative course, which had a special campus, which you'll explain to us in a minute, right?

Bronson Clark: Well, my bride, Eleanor, took our small daughter in arms and went down and met a parole judge. You couldn't do for winning on that one. So I got what they call a hot shot parole, which is you get a notice you're being released in three days. So that astounded me. I had a hospital assignment lined up in New York City, but when I met my wife, when I got out of there, took the train home with a funny hat that they give you from the jail, she informed me that the deputy director of the Bureau of Prisons wanted us to live in his house and I was not about to countermand my wife.

We tried that, you know, but Bronson was not inclined to keep his opinions to himself, and this man had two sons in the military. An explosion occurred, and we departed from his house.

I sought another parole, on a farm; he put his hand out and blocked it. I said, you know if I don't do something, I'm going back to the clink again. Well, I said, how about AFSC and going to the China convoy, the FAU [Friends Ambulance Unit]. So I was paroled to the American Friends Service Committee. I did go to China and served in China for a decent period of time. Of course they say China changes your life, it certainly did mine.

When I got back from my experience in China, sometime later, I read in the newspaper that Harry Truman had given pardon to some conscientious objectors. So I called up the Department of Justice, and I said, "Is Bronson Clark on that list?" They said, "If you are Bronson P. Clark, you do have a presidential pardon." So that restored my civil rights. I only used it once, when we were in urban redevelopment in Cleveland. I was officer of the corporation. They said, our insurance company, "Have you ever been convicted of a felony?" My answer was: "No." Well, that was good.

Chuck Fager: I'd like to say a little more about China. And I gather it was a war zone, you had not only the Japanese but you had conflicts within China between the nationalists and the communists. That must've been something.

Bronson Clark: It was. The Friends Ambulance Unit was a conglomerate of British, Australian, New Zealand, Canadian, and so forth, conscientious objectors. And we ran a truck route hauling international Red Cross supplies up through free China and to the hospitals. We also had teams of doctors and nurses. We lost some people to typhus who were there working with us. But they chose me to go to Yunan and see if we couldn't get a team on the other side. I don't have time for the long story, but let me say that I went essentially to George Marshall's office. It ended up they gave us three airplanes, they came down and they opened up the warehouse. The United Nations outfit had been frustrated at not getting supplies into the other side.

Well, I went to Yunan, I was put in a cave with a man named Foster Hailey who was the military editorial writer for *The New York Times*, nice guy. I tried to change the editorial policy, I don't know....But he had set up an interview with Mao, and he said to me, come on along. So I met the great man. One of the questions Mao asked was "Why is it that you people support Chiang Kai Shek, who is bombing us, and he is reactionary, and the whole thing is corrupt?"

And Foster Hailey says, "I think we Americans have forgotten the origins of our own revolution." I thought that was a pretty good response from him. I kept careful notes on that interview and used them later.

A team did go in there. Peter Woodrow knows a lot about that; his mother was in there. And they got essentially cut off. Eventually a group of them marched out in 1949 when Mao and his crowd reached Peking. That was the beginning of the Mao era.

Chuck Fager: Thank you. Now back to Max. Max, we left you, having gotten your CO and having volunteered to go to Ramallah. I've heard you refer to that experience in Ramallah as being one that profoundly affected you. And I wondered if you could try to paint the picture for us a little bit. I've heard "Ramallah" the word a million times, but tell us a little bit about, if you can, real quickly, about the town, the school and the situation as well as the impact on you personally.

Max Carter: To understand the impact, I need to paint with a bit broader strokes the environment from which I came. When you grow up on a dairy farm – how many here have milked cows? – you don't go very far away from home. You can't go much farther than it takes to get back for the evening milking. That defines a circumference of the world that in north central Indiana at that time encompassed people just like me. So the circumference of my reality was defined by a certain kind of Protestant Christianity. And that was what you understand to be reality. Anything outside that circle is unreal, it doesn't exist. Or if it exists, it's got to be wrong because it doesn't equate with what you know to be real.

The Christianity that I grew up with, that was presented to me, was deeply Protestant, even among the Quakers, and we were thick with Quakers, but again, it was a Quakerism that at that time had been deeply influenced by a Protestant understanding of Christianity. By that I mean, they accepted human depravity, basic sin.

And the Vietnam War threatened this, even the CO's did, because [the reaction was] much like [that of] the early Puritans reacting to the Indians as representing that chaotic state in which people live in human depravity. It evoked the kind of awful response the Puritans visited upon the natives, those long haired hippie freaks, pot-smoking free love folk, the peace movement, freaked them out, because it represented human depravity, at its basic essence. They had accepted authority, a basic keystone of Protestantism; thus they supported the magistracy, the magistrate was right, the magistrate protects the innocent from the guilty. And so there's a deep respect for authority, for the country, patriotism and all of that.

And this understanding was deeply "anti-works righteousness." The peace movement was seen as "works righteousness." That is, you think you're going to earn your way into heaven by your peace work, and by your justice work, when in fact salvation is supposed to be a matter of faith. It's acceptance of Christ as your personal savior; it's not anything you do. It was also deeply apocalyptic. There would always be wars and rumors of wars. This world is not going to be a safe place until Christ comes again.

I literally grew up fearful of sunsets. Where was that coming from? If any of you have seen the paintings of the second coming, it's always on clouds of glory with sunbeams streaming down from these clouds. That was very literal for me. When you grow up in that kind of background, you know you're never ready. Because that thought you just had, or having just said "heck" or "darn" – honestly, because those were euphemisms for the worst things. You didn't dance, you didn't play cards, you didn't do any of that kind of stuff because that was leading you into sin. I mean, that was the kind of Christianity I grew up in.

When I was in Germany a few years ago I was trying to explain Indiana Quakerism to these Germans, and I had explained that I grew up with prohibitions on dancing and card playing and all that kind of stuff, but that I was a minority as a CO, and that many of my compatriots had joined the army.

This one German who had survived World War II and become a Quaker out of that experience, exclaimed, "Was? Tanzen forbieten und Schiessen erlauben? Das ist unsinn!"

Which means, "What? They forbade dancing and allowed shooting, that's crazy!"

But once I got out of that circle and was in the Middle East, surrounded by Muslims and Jews and other kinds of Christians who were serving in Ramallah with me, a whole other world opened up. I'd already taken very seriously the Sermon on the Mount. Like Bill Eagles, I had taken those Sunday School lessons seriously. I'd read my Bible, I knew what the Bible said. I was deeply Christian. I knew I had kind of a different take on that from some of the other folk in this Protestantized version of Quakerism and Christianity, but [most important] was the experience in Ramallah, being exposed to a broader world and to different takes on religion, on Christianity.

If you understand fundamentalism at all, and I was raised fundamentalist, it is a self-enclosed system that makes sense when you're inside of it. But remove one little chink out of that and it collapses. You've got to stay within it pretty much in order for it to hold up. But for me, too many of those keystones had been removed. And it just collapsed and with it my faith had collapsed. And I had to go to Earlham School of Religion to get it put back together. Which is contrary to what to happens to most people who go to ESR....Only partially kidding.

Chuck Fager: Thank you, Max. Garrett, I've reflected on what you've said about your Peace Studies work and your studies of these various conflicts, and also listening to these other panelists, it's occurred to me to ask: In the course of your studies, are there movements or personalities that you've looked at which you think of as being particularly influential either for yourself or for the field, that you could tell us a little bit about? I have to say, this field of Peace Studies is still very new and so, at least for me and many others here, it's still something we're not very familiar with. So in your studies – I'm not asking you to speak for the Peace Studies discipline necessarily, I give you a chance to get at least your masters degree before I expect you to do that – who and what are the icons, models, influential people and ideas in that discipline at least as you understand it now.

Garrett Colgan-Snyder: Well, I'll respond in terms of the way I understand it best, the people that are the model for much of what is learned and studied, at Colgate anyway, and from the teachers at the other universities where I've been. I was in [the University of] Bradford, which is in the north of England, this spring, studying there, because we have this Peace Studies trip that goes every other year. They have a very large Peace Studies program there, the first one in England. The ladies and gentlemen after which it is modeled are – much of it is modeled after the work of Quakers, of people who devote their life to service.

 Peace Studies, obviously by the name and by the associations that come with that name, is centered upon service. I'm not going to go out and make a million dollars. If I happen to find it on the ground, I might be rich. But other than that, I am expecting to be about where I am at Pendle Hill with my room and board and maybe a little pocket money.

 Personalities, more specifically, the gentlemen who founded and was the first chair of Peace Studies at Bradford University, [who was] a man named Adam Curle. He was very influential for the head of my department at Colgate University, a man named Nigel Young. I know he's written a lot of books, especially about the campaign for nuclear disarmament and the anti-nuclear movement in England. He spent some time in Berkeley in the sixties and the early seventies.

 My professor first started teaching under Adam Curle in '73, '74, I think. We've learned a lot about Curle's work and his ideas, and he takes a lot from Gandhi; the department at Bradford takes so much from Gandhi. They have a very very large collection on Gandhi, a separate peace library there. I know a similar peace library exists at Swarthmore College. I don't know if anybody's checked that out. It's overwhelming at times, because it's big and it's old and it's kind of stuffy.

But personalities like Gandhi and what he did, helping to liberate India; Martin Luther King – obviously these are just obvious examples from which Peace Studies really takes its beginnings. As well as Luddites, who are machine breakers, anti-development-arians, I guess we can call them. And a lot of radical groups, a lot of a radical peace groups, a lot of anti-government anarchists, which I will group with Quakers because I think if you are a Quaker and you are a conscientious objector it's hard – I mean it is hard for me to pay taxes, I don't pay that much taxes. Especially working at Pendle Hill I don't pay that much taxes, being a student I don't pay that much taxes, but it is hard for me to even live with the $70 I do have to pay every other year or something when I do make over $2500, which is the allowance for students or something like that. But Peace Studies does take a lot from anarchists...[break in recording].

As far as personalities, I wouldn't go much further than Adam Curle, maybe Petra Kelly – who was a figurehead of the Green Party in Germany until ten years ago, not even, when she was killed – Martin Luther King, Gandhi.

Chuck Fager: Okay, let's take a question from the group here. Yes?

Will, From Philly: I wanted to ask Max to educate me about Indiana Quakerism and what happened to the peace testimony there.

Max Carter: I want to defend my state a bit. Again, Quakerism there is very very mixed. Remember, Indiana was settled by Quakers of conscience streaming into there from the deep South in their opposition to slavery. What happened, I think, to bring them into assimilation with the dominant culture was, first of all, a civil war that was seen to end the very evil that many of them had fought on the Underground Railroad and in other ways in anti-slavery work. Indiana Yearly Meeting split in 1843-44 into "Indiana Yearly Meeting – Anti-Slavery," and "Indiana Yearly Meeting" – basically, Gradualists. Those were deeply felt issues, and half of the draft-eligible or military service-eligible young people in Indiana who were Quakers fought for the Union in the Civil War.

So already in the 1860's half of the young people had opted for military service and were not read out of their meeting afterwards because so many of them had. So that brings into the meeting a dynamic after the Civil War that you've got to deal with. On top of that, after the Civil War, for a whole variety of reasons, the revivals came through, the Wesleyan revivals, the Methodist revivals. And within a space of 20 years Friends had kicked over the traces and had thrown out the peculiarities and distinctives. They wanted to be in the world and adopted much of the world's ways. That started a gradual process as well.

But at the same time there were many Friends who maintained the Quaker distinctives, the Quaker Peace Testimony. Throughout the time when I was wrestling with these issues in the 1960's, the succession of editors of *Quaker Life,* there in Richmond, Indiana starting with Fred Wood, Xen Harvey, Earl Conn, were deeply pacifist, deeply engaged with social issues of the world, and you read the pages of *Quaker Life*'s issues of the 1960s and it's something. They were wrestling with all those issues. And many other Quakers were around who kept lifting up that standard. I doubt if there are any fewer CO's coming out of Indiana than there were out of Philadelphia Yearly Meeting. Philadelphia doesn't have a sterling record.

My take on Quakerism is, it's much like tofu: it has some substance, but it picks up its flavor from the culture it stews in. Quakerism in Indiana stewed in an evangelical Protestant culture and in Philadelphia it stewed in a liberal, humanist culture and it picked up the values of either one.

Chuck Fager: Tofu Quakerism, boy has my mind been expanded already! Chel?

Chel Avery: My question is for Garrett. A lot of what we talked about yesterday afternoon was the infrastructure that came in place in support of young men who were facing conscription and were needing to make choices and were needing to carry those choices out. And we're not in that kind of emergency time now and we don't have that kind of infrastructure in place. And I'm wondering, as you look at yourself, or maybe even more at your younger brother or your friends who aren't in this context of the Peace Studies group – what about the larger community you're in, especially the community of Friends, is it or is it not supportive of your decision-making about this, and are there particular ways in which...?

Garrett Colgan-Snyder: I think that is really important. I think that I should expand on the cultural undercurrent for young men and women my age. There is tremendous antiwar feeling at Colgate University. And Colgate is a conservative university. I'm not just talking Indiana Quakerism conservative, I am talking even more conservative than that. I don't know what's more conservative than that....It's a very conservative institution. The students come from very rich communities, most of them. Most of the white students come from very privileged backgrounds, very sheltered communities. They don't come from a liberal setting. Many Quakers are well off, but you get that balance with, at least in the Northeast, a very liberal ideology. So that doesn't exist.

Despite that, there is, even at Colgate, there's a tremendous push to stop any sort of fighting on campus. It's a push as much by the administrators and the teachers to get a feeling of peace within the community of Colgate. One of the things we're struggling with at Colgate is the conflict between the community of students of color and the broader Colgate community, which can be defined as white students who make up an overwhelming majority of the student body.

There is a lot of work going on to get peace there, to create peace there. And that extends to a wider culture. I don't know which came first, the chicken or the egg. I don't know whether that comes from a wider feeling, a wider antiwar feeling, anti-violence feeling, which I do get a sense is pervading many, most of the universities across the country. People my age are, because of the example set by conscientious objectors, people who did service work during the First and Second World War, Korean War, Vietnam War, there is tremendous feeling that it can be avoided.

There's a lot of disgruntlement with the American stance remaining as the police country of the world. There is no support at Colgate, no support to speak of, for actions like that taken in the Middle East or that taken in Bosnia-Herzegovina. We have a very active Peace Studies department that, despite its current staff of two full time professors (one was just hired in the Fall, so it was just one before that), educates the Colgate community in a way that none of the other departments are able to do. And that is because of the tremendous dedication and hard work of that one professor.

But I think that, going outside of the Colgate community, there is a push towards support. There is a lot of support existing for me. Although my friends, although they support me, if it came down to a draft situation, I don't think that as many as I would like to see would be conscientious objectors, or would go to Canada, or would go to jail. I think that's unfortunate. There is support for those who want to do it, and there's support to stop it from happening, but once it starts happening, I think there would be a lot of nationalistic feeling being revived. And that's what happens; it sounds like that's what happened in Indiana, that's what happened in Philadelphia.

And unfortunately I think that's what's going to happen again. And until we get by this, we Americans, against them Chinese, Japanese, German, French, Yugoslavian, English, whatever, that that's going to exist, and that's not going to go away. And that is perhaps the biggest problem for Peace Studies, is breaking down the us-them dichotomy. Once that is broken down, it's all elementary from there. It's all elementary. And that's the important, beautiful thing about Quakerism, is seeing the light within each person. Once you see that, it's really hard to see them as different.

Chuck Fager: Before I take another question, there was a point I want to get to with Bronson because it's something I've seen in his book, *Not by Might* – let me give you a plug for your book, it's worth looking at. Between your experience in World War II and becoming active with the Service Committee on concerns about Vietnam, you had an experience, a tour, in North Africa, that I gather from your book, was quite influential in shaping your understanding of what was coming in Vietnam. I wonder if you could tell us a little bit about that. I think it sounds like a telling perspective.

Bronson Clark: Eleanor and I and three of our daughters were in Morocco and later Algeria. The French were trying to hold on to Algeria and it was taking more and more dead Frenchmen to keep the farms going there because the Algerian underground was really working. De Gaulle takes a hit now and then, but he was smart. He eventually created a committee of what he called notables, and he passed his power over to that committee, which promptly gavit to the FLN and brought that war to a halt.

The Service Committee asked us early on to please get into Algeria and see about what's going on. Nobody had gone in there, so using conference for diplomats I went to call the Logoric in Rabat. He came out right away to see me. And I said I've got to have a *laissez-passer* to get over the border. He produced that in 30 minutes. So we went into Algeria. We picked up an Algerian connection right away, somebody we knew. And we came to the first regroupment camp. They went into a panic. They thought the French were coming back. It turned out those regroupment camps were all across Algeria. It was hard to believe, but it was true. The camps were called *l'abattoir* sometimes. I mean, the killings that went on in there when they could catch some Algerian resister was very significant.

So when the Vietnam War came along, I went to the number two guy in the Pentagon and I said I want to tell you that I've been in a society where the French had to dig these resistance people out of a bank along the river and pull them out of there one by one. And I think in Vietnam you're going to have an even more complex situation and you're not going to make it. He held up a volume that said "Classified," and said, "I can't show it to you, but I can tell you what it is. It's a comparison of the Algerian situation and what we're about to do." I said, "I'm sorry I can't read it because that would be very interesting, but I think you're going to make a mistake." His name was John McNaughton.

Chuck Fager: So, regroupment camps in Algeria really became kind of a model for what were called strategic hamlets in Vietnam, is that right? And had kind of the same outcome.

Bronson Clark: Yes, they had a lot of informers working for them, Algerians. Their life in Algeria, afterward– you'd see them in long lines in chains going by. They were not loved. It was sobering as to what you get into in a situation where there's a combination of nationalism and a desire for independence and it's hard to stop.

Chuck Fager: OK. Thank you. Let's see what other questions there are. Marian, way in the back.

Marian Anderson: This is a question for Garrett. I'm very interested in your discussion of your Peace Studies program, but I have a fundamental question. There are more problems than only nationalism and not having enough wonderful models....Because I've spent about the last 20 or 25 years of my life studying the economic impact of the military and industrial complex and sort of set it as my goal in life for about 15 years to show the American people that in fact, high levels of military spending did not create jobs, but it was the reverse, it destroyed jobs. And it was this very aggressive assault on the myth that militarism is good for you that I think is at least some help to the peace movement and a lot of other people who weren't even in the peace movement but were just worried about the US economy and what was happening to the...

So this is kind of a long preface, but my fundamental question is do you study fundamental institutional causes for the continuation of the institutions that gain only by war?

I think there's another point I'd like to make in this conference; I might as well make it now. I think there's something else that we thought, the American people and the Pentagon, during Vietnam. It's very simple: you can't kill American soldiers. That would keep us out of ground wars. It does not keep us from bombing....And it certainly does not bring the military budget down dramatically, which, as you all have noticed, is $265 billion, which has absolutely nothing to do with anything in the world any more. It's like totally out of control in terms of reality. Even the Chairman of the Joint Chiefs of Staff has said, I'm really scraping the bottom of the barrel for enemies, you know, people like Qaddafi, that military budget of about....So if you're doing Peace Studies, is there some effort to work on the institutional causes for the continuation of militarism?

Garrett Colgan-Snyder: Well, the second semester that I actually started taking Peace Studies courses, which was during my sophomore year at Colgate, one class I took was called War, State and Society. What we did in that class was really study everything. Well, I'm not going to make any broad statements here. What we did in that class was we studied the origins of war, the origins of the current state system that exists and the government that we have that perpetuates the military industrial complex that you're talking about.

Unfortunately at Colgate, required courses for the Peace Studies major do not include economics, do not include statistics of any sort, which is a tremendous deficiency. Unfortunately because of the history, the education of the head of the department, who is English and he studied in England, he focuses on European history; he focuses on the difference between the European experience and the American experience, which is important, especially trying to understand where we are at this point in relation to this century, in relation to World War I and World War II and the differences that that has created. Unfortunately, like I said, economics is not brought into it the way it should be. Now, economics is not his forte, and I'm not going to fault him for that, but it is something that I have come to notice, after taking economics last year, that it is tied up with everything that one studies in Peace Studies.

Economics is probably, I think I can safely say that economics is the reason, our current economic state is the reason, why service opportunities exist. Service opportunities would not exist if the economics were not oppressive, if the economics did not perpetuate a situation where we had the military industrial complex, we had people not in jobs and not getting what they should be getting from the government.

Unfortunately, World War II taught us that war means money, war means jobs. World War I taught us that as well. And that has stayed with us. [World War II], bringing us out of the Great Depression, was perhaps the best thing that could have happened for the economy at that point, but the worst thing that could've happened for our future development as a nation. If we had been brought out of the Great Depression in some other way or at least if it was believed that we were brought out of the Great Depression in some other way, because it's hard to argue even that we were brought out of the Great Depression because of the war – but if it was believed that we were brought out another way, we would be leaps and bounds beyond where we are now.

And you're right, believing that the military industrial complex creates jobs, keeps our economy going, is a farce, it's really killing us. In terms of finding enemies, unfortunately the American government is doing better than we would hope. It looks like the next major enemy that NATO is going to face up against is countries with an Islamic majority. NATO has switched its focus from Eastern Europe to Northern Africa and the Middle East. NATO is looking for a big time enemy. Not only to keep making money for the companies that happen to be on the committee for the existence of NATO, like Lockheed-Martin, but for the existence of the institution itself. Those politicians and administrators that are in that institution, they don't want to see that institution disappear. They're making money. I can't fault them for that. That's their livelihood. I'm not going to say, you give up your job, unless we can give them an alternative. We can, but they just don't believe that, which is unfortunate.

But creating new enemies is another big problem. And you're right, it does come down to economics to a large part. And that is tied up with the creation of us and them. Why would we need this military industrial complex and creating all these weapons if there was not an us-them dichotomy. So I see those two things as linked, as so linked that you cannot even tell the difference.

Chuck Fager: Max, I want to turn to you. You work out of a college also, and you have dealings with a lot of bright young Quakers. And I gather that you have some sort of Peace Studies program down there. We're supposed to be looking ahead as well as looking back this morning. So that's why I'm wondering if you can imagine this group being a generation and a half younger here, QLSP class of 40 or 50 here, based on your own experience and reflections and reconstruction of your religious outlook at ESR and whatnot, what do you want to tell your students as far as the future of peace witness as best it looks to you now? After all, you are in that position, sort of, aren't you?

Max Carter: Allegedly. As I shared with some folk around the meal tables this week, people were asking me, what are college students thinking, how they are responding? It's real hard for a lot of college students to get a handle on the peace issue. There is not the presenting cause like Vietnam. It's a much more amorphous sort of thing, like nailing Jell-O to a wall, to figure out what is the issue to grab hold of. I see a lot of students at Guilford who really are concerned. We are past the "Generation X" kind of slacker stuff, if that ever held at all.

I see students very interested in service. I think the new newsletter coming out of the Quaker Voluntary Service Training and Witness is really meeting a need. Students are looking for internships, service opportunities, ways of being of help because the world is presenting such awful problems to them that aren't addressed by easy answers, that what helps them is a project where they can go for a week or a few months and feel like they have actually done something. It helps to know that maybe I can't solve world hunger, but I can build this house. So that is one thing: we try to provide service opportunities to get students in the habit of thinking of service, of helping others.

Another thing we try to address is what I think was in some cases lacking in some of the peace movement and that was a deep spirituality that goes to the bone. You look at folk who burned out – those who got into peace action just out of political action and then you work for years and years and years and if your motivation was, I'm going to save the world or end the draft or end the war, and that's your motivation and a lot of stuff you worked for didn't happen, you burn out if there is not something deep and fundamental you are operating out of.

Some of that happened also in my case, coming out of it with a faith that wasn't very solidly based and that fell apart, but we're working on helping students reclaim a spirituality that's deeply personal related to historical faith, to biblical studies as well as Quaker studies as well as world religions, as well as opportunities for accessing that personally. I think it is important, is key.

As to academic study, certainly at Guilford we do have an active Peace and Conflict Studies Program, and as Garrett mentioned, as Marian mentioned, it does have to address economic issues and other issues – matters of race and class and perhaps the biggest peace issue our students have struggled within the last couple, three years has been local economics.

A lot of our students were arrested in protest against the K-Mart Corporation, which had a big distribution center in Greensboro that was paying very low wages to predominantly African-American or blue-collar workers, lower socio-economic class folk, and thinking they could get away with it.

Students and faculty from Guilford who marched in that were arrested, did their jail time and the analysis of that is that what these economic systems do is destroy local community. They destroy family, and that in John Woolman's analysis, that's where the seeds of war begin. You've got to look at the furniture of your own homes and the clothing you wear and your lifestyle.

Chuck Fager: We're getting down to about the last five minutes, so we will take a couple more questions and then kind of wrap it up. I see Wallace Collett, who I believe is widely suspected of having been a businessman at one time.

Wallace Collett: I think it might be appropriate to say a few more things about Peace Studies. I see it as a place where we can make a real impression on future leaders. And when I came to Haverford over fifteen or twenty years ago, I was shocked to find these Quaker colleges really had nothing to do with Peace Studies. And there are so many things that everybody in this room and our friends need to work with on institutional matters. This applies not only to Peace Studies, but on United Nations and so on. Over these years, with assistance we got Peace Studies programs started at Haverford, Bryn Mawr and Swarthmore. And what a wonderful potential there is.

This was in the late '80s. I won't go through all the history, but with some more intense work of interior lobbying, like political lobbying, I think that we'll be able to get those three colleges to take on the responsibility of establishing a real Peace Studies department that will have a scholarship, a kind of study that you were talking about. To get them in before the students will help... would be very exciting material. And Garrett, in my opinion, you're in the best Peace Studies program in the country, at Colgate....I can tell you that the best programs are not in Quaker colleges....Looking at Max's...how much the problem is getting adequate funds for Peace Studies at Guilford?

We need to have a lobbying for Peace Studies and we ought to do it in such a way that all of the witness, all of the wonderful witness from the period here of these three days...how that can be displayed....There's a job to do in the Quaker colleges to get Peace Studies into a real discipline that will appeal to our great professors of history and chemistry and so on in the college. So keep that in mind. There is so much to do in institutional work....There was a struggle always to get that institution, that great institution, willing to focus on this major challenge we faced in that generation and there were similar things like that now, work with the Service Committee, and FCNL...to work on these issues. Period.

Chuck Fager: Thank you, Wallace. Did you have a question, David? Thirty seconds.

David: I want to read into the record two names that have not been mentioned thus far, which have to do with economics and Peace Studies. One is Elise Boulding. The other is Henry Niles, and the whole contribution to doing what Wallace could tell us more about in Business Executives Move for Peace in Vietnam.

Chuck Fager: I'd want to add Kenneth Boulding, Lewis Fry Richardson. And while we're beating up on Quaker colleges I think fairness requires that we take note of the fact that there is a Quaker college that does have a Peace Learning Center. It's George Fox University, out there in Oregon. I know Ron Mock, who is the director, and he's a fine guy. I think his program is way too small, but the difference between being small and not being there at all is pretty significant. Oh, yes, I also have to say that I think it's a scandal that we have three Quaker-founded colleges in the Philadelphia area and there's not a Peace Studies Program here; of course, you can't get a degree in Quaker Studies at any of these colleges either, which is a particular pet peeve of mine.

Friends, I think we're getting close to time. So, I want to thank our panelists and our audience.

Plenary Presentation:
Conscience, Citizenship and the Road Ahead

July 19, 1998

Peter Goldberger

Before I begin to talk on my assigned topic, some personal comments and thanks are in order. I discovered the Friends in 1966 by reading a book I took out of my high school library on world religions. I come from three or four generations of secular humanists, culturally and ethnically Jewish but totally nonreligious. No one has been observant on either side of my family in this century, so far as I know.

Frankly I was curious about this religion thing that seemed to be so important to so many other people and their families. So I did some reading. And in this book I discovered a little group of people whose beliefs and practices sounded like what I was coming to believe myself was fundamentally right about human beings and about living in this world.

Around the same time, I was doing some research on where I might consider applying to college. And strangely enough, the two places that seemed most interesting and right for me were a little place called Haverford and another one called Swarthmore. And look who started those colleges and ran them! So I went to the phone book and discovered there was a local Meeting – Ridgewood Meeting, in northern NJ – and I went there on a Sunday morning in mid- to late 1966 to see what was what. Well, I was basically hooked on the people I met and their approach to living the good life, that is, a life that is rightly ordered.

That's where John Mott became my draft counselor. Of course, I didn't know he had been a co-founder of CCCO, nor that I would later become a Board member of that organization, co-chair of the Committee, and later (and still) its general counsel. That's where I first heard Jeremy Mott speak, either just before or just after he had walked off his alternate service job to become a public resister. Believe me, he was as compelling and impressive a speaker then, at age 21 or whatever he was, as he was yesterday in this room, and that's saying something.

So the seeds were planted in Ridgewood, but Haverford College and draft counseling made me the person I still am (or try to be) today. That is, a person who cares about the impact you make in the world, who thinks individuals matter, and who thinks that right and wrong matter in the real world, and in your own life, including your work life.

And a person who takes joy in analyzing what other people consider legal technicalities and using them to assist the folks I care the most about, so they can have more freedom in their lives. That's why at Yale Law School I not only continued draft counseling, and volunteered to work for lawyers defending draft refusers, but also immediately joined the student group that gave legal aid to prisoners at Danbury Federal Prison. Danbury is where I first heard of John Bach – who I had the pleasure of meeting in person for the first time, 25 years later, yesterday – and where I met my wife.

I still do the kind of work I began doing at Danbury in 1973, federal post-conviction criminal defense, mostly representing prisoners on appeal, looking for the essential good in people condemned by society for doing wrong (or at least for breaking the law) and trying to use a superior knowledge of legal rules and procedures to help them win their freedom, if not immediately, then at least sooner, so they can have another chance.

That's also what inspires me to continue working with peace activists, conscientious objectors, and war resisters, both because I love and respect them, and because I have the privilege to possess some special skills that I can use to help them better achieve what God or their own conscience leads them to do to make this a better world, or to avoid or minimize the punishment for having done that. Just as it is and has been an honor to be able to lend some mundane technical assistance to living prophets like Robin Harper and Priscilla Adams (as well as non-Quaker prophets like Marian Franz and the Berrigans), and a privilege to know these special people, it's an honor to have been asked by you – and particularly by Chel Avery – to speak here as a person who is not a Quaker, and who is not a Christian, about "conscience, citizenship and the road ahead."

To talk about conscience and citizenship is to talk about law and our relationship to the law as individuals in a society. There is truth in each of two fundamentally opposing views of the role of law in society. On the one hand, law is a deeply civilizing force. It is a device by which a community channels and resolves conflicts that would otherwise lead to violence. The institutions of law provide a place for people in conflict, after private efforts fail, to take their problems to a neutral, respected, government-supplied forum to be resolved with impartiality and finality. In that forum, the conflicting parties can be represented by lawyers, who get between the actual adversaries, deflect and depersonalize the conflict, and mediate their dispute within the legal forum. At least we would like to think so.

Of course, that "government-supplied forum" part leads immediately to the other side of this coin: the system of law is the device through which the state exercises power over the individual, by monopolizing the legitimate use of violence and threats of violence, including the power of arrest and imprisonment. Behind every courtroom sits a jail cell. The law is not only a form of nonviolent conflict resolution; at the same time it is also violence in sheep's clothing.

Thus, as between one individual and another, law supplies the rules we turn to when we can't agree among ourselves how to resolve a conflict, and these rules are ultimately enforced by government power. And as between the individual and the government, law supplies the rules that control the individual's dealings with government power. It follows that in a system of genuine law, though not in a system of sham legal formalisms, the government itself is bound by law, which is the essential protection against totalitarianism.

Historically, Quakers have recognized this civilizing, conflict-controlling, violence-reducing feature of an established legal system, and have been obedient (though not subservient) to law, even basically conservative and establishment oriented, whenever they could be.

But of course, there is a hitch. Not a little hitch, but a big hitch. That thing about the Inner Light, about That of God in Every Person.

Sam Caldwell made me realize that this idea is the first and only principle of Friends theology that is based on faith, from which everything that Quakers do and all else that they believe, including the Peace Testimony, essentially follows as a matter of rational thought. That basic belief in the sanctity of the individual must inevitably, at least on occasion, come into conflict with even the most just and well-ordered system of government and law. That is because government and law will always be designed to work better for some than for others. Even the best systems, the ones that really strive for the greatest good for the greatest number, for the highest level of democracy and civil liberty, and for fairness through predictability, uniformity and equality, cannot account for every individual's situation, nor for each individual's conscience. And legal institutions will always be at least somewhat behind the need for constant social change – sometimes way behind. The only governmental system fundamentally consistent with the idea that God speaks to each individual directly and equally is, as the saying goes, "Every man a law unto himself." And of course that is no system of government or law at all.

That is why the interrelated issues of civil disobedience, conscientious objection, and legal protection for the free exercise of religion are of such special interest to Quakers. I'd like to speak a little about each of these three connected topics: civil disobedience, conscientious objection, and the principle of free exercise of religion, as they relate to the tension between conscience and citizenship.

Notice that civil disobedience is a way of describing or defining nonviolent direct action by its relationship to law. Simply to refer to "civil disobedience" is to acknowledge the importance of the law in our system of thinking about direct, often faith-based, action.

We do not tend to think of a person who simply goes about doing what she or he must, because that person believes it is right, without concern for how the law regards it, as engaging in civil disobedience. Examples, to my mind, would include the Quakers who held meetings for worship in the early years when or where those meetings were forbidden, or some of the actions and ministry of the Catholic Worker. When direct action anticipates or even seeks a confrontation with authority, on the other hand, and particularly when it seeks to achieve a change in the legal order, only then do we tend to think in terms of civil disobedience.

Viewed this way, many social and political philosophers, including some who are basically very conservative, accept civil disobedience as an essential aspect of democratic input in social change and law reform. This point of view tends to place value on the cheerful or at least willing acceptance of legal penalties by the resister as an essential part of accommodating civil disobedience within the legal system.

Civil disobedience can also be viewed, of course, less as a form of democratic input in the political process than as a form of individual witness against unjust laws. This attitude is common among tax resisters, for example.

We tend to think of civil disobedience as a form of protest against unjust laws, waged by breaking those laws openly. This is not always so, depending on the nature of the law or policy in question.

First, the easy case. Some laws demand action by the individual, and if that law seems to be unjust, then the conscientious individual may feel obligated to violate that personal legal obligation. The draft laws fell into this category when an individual was called upon personally to register or to submit to induction. If you don't believe that any individual should be compelled to train for killing others against his or her will, then there is no valid function for the draft law.

Very few laws demand personal action in this direct way, however. Refusal of special military taxes by some early Friends fell into that category; so does organized abolitionist resistance to the fugitive slave laws. But Thoreau's refusal of the poll tax, or the tax laws violated by tax resisters today, in my opinion, are not analogous to conscientious violation of the draft laws, because it is not the tax law or the process of compulsory taxation that is evil, but rather the uses to which the government puts much of the money collected. In such cases, the civil disobedience does not involve breaking an unjust law in the same sense.

Laws demanding that the individual refrain from certain conduct are far more common than laws demanding action from the individual. Sometimes those laws can be legitimately seen as evil in themselves, such as laws that forbid harboring deserters or illegal aliens. When Elizabeth Cady Stanton was arrested for attempting to cast a vote in her and my hometown of Tenafly, New Jersey, she was committing civil disobedience by deliberately violating an unjust law that forbade certain action. But more often laws violated by civil disobedience are not evil in themselves but simply happen to stand between the divinely or conscientiously impelled nonviolent action and the evil institution it seeks to confront. Participants in the southern civil rights and desegregation movement faced arrest for disorderly conduct and parading without a permit and trespassing more than for violating any specific Jim Crow law. It is not wrong for society to have a trespassing law as it is to have a draft law. Similarly, when the "ultraresistance," either led or inspired by Philip and Daniel Berrigan, invaded government buildings and burned files used to administer the draft, they were deliberately violating laws against burglary and destruction of government property. Those laws are not unjust or evil, but it was nevertheless a form of civil disobedience to violate those laws when they were marshaled to protect a great official evil, such as the perpetration of the Vietnam War.

Professor Hugo Bedau, a progressive social philosopher at Tufts University, writing in the late 1960's, attempted to define civil disobedience so as to distinguish clearly it from other lawbreaking. Academic efforts of this kind are not satisfying, and can be frustrating. He proposed that to qualify as civil disobedience, violation of the law had to be conscientious in motive, reformist in objective, nonviolent in tactics, public, and willing to accept the established legal consequences. I question Professor Bedau's efforts to reach a clear definition, because the civil rights and Vietnam protest experience, which inspired his study, challenges much of this attempt.

We might be able to agree that the most massive and most effective popular resistance to an unjust law in American history was neither conscientious in motive nor nonviolent, and that it probably should not be viewed as civil disobedience; I am speaking of the popular rejection of Prohibition. But the Underground Railroad was not conducted openly or in public; its members did not seek out punishment or hope to fill the jails. They wanted to rescue slaves. The same is true of the illegal abortion network known as the Clergy Consultation Service in the years before *Roe v. Wade*. Yet both efforts affected public perceptions of right and wrong and helped bring about reform. I would view them as civil disobedience.

Not everyone would agree that the Berrigan-inspired Plowshares actions, involving physical destruction of nuclear weapons components and delivery systems, could be called "nonviolent," although they involved violence against property only. After all, so did most radical bombings, which almost no one would call nonviolent. Yet I would call the Plowshares actions civil disobedience. Finally, American civil activists have almost *never* accepted the Gandhian principle of willingly accepting legal punishment, even demanding the maximum punishment. Thoreau did, but many more have followed in the tradition of Anne Hutchinson, the Puritan heretic, who defended herself in a Massachusetts colonial court by arguing that she had done nothing wrong and simultaneously that the court had no authority to judge her. Lawyers for arrested civil rights protesters fought vigorously against their convictions and sought to get as many as they could out of jail as soon as possible. Many Vietnam draft resisters mounted legal defenses, both traditional and non-traditional, although from what I can tell none or almost none of the World War II resisters did; yet draft refusal did not lose its character as civil disobedience from the process of seeking to avoid punishment by a dishonest, warmaking government for doing what was right.

As I started out by saying, civil disobedience defines itself in relation to the law; so does conscientious objection, which is the demand for an *individual* exemption from legal compulsion on grounds of personal conscience. Conscientious objection, by its nature, does not seek to change the law in question, but only to excuse the individual from complying. Conscientious objection, as I define it, does not assume legal recognition. The World War I resisters who were forcibly inducted into the Army and then court-martialed and imprisoned, or worse, under military authority were nevertheless CO's. Despite what some people might carelessly assume today, "conscientious objector" is not a government-assigned classification; it is a personal stand. I say I was a conscientious objector under the Vietnam draft, although I went from 2-S to 1-H, and was never classified 1-0. Dan Seeger would have been a CO whether or not the Supreme Court had acknowledged his unconventional claim under the statute. Nevertheless, there has been a continuing legal struggle to establish recognition for CO's under military conscription laws, and then under the laws that define the categories of enlisted personnel eligible for discharge, and once established, to expand those definitions.

Because of this emphasis in our concept of conscientious objection on what is acceptable to the individual, the refusal of a legally unrecognized CO to accept induction, or to obey orders within the military, cannot always be described as an act of civil disobedience. A purely personal witness, laudable though it may be and worthy of great respect and full support, does not seem to me to be a form of civil disobedience, as contrasted with an individual's assuming a conscience-driven role in a concerted effort at social change.

There is a further fascinating complication under our American system of law to this effort to understand the role and nature of civil disobedience, which arises from the power of the courts to interpret the law, both statutory and constitutional. When Rev. Martin Luther King led an unauthorized march, having been denied a required parade permit under a local ordinance, when his lawyers advised him that they thought the ordinance was unconstitutional, was this a form of civil disobedience? When the Freedom Riders rode buses into segregated waiting rooms, knowing that the federal Interstate Commerce Act required those stations to be integrated, was that civil disobedience? The protesters contended and believed in those cases that their conduct was legal, and had a good sound basis for thinking so. That doesn't sound like civil disobedience. For a draftee to refuse induction after being wrongly denied CO status, like Muhammad Ali, was not civil disobedience either, though his claim would have to be vindicated in court.

When Dan Seeger refused induction, after his CO claim was turned down because he would not say he believed in a Supreme Being, was that an act of civil disobedience? He sought, with the support of CCCO, to become the "test case" that would persuade the courts to say the restrictive, religious definition of a conscientious objector was unconstitutional.

But he had no legitimate hope of winning that case in court, in my opinion; both constitutional precedent and the plain language of the statute were against him. The "test case" posture was, to all appearances, a mere protest gesture, simply *disguised* as a legal argument, no more likely to succeed than the so-called "Nuremburg defense" first used by Quaker lawyer Harrop Freeman on behalf of A.J. Muste's tax refusal in 1961. That sounds like a form of civil disobedience, despite the proceedings in court claiming the legality of the action. But somehow, miraculously, Dan Seeger and two fellow CO appellants won their cases in the Supreme Court in 1965. The Court gave a broad interpretation to the language of the Selective Service Act requiring that CO claims be based on "religious training and belief." Five years later, in the *Welsh* case, the Court went even further and ruled that deeply held nontheistic moral beliefs were covered under the Act. What had looked like civil disobedience suddenly was redefined, by the legal establishment, as legitimate conscientious objection.

You might think Dan Seeger should have won his case, if he was going to win at all, on Free Exercise grounds. The First

Amendment says that "Congress shall make no law respecting an establishment of religion, or prohibiting the free exercise thereof." Of the two Religion Clauses, the Establishment Clause is more in the news. School prayer and Bible reading, aid to parochial schools, public sponsorship of Christmas displays, all the popular controversies concerning the "separation of church and state" seem to involve Establishment Clause problems. But interpretation and enforcement of the Free Exercise Clause are no less difficult or important. The Free Exercise Clause, as the other side of the same coin, assures each adherent of a minority faith the right to practice his or her religion without interference.

On its face, taken literally, the Free Exercise Clause would seem to establish a general right of conscientious objection, at least for those with a religious basis. When a law requires everyone to engage in conduct that violates some people's religion, or prohibits conduct required by some people's religion, doesn't that law violate the Free Exercise Clause as applied to the religious objectors? For most of its history, the Supreme Court has answered those questions with a firm No. The Court has never wavered from the position that the Free Exercise Clause "embraces two concepts – freedom to believe and freedom to act. The first is absolute, but in the nature of things, the second cannot be."

A review of the interpretation and application of the Free Exercise Clause will demonstrate a tremendous reluctance throughout the years to give the Clause any bite as a protection for religious practices which conflict with generally applicable laws. The Court has apparently been concerned that the implication of the Free Exercise Clause, if meaningfully enforced, is that the conscience of each citizen may become a law unto itself. Yet respect for the Framers' drafting requires a presumption that they chose their words carefully and included no redundant clauses. If some special level of protection were not intended for religion, apart from other systems of belief, it is difficult to understand why the First Amendment would have two of its five clauses specially devoted to that subject. The Framers' choice of the inherently muscular phrase "exercise of religion" itself suggests that the Clause protects more than mere private belief; a level of protection beyond that already afforded to other forms of belief and expression by the Free Speech Clause must have been intended. In my opinion the bedrock principle of Free Exercise law is obviously wrong under the plain language of the First Amendment; but the Supreme Court didn't ask my opinion, so let's look at what they have said.

The earliest cases in which the Supreme Court confronted this problem involved enforcement of the criminal law against polygamy in the Utah territory, where early Mormon settlers had adopted that practice as a matter of faith. In the first of several polygamy cases to be considered, in 1878, the Court declared that although laws "cannot interfere with mere religious beliefs and opinions, they may with practices."

The Mormon cases essentially killed Free Exercise claims for half a century. In the 1940's, however, a series of decisions involving members of the Jehovah's Witnesses began to breathe life into the Clause again, by focusing on the free speech aspects of religious proselytizing. In the leading case, three Witnesses had been convicted of soliciting funds for religious purposes without a license and of breach of the peace, for playing an anti-Catholic recording on the street in a largely Catholic neighborhood. The breach of the peace convictions were reversed on the basis that, "in spite of the probabilities of excesses and abuses," an expression of opinion that is merely annoying to listeners may not be punished.

The Mormon cases involving the actual practice of polygamy have not been undermined, however; claims for exemption on religious grounds from obligations imposed by law have almost always fared poorly where there was no associated free speech claim. In *Gillette v. United States,* in 1971, the Supreme Court confirmed its 1934 holding in *Hamilton v. California Board of Regents* that there is no constitutional right under the Free Exercise Clause to a conscientious objector exemption from military training or service. *Gillette* thus held that Congress could limit CO status under the draft law to those who oppose all wars, like Quakers, and refuse it to Catholics and others who subscribe to a "just war" theology and are therefore selective objectors.

Similarly, in 1982, the Court upheld the extent to which Congress had limited the exemption granted to groups such as the Amish, who object to participating in the Social Security system. In passing, the Court also repeated the comment originally made by a concurring Justice in *Hamilton* nearly 50 years earlier, that the Free Exercise Clause would not support a pacifist's claim to an exemption from paying taxes that support warmaking or military preparations.

In 1963, just prior to the *Seeger* decision, the Supreme Court had announced a new standard for assessing religious freedom claims that seemed at first to herald a new day for Free Exercise jurisprudence. In *Sherbert v. Verner*, the Court reversed the denial of unemployment benefits to a Seventh Day Adventist, who was unwilling to hold herself available for Saturday work. The denial of benefits was unconstitutional, because it imposed a penalty on the exercise of religion and thus indirectly pressured her to forgo that faithfulness. The Court declared a new, so-called "balancing test" for determining whether government action violated the Free Exercise Clause: only the need to accomplish a compelling state interest can outweigh a burden on religious exercise, and then only if no less restrictive means are available to achieve the governmental purpose. This holding was reaffirmed in 1981. In that case, a Jehovah's Witness had left his factory job because he was directed to work on military equipment and was refused a transfer back to nonmilitary production work. The Court ruled he could not be denied unemployment benefits on the basis that he had quit without "good cause."

The high water mark for the "compelling state interest"/ "least restrictive alternative" approach to First Amendment Free Exercise claims was Chief Justice Burger's 1972 opinion for a near-unanimous Court in *Wisconsin v. Yoder*. In that case, the Court sustained Free Exercise claims of Old Order Amish parents to withdraw their children from school after eighth grade, as against the state legislature's attempt to compel attendance for all children through age sixteen. The Court's decision combines discussion of the primary role of parents, not the state, in guiding the upbringing of their children with an analysis of the state's failure to justify impairing the exercise by the Amish of their religious commitment to stand outside the "world." A year later, scrupulously applying the same test, a federal judge in Philadelphia ruled that the AFSC was protected by the Free Exercise Clause from having to withhold income tax from its war-objecting Quaker employees. Unfortunately, that decision was overturned by the Supreme Court within a year on procedural grounds.

For nearly 20 years after *Yoder*, the Supreme Court continued to profess adherence to the "compelling state interest"/"least restrictive alternative" balancing test, but never again did a claim for a religious exemption or even for accommodation prevail. Then in 1990 the Supreme Court shocked the religious community by dropping its pretense of promising accommodation for religious objections. In the notorious *Smith v. Oregon* case, written by Justice Scalia, it upheld the denial of unemployment compensation to Native American drug and alcohol counselors, fired because they admitted using peyote in their own religious ceremonies. The Court declared that the Free Exercise Clause did not require any religious exemption for generally applicable laws that were not designed to interfere with religion or discriminate against religious justifications. Under *Smith*, for example, an ordinance declaring that no church could have stained glass windows would be invalid, but there would be no Free Exercise violation if the law provided that no building in town could use stained glass, even if the only buildings with colored windows were churches.

The religious community saw the Supreme Court's interpretation of the Free Exercise Clause in *Smith* as a major threat to freedom of conscience. A remarkably broad coalition, with the Friends Committee on National Legislation (FCNL) among the original conveners, began the process of drafting and lobbying for corrective legislation. Remarkably, in the fall of 1994, a chapter was added to the federal civil rights laws called the Religious Freedom Restoration Act, called "RFRA." This statute attempted to restore and establish by legislative fiat the compelling state interest, least restrictive means balancing test that had been announced and applied by the Supreme Court in *Sherbert* and *Yoder* but hardly ever actually applied in any other case.

A struggle for power ensued between Congress and the Supreme Court. In the spring of 1996 the Court ruled that RFRA was unconstitutional, at least as applied to state and local government actions, because it exceeded the power of Congress to regulate the states under the guise of enforcing the Fourteenth Amendment. The White House and the Justice Department, to their credit, took the position that RFRA still stood as a limitation on the powers of federal agencies, however.

If the Administration is supporting RFRA and its application to federal agencies, wouldn't that seem to herald the dawn of a new day, legally speaking, for tax resisters? A succession of Administrations has opposed the Peace Tax Campaign, believing it poses a radical threat of selective tax resistance. It took some 20 years to get a hearing on the Peace Tax bill, and it has never come up for serious discussion or a vote. Does RFRA make the Peace Tax Fund Bill unnecessary and redundant? What about the effort to codify the right to a conscientious objector discharge in statutory form? That right has existed only since 1962, and only in the form of regulations promulgated by the Secretary of Defense, which are therefore vulnerable to fairly easy watering down or repeal at any time. Is a military CO law unnecessary if we have RFRA?

The answer to these questions lies in how the courts will apply and enforce RFRA. So far, three Quaker tax resistance test cases under RFRA did poorly at the trial court level, although all are suddenly in a hopeful posture for appeal at the same time. Those cases are Gordon and Edith Browne's challenge out of Vermont, and Rosa Packard's out of Connecticut, both headed for the Second Circuit federal appeals court in New York City, and Priscilla Lippincott Adams' appeal from Tax Court, which is in the Third Circuit appeals court in Philadelphia. My office is representing Priscilla and Rosa, while Quaker lawyer J.E. McNeil, from Washington, D.C., represents the Brownes.

In each of those cases, the judges showed a truly stunning

level of resistance to the request that they apply RFRA as written. All three judges, including the Vietnam-era Swarthmore graduate who was the Tax Court judge assigned to Priscilla's case, ignored RFRA's requirement that the government prove *with evidence* its claim of inability to accommodate the individual objector and simply *asserted* that accommodation of conscientious objection to taxation for military purposes is impossible. Of course, we all know that is not true. The Peace Tax Fund idea, for example, could work. And the government itself permits taxpayers to check off whether they do or do not want $3 of their income tax to be put into the Presidential Election Campaign Matching Fund. It could ask the same question about the Pentagon and nuclear weapons budget. Perhaps the appellate judges will rise to meet the challenge, because the military needs citizens' taxes now, in this era, far more than it needs their sons' or daughters' arms to carry weapons.

This is a new and different time. Every time is a new and different time, of course. But the ways in which this time, and the coming age, are new have major implications for the age-old collision between citizenship and conscience. Warfare, like everything else, is becoming increasing hi-tech, particularly for the United States and other industrially advanced nations. That fact, combined with interventions in low-intensity wars and so-called "peacekeeping" missions, suggests that a smaller and more professional military may be a permanent fixture on our landscape – at least so long as we cannot abolish it entirely.

There is essentially no draft, and will perhaps never be again. Of course, there is the political refusal to abolish Selective Service, with the resulting cruel dilemma of an obligation to register for no legitimate governmental purpose at all which confronts conscientious male youth, particularly those who are religious pacifists. Under RFRA, properly applied, these young men should be viewed as exempt, because the government could never demonstrate a compelling need to register them, but I wouldn't bet my law license on a court's agreeing with me. And of course we face the continuing need to nurture, counsel, support and defend the relative handful of volunteer military members each year who have religious maturing experiences and become conscientious objectors.

But it will never be 1968 again, and those direct confrontations between a legally enforceable direct military obligation and the demands of the individual conscience are not what we are looking at in the coming age. The challenges we now face, and will be facing more and more in North America, arise out of the fact that we live in an increasingly integrated and powerful military-industrial-communications-entertainment-information complex, controlled by a relative few major corporations with close ties to the government, including the Pentagon. Realistically, very few individuals will be in any kind of position to say No entirely to that world by opting out. Instead, there will be many more opportunities and obligations of resistance, often requiring the individual, and groups of like-minded individuals, to be attentive to more subtle occasions of compelled complicity in violence and war making.

Massively interlinked computer networks, accessing and exchanging information, offer tremendous opportunities for education and empowerment, but also threaten an unprecedented loss of privacy. Without enough privacy, can there be real respect for each individual and for individualism? Will there be a sufficient opportunity to listen to that still, small voice of conscience? Quakers have a historic calling, perhaps a divine calling, to see that these questions continue to be answered affirmatively.

The individual search for the right answer, not just the expected answer, to important questions is not merely a source of constant conflict with the duties of citizenship, as I have been emphasizing. Rather, when individuals listen to and act on their consciences – often not simply as individuals but as groups of like-minded persons – they have a power to affect the course of events that we do not fully understand. Exercise of this power is both a religious obligation to Quakers and the fulfilment of a duty of citizenship – the duty to participate in the democratic process and to be involved in the "actions and passions of your times." Neither that religious obligation nor that political duty will ever change.

Vietnam and the Branches of Friends

Plenary Presentations:

Arthur O. Roberts: Evangelical Friends International

Bruce Birchard: Friends General Conference

Johan Maurer: Friends United Meeting

July 20, 1998

The Vietnam Era and the Evangelical Quaker Community

Arthur O. Roberts

July 20, 1998

INTRODUCTION:

I commenced a teaching career at George Fox College in the fall of 1953, following completion of a Ph.D. program at Boston University. In returning to my alma mater I also returned to that sturdy Northwest Quaker community in which I had my spiritual and cultural roots. From childhood I had worshiped with other Quaker families in Greenleaf, Idaho. For this settlement, Quaker farm families had chosen the middle name of the Quaker poet whose last name, Whittier, had been chosen earlier by Quaker migrants to the fertile valleys of Southern California.

In Sunday School I received Bible teaching, reinforced by classes at Greenleaf Friends Academy, by family worship, and by youth meetings in quarterly and yearly meetings. One summer, at Quaker Hill Camp, in the central Idaho mountains, I experienced Christ as my Savior in such a wonderful way that when later I read Fox's testimony I knew that the One who spoke to his condition had also spoken to mine. In the fervency of spiritual discovery I sang a chorus, "I have decided to follow Jesus, no turning back, no turning back." Sixty years later these words still move me to tears. "No turning back!"

To this Quaker lad, following Jesus was why Quakers had a peace testimony, and why they sent missionaries to Bolivia and Africa, and why they dealt fairly with their neighbors. A text from the book of Hebrews expressed our spiritual aspirations: "Follow holiness and peace, without which no one shall see the Lord."

Discerning in me a call to the ministry, Greenleaf elders nurtured that calling (as did my family) until it was affirmed by Northwest Yearly Meeting in a recording process following graduation from Pacific College (now George Fox University). My father's people had left Wales to join other persecuted Quakers in William Penn's colony. With other Welsh migrant families they clustered in settlements with names drawn from the old country, such as Bryn Mawr and Merion and Gwynedd.

In subsequent years, expanding Roberts families migrated to New Hampshire, Virginia, Indiana, Iowa, and finally to Idaho, seeking fertile soil to farm and Christian communities in which to rear their children. Northwest Yearly Meeting contained many families with similar westering histories and concerns, many coming directly from Iowa. My grandmother and great-grandmother were recorded ministers, in the non-pastoral tradition. So from childhood I had a strong sense of Quaker tradition.

When World War II erupted I registered as a conscientious objector, as did many of my friends. Our church leaders, locally, and at the yearly meeting level, urged, taught, and facilitated this testimony. Some of my pals chose alternate civilian service; others chose non-combatant service in the armed forces. A few were regular enlistees or draftees. None of my friends went to prison. As young frontier-type Americans, we were generally optimistic about our nation, and pleased that conscientious objector status had been legally acknowledged. I was exempt from service because of ministerial status (serving as a pastor). This exemption bothered me a bit later – what were my sacrifices compared to those drafted into the army or into Civilian Public Service camps?

Those of us who struggled with our consciences during this war, like Bonhoeffer but to a different conclusion, weren't sure how to combine or prioritize the Biblical mandates for peace, justice, and holiness. To many of us, subsequently, the Vietnam War posed no such agonizing dilemma. How could anyone support this Asian war on moral grounds? But our children lived in different times and under different influences. To them the issues were new and confusing. And these different times are the ones I address now.

First I will comment upon the impact of the Vietnam era upon the George Fox College community, then upon Northwest Yearly Meeting, and finally upon me personally.

A. *The impact of the Vietnam era upon the George Fox College community.*

As mentioned, I came to George Fox in the fall of 1953, where I taught courses ranging from Literature of the Bible, to Social Theory, to Logic. For many years I also taught History and Doctrine of Friends, a requirement for Friends students. For the first two decades of my professorial career most students were Quaker, in a small student body drawn mostly from the Northwest states. Between 1968 and 1972 I served as academic dean. Vietnam was largely a blue-collar war, a circumstance abetted by generous student exemptions. Our student body was impacted by the war and by counterculture forces of social protest, however, as were other campuses.

The motto of the college, established in 1891, is "Christianity and Culture." This reflects the optimistic mood of its founders, that faith offers the appropriate context for reason, that the arts and sciences are of intrinsic value, and that the Gospel as light and leaven draws civilization toward God's kingdom. This Christian liberal arts viewpoint characterized the college in the sixties, and seventies, also. We shared with other Christian colleges the conviction that "all truth is God's truth." The Vietnam era challenged the optimistic symbiosis between Christianity and culture. It forced a reconsideration of another faith stance: Christ against culture. As the war dragged on to its slow conclusion, and the idealism of the protest movement degenerated into secular cynicism and moral relativism, the question arose insistently: Which culture are we against? Establishment or counter-culture? Or both?

At neighboring Reed College in Portland, protest was more radical than at George Fox College. At Reed, it seemed, students spent more time arguing and marching than studying. They littered the campus, and dressed in grunge. The physics department went begging for majors. (With the world burning why study quantum mechanics?) At George Fox, a radicalizing of social witness did occur, but much less stridently. Was it timidity, or concern that even a prophetic witness requires basic civilities? I think it was a concern to sustain Christian values even in times of social turmoil.

Our students joined others, however, in protest marches in Portland. They put bumper stickers on their VW's. They flashed the peace sign on the way to student prayer meetings. They read the *Post-American* and the *Wittenburg Door*. They argued about, and made commitments to, simpler life styles. Some brashly upbraided their local church leaders for inadequate Christian social witness. Sensitivity sessions were in vogue on campus. "Letting it all hang out," was a phrase depicting a counter-cultural zeal for openness.

For a time my wife and I hosted in our home weekly worship-sharing meetings for young couples, some married, others soon to be. We would sit on the floor in a circle. There were some wonderful times of spiritual communion, but also some troubling aspects to this worship. My wife and I were abashed at the uninhibited confession of personal problems, couples reporting on difficulties in sexual intercourse, for example. Public confession went beyond the bounds of a prudent respect for others. It seems that polite reserve was suspect, as signifying hypocritical, authoritarian, order – an assumed antecedent to strife. One year certain graduates (wearing stylized granny dresses and ripped jeans) protested the pomp and ceremony and the regalia of commencement activities. After some debate the faculty affirmed the values of tradition even in revolutionary times.

One issue involved public symbols. The stage of our auditorium included an American flag. Because worship occurred there its presence was protested by some faculty members. Traditionalists insisted it should remain. The issue was resolved by purchasing an Oregon State flag and a United Nations flag and placing all three flags on stage. But above the three flags were placed two very large banners. One banner depicts the Lamb of

God. It symbolizes God's mode of conquest. The other depicts the descending dove. It symbolizes both the descending of the Spirit at Pentecost and the return of peace to a damaged world.

Curricular shifts occurred as a result of the Vietnam War. Vocational preparation at the college now included a fuller appreciation for service as one of the three components of Gospel witness (along with proclamation and fellowship). Social work became a leading major. The number of pre-med students increased.

Once in a chapel talk I encouraged students to be positive, instead of negative, in their peace witness. Find something constructive to do, I urged. In response, the president of the student body, Fred Gregory, and two other graduating students, Jon Newkirk and Jerry Sandoz, volunteered to go to Vietnam. Dorlan Bales joined them later. Fred Gregory has shared with me his reflections, in a paper, "Vietnam Remembered," which he anticipates editing and enlarging for publication.

During the years 1966-68, these young men went out under the umbrella of the Mennonite Central Committee, and worked with Vietnam Christian Service. Gregory's activities included establishing a feeding program and developing a vocational school for displaced children in Quang Ngai, medical assistance, and in the central highlands (at Di Linh) assisting with craft exports for tribal people suffering from Hanson's disease (leprosy). Fred's life was threatened by American military personnel who assumed he was giving information as well as aid to the enemy. On several occasions the house in which he lived lay in the line of fire.

The other George Fox College students worked in separate areas of the country, but were engaged in similar relief work. They were exposed to similar dangers. Jerry Sandoz, for example, hunkered down in a house riddled by crossfire during the Tet offensive, out of contact with anyone for eight days. "All of us volunteers," said Gregory, "spent many a night on the floor to avoid getting hit with incoming rounds of mortar or small arms fire." Some excerpts from Fred's manuscript illustrate the impact of the war upon a Christian college student leaving a friendly and secure environment for a dangerous and insecure one:

"George Fox College and Northwest Yearly Meeting embraced our going to Vietnam. We were 'sent' by the Yearly Meeting on this peacemaking mission. Accordingly we were invited to speak in many Meetings and at Yearly Meeting about our prospective service. I remember the great feeling I had of being cared for and encouraged during those days prior to leaving....

"On one occasion plague erupted in the camp. When I learned of it I went to the house where two boys lay very sick and dying. They had been isolated from others in the camp for fear of the disease spreading. I brought the team VW van out to the camp and, much to the surprise of everyone, carried them to the car and took them alone to the hospital, where American military doctors were able to treat them. The boys eventually recovered to normal health, and became students in the mechanics classes of the school we had started....

"I became very good friends with the town baker who baked the bread for the feeding programs. He and his wife had three daughters and no son. The wife later described me as her American son. I learned of their flight from the north in 1954 to flee the communist takeover of that part of the country. They were Buddhists. I learned of their hopes and fears. From them I learned the grace of hospitality: I could not go to their house without at least being served tea. I learned of their fear of the communists, but also of the American-run war. I learned from others that they really had no fear of Ho Chi Minh. What they feared was having to live in the middle of the fighting. At night they had to be beholden to the Viet Cong. In the day they had to be beholden to the South Vietnamese Army and Americans. They could not win....

"We lived about six miles from Mai Lai, where the infamous massacre took place. It was during this period of time that I started a feeding program for rural people who had been forcibly moved from their villages to a desolate field outside of a little District Headquarters about 10 miles from town....

"Many of the people had hidden in caves to elude the American soldiers brought to their village by helicopter. When discovered, they were forced out of hiding with CS gas thrown by the soldiers. When I saw the people who were gassed, they were coughing blood, as their lungs had been seared by the toxin. Most of the old people gassed died within days or a few weeks.

"When confronted about gassing people, the young American soldiers would often weep upon realizing what had happened. 'I was told that this gas would not harm the people' was an all too frequent response. More than one young foot soldier talked to me about betrayal and lying by his superiors....

"General Westmoreland, and many other high ranking American officers, along with General Ky and General Thieu came to town eventually to celebrate the 'victory.' It was soon after the celebration that the rumors changed to factual details of the Mai Lai massacre. Our Vietnamese friends had been telling us stories that they had heard from Mai Lai.

"By now I was becoming cynical and bitter at the Americans and the lying. Later, in another location in the mountains, I watched an American major write a 'kill' report which went into the weekly briefing report that was made in Saigon about the number of enemy killed. He was writing a good report to enhance his own performance review, and it seemed to have little to do with reality....

"During this time I also became acquainted with some Protestant missionaries who were close to the American military in one way or another. Some had what I believed to be a heretical understanding of God and what He needed to accomplish His work. One missionary sincerely thought the US should drop tactical nuclear bombs across the DMZ in order to build a barrier between the north and south. He believed God needed the war to accomplish His work of evangelization of the Vietnamese people. He truly believed that this was the Lord's war!

"To this day, I have great reservations about that denomination, because of what was too often a colonial, conquering spirit displayed by their missionaries. I know that many of the younger missionaries today would shudder at their elders' attitudes....

"The dark side of my successful coping was, later in life, understanding and having to face the reality that I had become addicted to excitement and the possibility of death. Although I helped thousands of people to live, I became hooked on the thrill of danger. I have since made deliberate decisions to avoid those situations if at all possible. The longing to engage in a 'complex humanitarian crisis' (today's jargon) is still with me. More that one close friend has been killed in the line of humanitarian duty. We call them heroes, when maybe they just lost perspective, and then lost their way....

"My last few weeks in Saigon were stressful. At night I would hear fighting in the far off distance, and imagine that it was getting closer with each minute. My nights were filled with fear....

"Vietnam changed my life forever. I didn't know the extent of the change until years later. My vocational direction was altered. I am yet today working with the poor overseas. I have great empathy for the tens of thousands of Vietnam vets who are not able to function normally in society today. What they were asked to do by the US government was not right. They were asked to put aside values they had been taught in order to execute the war. Killing children, elderly, animals as well as the identified 'enemy' required changed values. Young men had been asked to put on hold normally held values and morals in order to fight a war where the enemy was hard to define or identify.

"It is no surprise that sexual promiscuity, drug and alcohol problems emerged to the degree they did. The damages of war go far beyond battlefield casualties. Unfortunately, most war casualties are not combatants. Vietnam changed the balance of who gets killed and maimed, from combatants to civilians. The legacy of civilians constituting most of the victims of war continues....

"Peacemaking during war and compassionate care for innocent civilians is needed more than ever. But such actions are very risky, as the 'old' rules of war mostly do not apply today. Aid workers are no longer off-limits from hostile action. New strategies are required for dealing with the innocent in times of war. Friends and other peace groups need to form an army of peacemakers to counter destructive wars.

"It is time to speak of the Vietnam War in the public

square, in order to heal the broken and to learn lessons for the future."

Fred Gregory has understated the personal vocational impact of the Vietnam War. He has spent thirty years in relief administration, currently serving as president of Esperanza International. This agency helps poor women in Latin America break the poverty cycle through micro-credit programs. In 1972-74, under the aegis of the World Relief Commission, he formed an indigenous development agency in Bangladesh that today is self-supporting, with 900 employees. For many years he was associated with World Concern, serving as president from 1987 to 1995. Fred has returned to Vietnam twice in the past ten years.

The other members of that George Fox student volunteer team also found careers in relief and service activities. In Vietnam Jon Newkirk became aware of the plight of those who till the soil. Subsequently he became active in social justice issues, working with Methodist and Presbyterian groups in Washington DC, and for a time in Albany, New York, in the Governor's office. He holds a professional degree in agricultural economics. Jerry Sandoz has spent thirty years as a service missionary in South Korea. Dorlan Bales left academia to develop "Friends of Jesus," a ministry to poor families in Wichita, Kansas.

This is how four George Fox students heeded a professor's exhortation to "do something constructive" by way of a peace witness. Or, more accurately, how they heeded the Holy Spirit, and let the Vietnam experience become a catalyst for many years of Christian service.

B. *The impact of the Vietnam era upon Northwest Yearly Meeting of Friends*

The Vietnam War forced Northwest Quakers to reexamine the nature of their peace witness and their views about government. My colleague, Ralph Beebe, made a study of the Yearly Meeting representatives in August of 1967 and found that 45.5 percent favored escalation rather than "a continuation of the existing policy of limited warfare with gradual escalation" and another 45.5 percent favored "de-escalation of the war even if the North Vietnamese and Viet Cong did not reciprocate." This study pointed up the fact that in practice some Friends separated personal and public ethics – a variant of Luther's two-kingdom theory. Beebe also did a study of churches in Eugene, Oregon, in early 1968. The Free Methodist and Nazarene churches took very hawkish positions and the Eugene Friends Meeting took a very dovish stance. Eugene Friends Church was very much like the other evangelical churches on doctrine, but very much like the unprogrammed Quaker meeting in regard to Vietnam.

Along with other Christians, Friends of the Northwest faced a growing polarity. Some in the community of faith became increasingly nationalistic. These persons feared anarchy and/or communism and its social consequences. They favored strong support for government regardless of a flawed foreign policy. For others the war served as a wake-up call to greater prophetic faithfulness in calling nations to account against God's standards of righteousness rather than to some geopolitical calculus. This tension became exacerbated by the stridency of the protest movements, and by symptoms of social degeneration. When I began to grow a beard in 1967, one dear Friend labored with me, "You look like a hippie, Arthur!" A few days later, however, perhaps with Sallman's painting in mind, she admitted that Jesus probably wore a beard!

There were good reasons to fear anarchist tendencies in the anti-war counterculture. Some religious movements succumbed to pop or drug culture. Once I attended a meeting with a "Jesus freak," David Berg, in Seattle. We sat on the floor, holding hands and singing gospel songs. But later in this movement, sadly, spiritual ecstasy subtly yielded to sexual ecstasy. Then "flirty fishing" became promoted as an evangelistic tool (win a convert by having sex with him). Having rationalized sexual immorality these "Children of God" turned tyrannical. "Jesus people" became idolatrous. False gods triumphed. The warning of the Apostle Paul comes to mind, "Satan himself masquerades as an angel of light" (2 Cor. 11:14).

Even some persons within a significant inter-yearly meeting movement, Young Friends of North America, succumbed to self-deception. The slogan "make love, not war" became a license for sexual promiscuity, and the movement floundered.

Despite conservative resistance to the counter-culture, for the reasons noted above, within Northwest Yearly Meeting, in the truest sense of the word, a "radicalizing" of the Gospel witness occurred. The Biblical exhortation to honor governance, Romans 13, was paired with the Biblical warning against diabolical governance, found in Revelation 13. Ecumenically, the National Association of Evangelicals became less important to Northwest Friends than contact with historic peace churches. Mennonites such as John Howard Yoder gained a hearing. The fiery Jim Wallis, dressed in a coarse denim shirt, became a prophetic voice. Ministers and other leaders read his magazine, first known as the *Post-American,* and subsequently as *Sojourners.* Baptist sociologist Tony Campolo became a sought after writer and speaker.

This is how I summarize the impact of the Vietnam era upon Northwest Friends.

1. *The Church deepened its understanding of sin and grace.*

This included an acknowledgment of structural as well as personal sin. Our Quaker doctrine of Christian perfection was challenged, and had to be reformulated against Biblical standards. The complexities of evil challenged both extant (and often bifurcated) expressions of Quaker perfectionism: personal sanctification and social witness. Under the challenges posed by the Vietnam War and its social upheaval, doctrines of personal heart purity and social benevolence both became vulnerable to charges of spiritual pride and legalism. Faced by crumbling moral authority and the complicit character of evil, the church acknowledged that holiness is a gift of God and not a personal or social achievement.

Northwest Quakers, in humility, re-emphasized forgiveness and the healing of hurts. Did this renewed emphasis upon grace constitute what our forebears dubbed "preaching up sin"? I don't think so, although it is the case that formulaic holiness teachings (e.g. Wesleyan "second definite work of grace") gave way to less triumphalist salvation claims. Northwest and other Friends are still reformulating holiness theology, and there was a wide and positive response to my "New Call to Holiness" first presented at Malone College in 1991 and variously published since then.

2. *The Church broadened its missionary witness.*

Missionaries coined a new term for accommodation to culture without compromise of Christian convictions: contextualization. They saw the need for a Christian witness within the context of culture, for during the Vietnam era, especially because of media coverage, a plurality of world cultures was revealed. And the culture of the sending nations was no longer viewed as necessarily beneficent for people throwing off colonial power. Missionaries understood more clearly the triune nature of Gospel witness: proclamation, fellowship, and service – and their own cultural biases.

3. *The Church became more forthright in peacemaking.*

As during other wars, the churches urged youth to register as conscientious objectors. Yearly Meeting letters to the federal government urged peace. That Oregon senators Wayne Morse and Mark Hatfield opposed the war encouraged Friends to do so more forthrightly. Specific peace efforts occurred. For example, a Northwest Yearly Meeting leader, Norval Hadley, helped initiate the New Call to Peacemaking, which movement engendered significant Quaker and other peace church participation in the 1970's and created a more vocal national witness for peace and against war.

In 1973 a conference at Winona Lake, Indiana, brought together persons from Anabaptist, Wesleyan, and Quaker backgrounds to discuss war and holiness. A Church of the Nazarene theologian defended holiness as essentially inward and attitudinal.

A soldier, he claimed, could bayonet an enemy while retaining perfect love in his heart toward him. A Free Methodist theologian, who had served in the military, shook his head at this claim. No, said he, such detachment of attitude from action isn't possible. He would rather accept a just war position than try to maintain a theology of perfection based upon such Jesuitical premises. He opted for a theology more Calvinist than Wesleyan – choosing among lesser evils – rather than to claim that in official killing one could maintain sanctified inner serenity in accord with Divine will. The latter course seemed to him more Stoic than Christian.

We Quakers and Mennonites argued for passive, or non-violent resistance, as the means for Christian faithfulness. But we had to acknowledge that our pacifist position, as experiences had shown, could lead to self-righteousness. [Material for the preceding paragraph is taken from my autobiographical reflections, *Drawn by the Light* (1993).]

C. *The impact of the Vietnam era upon me personally*

1. *I experienced how the Holy Spirit brings reconciliation.*

The Vietnam War impacted our family significantly. In 1965 our son dropped out of college and enlisted in the Navy. This may have pleased his grandfather – a World War I veteran – but not his parents! Our son was sent to Connecticut for schooling and in due course assigned to a nuclear submarine as a torpedo man. The submarine engaged in hide and seek with Russian vessels in the China Sea, but not in combat. At the end of his four year stint he had a run-in with officers, for in a drill he asserted he would never launch upon a city or civilian target. After some uncertainty he received an honorable discharge. The social and cultural conflicts of the era impacted him greatly, and the post-war years were difficult.

Our family bonds weakened but did not break, and gradually they strengthened with his, and our, maturity. A few years ago, while he and I were walking in the woods near his home, out of the blue he said "Dad, I've recommitted my life to Jesus

Christ." What a reconciling moment! What answers to years of prayer! My son and I continue to differ on issues but together rejoice in rekindled love, and in God's all-encompassing grace.

He shares the hurt and sometimes the cynicism of other Vietnam War veterans. He is generous to a fault, and his trust is often betrayed. Politically he is libertarian, wary of the federal government even more than of big corporations. He wants life to be simple but has not found it so. He is a (reluctant) just war advocate, not a pacifist. His concern for infantry veterans is passionate, very similar to that of Fred Gregory, as noted above.

From my son I have learned that persons who zealously support "good" causes may be misled in assuming they represent the "public interest." They may actually represent a privileged elite. For prophetic witness to be Biblical it should represent equity and justice, not special privilege. People, said Jesus, are of more value than sparrows. More than marbled murrelets, maybe? Our son lives ten miles inland from the Columbia Gorge, and with other residents bears burdensome land restrictions supposedly "in the public interest" but actually excessive of need and repressive for working people. My son is a blue collar, Harley Davidson riding conservationist, and one-time sawmill foreman, who broadened his academic father's vision of the people whom social policy ought to serve.

Currently, with sixty other property owners, my wife and I are trying to protect our long-entitled properties against a few litigious "eco-terrorists" who claim a trail should replace our beach front homes. The Vietnam era fostered a liberal penchant for "doing causes," no matter how impractical or disruptive. Are Quakers caught up in such power games activists in "ego trip" causes? I hope not!

2. I understood patriotism at a deeper level than before.

In 1970 my wife and I visited Sweden. I will never forget a huge painting in Stockholm's Museum of Modern Art. It depicted the White House with a tongue of blood running down the steps.

The painting disturbed me, and I went home determined that the good things about America should prevail, not its violence. (We had considered emigrating to New Zealand.)

Philosophically I understood that governance at its best is a nonviolent way to meld the needs of the individual and the group. William Penn had once said that if people will not be ruled by God they will be ruled by tyrants. So I took seriously the Puritan/Quaker understanding that political leadership can be an instrument of Divine purpose. People of godly faith are, as Jeremiah said, to seek the peace of the city, even one that holds them captive "because if it prospers, you too will prosper" (see Jer. 29:7).

So I ran for the Oregon legislature but lost in the primary election. But in 1972 I achieved some political participation by helping Mark Hatfield in his election campaign. He stoutly defended his anti-war stance whenever challenged. The people of Oregon re-elected him. They admired his forthright position, whether or not they agreed.

Some years later, in a convocation address, Senator Hatfield urged George Fox College to strengthen its peace witness. This concern bore fruit in the establishment of the Peace Center, led first by Lon Fendall (a one-time Hatfield aide) and then by the current director, Ron Mock. My own participation in democracy included six years on the Newberg Planning Commission, and in retirement years several years' service on the Yachats City Council. Currently I serve as mayor.

3. *I adopted new lifestyle symbols.*

During the late sixties and early seventies professors opted for non-establishment lifestyles. Traditionally we academics delight in non-conformity, in tweaking the establishment. The Vietnam War gave such non-conformity added symbolic clout. For the classroom, suits and ties were out, casual clothes were in. As a Westerner at home in causal attire, I welcomed this "dressing down," this freedom from the business model of dressing for success.

Television popularized the new styles. Some symbolic forms consisted of socio-dramas, such as sit-ins, teach-ins, and protest marches. Others were audio: Peter, Paul and Mary singing "Where have all the flowers gone?" Still other symbolism was visual. Clothing and accessories constituted symbolic statements.

For Christians it meant that Biblical earthiness replaced Platonic essences, and the doctrine of creation became basic to the doctrine of redemption. One of my visual symbols was this shirt depicting ancient Christian triune and cruciform symbols. It's my church history shirt. My wife, Fern, made the shirt from flour sacking and carefully hand-stitched the symbols. Inuit Friends from Alaska Yearly Meeting had given me ancient ivory during the years I researched their history. I carved this ivory into various accessories, such as the pendant I am wearing.

4. I developed my poetic talents.

The Vietnam experience stimulated a continuing excursion into the writing of poetry. Several poems focused directly upon the war. These included "The Age of Metal," "My Lai Manifesto," "Herod's Christmas, 1972," "Return of the Prisoner," "A Christian Postscript," and "The Exiles." The "exiles" depicted were a Roman Catholic, a black Baptist, a non-cooperator, and a seeker. The last stanza, about the seeker, reads:

Under ground from Ur
by psychedelic bus
he found a country where
faith lies latent in despair –
driven, not called out.
Is the land of promise
communal living, pot?

He's sure it is not
napalm and the draft.

Through organic gardening,
goats, Garfunkel tapes,
guitars, Woodstock,
Goodwill shirts, babies,
love has nourished him
and prepared a harvest–
by the Jesus people.

[These poems were published in *Listen to the Lord*, in 1974, and some were republished in *Sunrise and Shadow* (1984).]

5. *I gained spiritual insights.*

At Reedwood Friends Church, Portland, Oregon, on May 19, 1974, I presented in sermonic form what I had arrived at philosophically, and had begun teaching in ethics classes. This position I labeled "situation grace," to contrast it with Joseph Fletcher's "situation ethics," which had been used increasingly to rationalize questionable conduct on the basis of good intentions. Bonhoeffer's "tragic moral choice" had also degenerated into a "do your own thing" relativism.

Some lines from that talk are appropriate. They reflect a long search to understand how God in Christ not only forgives us our sins but also delivers us from their power, so that we do indeed participate in God's holiness:

"Situation grace acknowledges that hard circumstances confront us and that we are limited, finite, and fallible. It also acknowledges God as sovereign....We live within limits. Thus grace. We do not have to accept God as some inexorable force, but as a Father who gives us new starting places; over and over again, if necessary. The discovery of Jesus' way is like finding the world's most valuable pearl, like finding treasures hid in a field, like a full day's pay for an hour's work. Jesus' statements in the Sermon on the Mount are not intended to put morality out of reach, but rather to teach the ways of love..., not designed to make us super-puritans who develop increasing scruples on this and that, but rather to accept the meaning of grace and to reverence a holy God. Sanctification is the work of the Holy Spirit and not our own achievement. Therefore my stand on morality is this.

"First, I accept the Law as greater than all codes. I honor the decalogue as establishing boundaries of morality and all the other Biblical statements as ways by which I should love my neighbor as myself. I recognize that God's will is greater than rules. He is, after all, the Heavenly Father and not some traffic cop hidden in the willows....

"Second, I accept love as the best word. This is the way to hold God's ethical choices together. I would rather fail in love than to accept hate or violence or greed. I will do all I can to apply love within the structures of society, family, commerce, nations....

"Thirdly, I will acknowledge grace. After all, I have limits of knowledge and limits of power. I will therefore be more compassionate toward those whose power and knowledge is less than mine, or whose circumstances differ. I will seek to follow those who are exemplary and be less censorious of those who are not. I will not confuse grace with relativism. God's way is good. He gives good gifts. As a giver and as a receiver I would be like Christ....

"Fourthly, I will accept discipleship in God's kingdom now with all the risks and dangers involved, not calculating consequences by human wisdom but joyously sharing in life, shedding light and sprinkling salt wherever I can. I invite you to join me in the jubilee of God. Let the Light shine!"

[Excerpted and adapted from *Drawn By The Light*, Chapter 8]

CONCLUSION

These, then, are my perspectives upon how the Vietnam era impacted my primary faith community – George Fox College and Northwest Yearly Meeting – and how it affected me personally. In retrospect, the era tested whether and how we could be faithful to

Jesus Christ, both in deed and in truth. As with others, I am sobered by the experience. I have felt the cold shadow of the Cross. I have sought more diligently the nature of Christian discipleship, gleaning insights from the classics of spirituality and from the Bible – and from prayer and compassionate caring. The Vietnam era made me more aware of the cost of such discipleship.

It Was a Hard Time, and Friends Were There

Bruce Birchard
Friends General Conference

Much of what I had originally considered saying in my talk has been covered very well by other speakers. I've done a lot of writing and re-writing since this conference began! When I finished last night, I had two very different parts to this address. I shall begin by recounting some incidents from my own experience during the years of the Vietnam War. I've decided to do so in part because, at the time, I was a very new Friend, very unsophisticated, and my experience may have been closer to the norm than that of other speakers who were more "mature" in their Quakerism and/or their political awareness at the time. I will limit my recollections primarily to those which relate specifically to Quakerism and my growth as a new, young Friend.

In the second half of my talk, I will do two things. I will share my thoughts on the issue of effectiveness of our peace work vs. witness "because we can do no other." I will also briefly explore where we Friends might go as we continue attempts to live in the spirit of the Friends' peace testimony, perhaps adding still more limbs to the strange "Questing Beast" which Jeremy Mott described so well in his talk.

The Vietnam War and my Coming to Quakerism

I should begin by explaining that I grew up in a rural, conservative, and patriotic small town in northwestern New Jersey.

Five of us kids in my neighborhood played together, mostly around the brook or in the woods. Our favorite game was one we simply called "Guns." We had a little club and called ourselves "The Junior Marines." My family belonged to the Presbyterian Church, where my father taught Sunday School and sang in the choir. I learned the Apostle's Creed and joined the church when I was 14 years old. I never heard of Quakers or pacifists, but my high school English teacher was an ex-Marine who fought in the Pacific, and he would not allow the boys in his classes to glamorize war. Once he told me a bit about what it was like to live in terror, kill other men, and then shoot the corpses, because one of them might still be alive and suddenly shoot you as you walked by. In 1963 I graduated from Hackettstown High School and went off to a college no one in Hackettstown had ever heard of: Wesleyan University in Middletown, Connecticut.

Spring, 1965: I'm sitting on the lawn in front of Olin Library with two friends. We've been talking about the fighting in Vietnam, and how terrible it is. One friend mentions that he is writing to his draft board to tell them he is something called a conscientious objector, and he tries to explain what this means. I don't understand real well, but I don't forget this conversation.

Good Friday, 1966: I've been attending Middletown Meeting for several months. Now I'm at Beacon Hill Friends House in Boston with my professor and Clerk of the meeting, David McAllester, and another hundred or so Friends. We're being told about the silent vigil we'll soon be holding in front of Mary Dyer's statue, across from Boston Common. We are to remain totally silent, hold our signs, and ignore provocations. There are people of all ages in this group. It feels right. I feel the strength of the group, the experience of the older Friends, the centered, religious tone of the vigil. Back in Middletown I begin attending many of the weekly Wednesday noon antiwar vigils on Main Street. It's usually ten or fifteen people, a lot of them from meeting. We get hassled some, but I feel clear and confident with these Friends.

April, 1967: I'm in the common room of my college dorm, meeting with three Friends from Middletown Monthly Meeting.

They are the clearness committee which has come to talk with me about my letter requesting membership in the meeting.

"Tell us about why you want to join Middletown Meeting," they suggest. "There are two main reasons. First, I have rejected many of the teachings of the Presbyterian Church in which I was raised, including the claims of Christianity to an exclusive knowledge of religious Truth. However, I continue to be concerned about religious matters, about what God is and is not, about how I live my life. I would like to be part of a group that would support me in my searching without insisting on adherence to specific Christian dogma. And secondly, Quakers seem to act on their beliefs; their lives are generally consistent with what they say they believe, which does not seem true of a lot of other Christians."

As the discussion proceeds, I feel compelled to acknowledge that it is odd to be asking for membership in Middletown Meeting when I will be graduating from Wesleyan University in another eight weeks and moving to Chicago in the fall to begin graduate work in Anthropology at the University of Chicago. I explain, "It would seem to make more sense for me to move to Chicago and join the meeting there. But it would take time for me to get to know the new meeting, and for them to know me, and I could not submit an application for membership until this happened. As you know, I have decided that I will not go into the armed forces, and I may request classification as a conscientious objector, and it might help if I'm a Quaker." It is embarrassing to speak of this, for it makes my application for membership seem so, well, convenient and instrumental, but this did influence my decision to apply for membership rather than waiting another year.

Thankfully, these Friends are sympathetic and supportive; they don't make me feel bad or small. My application for membership is accepted. Soon I am a member of Middletown Meeting. Now I'm a Quaker.

Fall, 1967, 57th Street Meeting, Chicago: Meeting for worship has just ended. I see another young man, and I've heard that he knows a lot about the draft. I approach him. "I've been thinking a lot about the war and the draft. I know I'll lose my II-S deferment next summer. I know I won't ever go in the army, and I know I won't leave the country. I'm trying to decide what to do. I recently became a Quaker. Do you think I could get classified as a conscientious objector?"

He looks at me with, well, disdain. "Yeah, you probably could – if that's what you want to do." Then I realize – he's a draft resister. He's one of those really courageous men that I admire for their refusal to cooperate in any way with the system, and he'll probably go to prison. I feel very small. It takes me several weeks to get up the courage to approach another member of meeting who, I'm told, is a draft counselor. He is more sympathetic, and I soon begin work on my letter to Local Board #45 in Philipsburg, New Jersey.

Christmas Eve, 1968: Another vigil, but this one is different. We're in front of the Presbyterian Church in Hackettstown as people file in for the Christmas Eve service, and there are only six or seven of us, including my father, my mother, my brother and me. This is the church I grew up in. Some people know me; most know my mother and father. I admire them – witnessing in this way to their friends and neighbors, most of whom support the war and the sons of Hackettstown who are over there fighting and dying.

Four years ago, my father eldered me when I wrote a letter to the Hackettstown *Gazette* in support of the civil rights struggle. He agreed with me, he said, but I needed to understand that they still lived in Hackettstown and I didn't. Could I be so considerate as to show them anything I wanted to publish in the local paper before submitting it? Now here he was with a draft resister and an antiwar sign in front of his church. We did not get many smiles. I've often said that a major part of the antiwar movement took place in people's kitchens, because that's where I explained to my parents why I wouldn't go to war. They understood, and they supported me. It must have been hard for them at times. It probably helped that I had become a Quaker. There was a faith basis for my position. My parents understood taking a stand based on religious principle.

Early February, 1969: On the plane to San Francisco. All my appeals for classification as a conscientious objector have been denied, and I got my induction order a few weeks ago. I told the director of the Indian Education Study that I would refuse induction, and that this would mean a trial, and quite possibly a prison term. I'm prepared to accept this, because I don't see any other alternative, but prison scares me, and I don't want to do any more time than necessary. As an experienced draft counselor, I know that the Ninth Federal District Court in San Francisco is giving the lightest sentences to draft resisters. Could he transfer me to the field office in San Francisco for a few months so I can commit my special crime within its jurisdiction? Then I'll have many months back in Chicago to finish up the work before I have to go back to San Francisco for trial. He is glad to help me, and I'm on my way.

Just a week ago, I broke up with my woman friend of one and one-half years. Another woman, a draft counselor and antiwar activist, wants to begin a relationship with me, but I'm just not ready. Emotionally, I'm in little pieces. The director of the field office in San Francisco has offered me a place to stay in his home. I will spend most of my nights in his family's living room on a sofa, behind a screen, for two months, and continue my work on the Indian Education Study in his office during the day. Now, on the plane, flying over the Rockies, I open an envelope which my friend Peter gave me when I left our apartment this morning. In it I find a poem which Peter wrote for me. It's about me, and he compares me to Sisyphus. I begin reading; I realize how much Peter understands and cares about me, and I start to cry. It's a hard time, but friends are there.

I should end this section by explaining that, after informing Washington that I would refuse induction and pointing out several procedural errors in my case, my induction order was postponed. I returned to Chicago. I went through a couple of steps with my local board, which then issued me a second induction order. I returned to San Francisco, but also wrote to General Hershey, head of the Selective Service System. My second induction order was canceled, I returned to Chicago, but my local board and New Jersey State

Appeal Board still refused to recognize me as a CO. I requested an occupational deferment; my local board denied this also, but on appealing this decision to the Illinois State Appeal Board, I was classified I-O. Subsequently I performed alternative service as a day care teacher in an inner city Chicago Head Start program, which was a good experience for me and, I believe, the kids with whom I worked.

Are We Called to be both Faithful and Effective?

In opening this conference, Lou Schneider asked: "When war threatens, is there a pragmatic extension of conscientious objection which strives to be effective not only in opposing the war, but also in preventing war? Or is the integrity of the witness alone, without any consideration of efficacy, its own reward?"

During the war in Vietnam, I and most of the Friends I knew were determined to stop the war. The killing and destruction were so terrible, we felt a responsibility to end it. It was not enough "simply" to offer a witness. In his talk, Jeremy Mott stated that this was the first time that Friends acted as if the peace testimony required us to act in nonviolent ways that could force our government to end the war. I concur.

What led to this new development? In part, I believe, it stemmed from a development in our political culture to which we were, indeed, conformed. The early sixties was a time of great hope. There was a conviction among many that we really did have the power to change our society. We were inspired by the nonviolent struggle of Black people and their white allies for an end to Jim Crow segregation and violence, and for civil rights. Principles of Gandhian nonviolence were adopted and expanded as African Americans in particular built a direct action movement, taking huge personal risks to confront an oppressive, violent system and to live as if that system were dead.

Edward P. Morgan, in *The 60's Experience*, argues that the social movements of the sixties were informed by four basic values: equality, personal empowerment, community, and morally-based politics. These values were the basis for a cultural revolution emphasizing personal relationships ("the personal is political"), building community, and the radical democratization of society based on equality and justice. None of these values were inconsistent with the testimonies and practices of the unprogrammed Friends I came to know in the early sixties, and I believe that Friends took them up with conviction and applied them in many ways.

The idealism of the early Kennedy administration also contributed to a belief in liberal circles that we had power and could effect change. As the US war in Indochina expanded, our idealistic picture of a sympathetic government responsive to moral persuasion was shattered. Yet we still understood, as public opposition to the war grew in the late sixties and early seventies, that our government could not continue this war indefinitely. The terrible reality was that the Nixon administration was dragging it out as long as possible, even escalating the violence against the Vietnamese people. Again, we were desperate to be effective to end this horrific violence – and with good reason.

This may have had a long-term impact on the Religious Society of Friends. Many of us who came to Quakerism in the sixties lacked the deep spiritual experience of being called to a faith-based witness which no rational observer would expect to "succeed." Many of us thought more "politically" than "faithfully" about how to work for peace and justice. Fortunately, other Friends "kept the faith." I'm encouraged by what I've heard here these past several days. As a religious society, we still have a deep understanding and experience of faith-based witness. We need to do more within our faith community to share that understanding and experience. This is important, both to maintain the "Religious" foundation of our "Society of Friends," and because this kind of witness can have tremendous power.

The authors of *Speak Truth to Power* put it well in 1955:

"We have tried to face the hard facts; to put the case for nonviolence in terms of common sense. Yet, we are aware that [those] who choose in these terms alone cannot sustain [themselves] against the mass pressures of an age of violence. If ever truth reaches power, if ever it speaks to the individual citizen, it will not be the argument that convinces. Rather it will be [our] own inner sense of integrity that impels [us] to say, 'Here I stand. Regardless of relevance or consequence, I can do no other.'"

Please note, however, that even the authors of this statement justify the importance of the "inner sense of integrity" in supporting our witness for nonviolence by stressing that only this kind of witness has the potential of convincing others, particularly those in power.

To return to Friends' efforts to end the Vietnam War, it was not that we were wrong to be concerned about effectiveness. To be unconcerned about effectiveness would have been irresponsible! But there does need to be a balance. We need to live with the tensions within this faith-effectiveness dilemma. At times, we must witness without obvious effect because we can do no other. However, it is often possible to be both centered in our faith, in our understanding of divine Truth, and to be effective. Jesus was a model of faithfulness to God's leadings. He also went to great lengths to communicate and witness with effect.

The Future of our Work and Witness

With this concern to be both faithful and as smart as possible about how to reduce war and violence, I want to venture some thoughts about the future. I shall start with the place of conscientious objection to war in our witness and struggle. What is the place of conscientious objection in a nation which can wage devastating "limited" wars abroad – and sustain the conditions for terrible violence at home – without conscription?

What are the chances of building a sixties-style antiwar movement when our government can wage these wars without risking the lives of large numbers of US citizens, both through the use of very sophisticated weapons and war technologies and through the use of proxy forces? We should also understand that the twenty-first century world will be dominated by economic forces based in the "developed" nations which are likely to find major wars in most parts of the world inconvenient, but which will sustain and create terrible injustice, violence and suffering.

The logical extension of our work for conscientious objection to military service seems to me to be war tax resistance. Our money is more important than our bodies. Of course, we are nowhere near being "effective" in reducing war and militarism by withholding our tax payments. This is really a faith-based witness, undertaken by Friends who can do no other, who cannot abide the thought of paying for guns and bombs that kill people. Could it be effective if, say, 10,000 Friends, with strong support from their monthly and yearly meetings, refused to pay taxes for war? Could the power of such a concerted, corporate witness actually shake the foundations of militarism?

Maybe. Would the passage of a Peace Tax Fund make such an outcome more likely by making it easier for more people to demonstrate their opposition to war and militarism through tax refusal, or would it co-opt what could be an effective witness and/or open the gates to tax refusal for many other causes? I don't know.

At any rate, I believe that we are unlikely to face conscription again in the United States, and that a major focus on support for conscientious objection to military service would be a mistake. Certainly we want to be very clear about our testimony against participation in war and military forces. And we want to support men and women in the military who find that they are conscientiously opposed to further military service.

But our greatest need is to develop a broader, positive pacifist witness. How should we live so as to remove the seeds of violence from our personal lives, from the life of our religious society, and from our culture, nation-state, and world? Many Friends are in fact developing such a witness and such work. This certainly includes the exciting and important efforts to teach nonviolent conflict resolution to prisoners in the "Alternatives to Violence Program," to school children through programs such as "Help Increase the Peace," and many others. It includes countless grassroots efforts to contain and lessen the violence that plagues so many neighborhoods in our cities, suburbs, towns, and rural areas.

Some of the work is cultural, and authors, song-writers, musicians, and other artists are all an important part of this movement. Lady Borton, Peter Blood, and Annie Patterson are examples of such workers. On the international level, the work of various peace teams and nonviolence trainers should be supported and increased. We have heard David Hartsough speak of the need and the opportunity, and this should become an important part of Quaker international witness and work.

I believe another front in the struggle to end the mass violence of war is the work to overcome old hatreds and to build international and cross-cultural connections. We know the power of the state and compliant media to generate effective enemy images and stir up war fever, as we saw during the war in the Persian Gulf. We are horrified at how easy it is to stir up ethnic and religious hatreds to devastating effect – in Ireland, in Bosnia, in Kosovo, in the Middle East, in many African nations. Can we prevent and overcome such hatreds with patient and innovative efforts at bridge-building?

This kind of effort was particularly important in the European movements for disarmament, when citizens of many countries on both sides of the rusting Iron Curtain worked "from below" to end the Cold War, to initiate some measures of disarmament, to build institutions of "civil society," and, in the process, contributed to the collapse or weakening of many totalitarian governments. I believe it was also important in the struggle to limit and end the US-sponsored wars in Central America. As people, including many Friends, traveled to Nicaragua, and as some courageous Central American refugees took public sanctuary in US faith communities and spoke of their experiences, it became harder for our government to continue supporting the killing there.

There are many negative aspects to the shrinking of our world into a global village, but the fact that our children can and are communicating with, traveling to, making friends in, and marrying people from Asia, Latin America, Africa, the Middle East, and other parts of the world builds bonds which should make at least some wars more difficult to initiate and sustain.

I have also become convinced of the importance of developing major service programs for children and young adults. Such programs should enable Quaker and other young people to work with poor and oppressed peoples and with the victims of many forms of violence, both at home and abroad. They should be clearly faith-based and incorporate regular worship. These programs should be developed with an understanding that the friendly and cooperative relationships formed, and the often intangible learnings gained by both the "servers" and the "served," are often more important than the physical results.

Such programs should be explicit in their commitment to overcome racism, sexism, homophobia, and the growing economic inequalities within our country and our world. In other words, they should combine clear commitments to both nonviolence and to justice, including economic justice. They should provide opportunities for seasoned pacifist Friends to worship and work and talk with young people. There should also be encouragement and support for young people to seek and develop their own leadings and programs, which will be different from ours.

Conclusion

These are a few elements in what could be a strong, faith-based, and potentially effective Quaker peace program. Friends are already involved in each of these elements, but there is so much more we could do with strong support. Many of you may have additional elements to add. Of course, we cannot know the impact such efforts would have, but we are called to proceed in faith. In the end, we need at least to stand in love with the victims of violence and injustice and know that this has an impact. For hundreds upon hundreds of millions of precious, individual people, it is a very hard time. Friends must continue to be there.

"Was There a War Going On?"

Johan Maurer
Friends United Meeting

Thank you for the invitation to be part of this important and inspiring event. Based on what Chel Avery and Dan Seeger asked me to try to contribute, I'm drawing on both autobiographical and institutional memories, which in connection with the Vietnam War era almost do not overlap at all in a chronological sense. However, at one important point in my life, and partly under the influence of the currents of wartime, I joined my personal story with the Church's story, specifically with that of Friends United Meeting, and hopefully the autobiographical part will help to explain why.

I am a product of World War II. Probably all of us could find a way to say that about ourselves. Here is my way: My father was born and grew up in Norway, which in that war was invaded and occupied by Germany. As a wartime teenager whose own father was a lieutenant in the secret resistance army, my father learned the vital importance of not saying and asking too much. He saw Russian prisoners of war, the results of Allied bombing raids on Nazi installations in Oslo, teachers arrested for refusing to teach what they were told. His father, the lieutenant, was by far not a pacifist, but he taught functional nonviolence during the war: violence and terrorism only exposed the resistance to unnecessary danger.

My mother, on the other hand, was born and raised in a German family in Japan, where as a wartime teenager she saw the results of Allied bombing on residential areas and schools. She was taught the Nazi theories of Aryan superiority, adjusted to include the Japanese. German and Japanese philosophies of authoritarianism meshed nicely, to the point that I sometimes say that the only religion I was raised in was the cult of obedience to established authority.

The end of the war began a seething rearrangement of world populations, as some refugees returned home, other people became the new refugees of postwar chaos and empire-building. My mother's family was forced to leave Japan and return to Germany, where my mother began university. After a year, she decided that the USA was where the future was, despite its Army Air Force having bombed her own school. My father also joined the exodus of European young people leaving for North America; so did his sister and at least two of his cousins. For many young people, World War II proved that Europe was too small, too brittle and too corrupt. So out of that context of people on the move, my parents met at Northwestern University in Evanston, Illinois, married, and moved to my father's old home in Oslo to begin their family. I came along in 1953, but soon afterwards my parents went back to Evanston, where I did not rejoin them until four years later.

I may have been a product of World War II, but my parents were not led by their wartime experiences to prefer the ways of peace. From a young age, I heard them, in their angrier moments, refighting World War II – arguing, for example, which of them had seen the bloodiest scenes, the most dead bodies. My mother, having seen the flash of Hiroshima and having endured years of regular leukemia scares, held the trump. Perhaps the lessons of peace did not sink in because they had no religious faith to take the place of the cult of obedience to authority. They were impressionable newcomers to the USA as the fear of communism sank deeply into the national psyche, and my mother was still a deeply convinced racist and anti-Semite.

Parenthetically, how does this make me qualified to speak about the Vietnam years from a Friends United Meeting perspective??? In fact, during almost all of the war I was not even a Friend. However, the more I meet and love Friends in my constituency, the more unique each seems to be; there are no "typical" FUM Friends, and so I offer myself as the "sample" I know best of those Americans who were affected by the war and (in some ways that link up with those effects) find their spiritual home in FUM. My task is assisted by the fact that I began a diary on January 1, 1968, which recorded and documented my transformation from a loyal supporter of a cult of obedience to a pacifist and Friend. After I finish these autobiographical remarks, I will talk about some of the other FUM people who responded to my query, "How did the war affect FUM, and how did it affect you?"

On January 7, 1968, I wrote in my diary, "The more I read newsmagazines and listen to news on the radio, the more I become convinced that (1) the Vietnam conflict is necessary; (2) President Johnson is a fairly good president." Later that spring, my thoughts were in support of Johnson and Humphrey, and against Robert Kennedy and Eugene McCarthy. I was sure that the April 26, 1968, "International Strike" of students was a cynical communist plot and felt glad when the participation of my own Evanston Illinois Township High School student body was low. I was happy to hear official statements on how great the American position in South Vietnam was.

Meanwhile, at home, on July 6, 1968, at age thirteen, my sister ran away from home for the first time in a long series that resulted in hospital and jail time, a foster home, institutionalization at the Illinois State Psychiatric Institute, and ultimately her death at the hands of a drug dealer on March 28, 1970.

Back to 1968. When August came around, bringing with it the Democratic National Convention in nearby Chicago, I got my first chance to hear the efforts of the "doves" to express their views, and I was impressed by their logic. Nevertheless, I thought that righteousness was on the side of Humphrey and the supporters of a continued war, and I was happy to hear that he won the nomination for President. Part of my continuing doubt about what seemed like left-wing alternatives was caused by the spectacle, during those very same days, of the Soviets cynically crushing the Prague Spring in Czechoslovakia, and trying to install their puppets in place of Alexander Dubček and his team.

My diary recalls my delight on October 30, when I read an item in *US News and World Report* stating that the communists were on the brink of defeat in South Vietnam. On January 2, 1969, I wrote, "There was another Paris peace-talks session, nothing gained. The communists seem to have taken a stand in Paris that is out of proportion to their military position."

When did the first real doubts enter my mind? Back on April 4, 1968, I wrote that this day, when Martin Luther King was murdered, was a "day of shame for the US." Two days later, I recorded my distress at the outright racism expressed by my mother, who abused the memory of Martin King and scolded me viciously for defending him as one of my heroes. Then on January 15, 1969, I participated in a school assembly, and a walkout and march downtown in Martin King's memory. There were antiwar protesters involved with the march – I remember some of them sitting on a truck bed with Vietcong flags, looking like Che Guevara look-alike contestants. I ignored them disdainfully.

However, in noting President Nixon's Midway withdrawal announcement in my diary on June 8, 1969, I remember thinking that it was something of a token withdrawal (25,000 men out of a total of over 500,000). By June 14, I was ready to write in my diary that I didn't "want to ever kill anyone for any reason." In further entries about hostilities in Vietnam, I seemed to have adopted a practice of putting the word "enemy" in quotation marks. On September 2, 1969, I noted the sobering news of a 15-year-old boy shooting himself on the steps of the Capitol in protest against the war. Two weeks later, I wrote, "I feel myself pushed more and more into the ranks of the 'nonviolent revolutionaries.'"

In December 1969, my parents and remaining sister went to Germany, leaving me at home alone. (My run-away sister was at the Illinois State Psychiatric Institute.) For some reason, I had been told not to go to school, so I had a lot of time on my hands to think.

The December 1969 issue of *Reader's Digest* gave me much to think about, which I duly recorded. The editorial was entitled "Patience" and counseled that the US simply needed "courage, unity and above all patience." I wrote that it didn't take much courage for a small circle of leaders in a huge superpower to send young men to kill others in a relatively small country far away. But the very act of doing so provoked irreconcilable conflicts and prevented unity.

The patience called for by the editorial was based on Joseph Alsop's article in the same issue, entitled "The Vietcong is Losing its Grip." It was the patience to wait it out while the US military machine ground up generations of gun-bearing communists. As Alsop pointed out "... Only about 125,000 able-bodied youths annually reach military age" in North Vietnam; yet, "to provide manpower for the Tet offensive and its two sequels, Hanoi in truth sent southward in that one year [1968] just under 350,000 men..." – according to Alsop.

Already, previous to that year, 400,000 men had been sent to the war. Alsop equated this to about 10,000,000 Americans. As I wrote, "His optimism is based on statistics that prove to me what a horrible carnage we are involved in." Both articles struck me almost physically with their "blood-red cynicism," and "seem[ed] to me [a nonbeliever at the time] to be an indication of how far we have slipped from the religious ideals we pay, many of us, fat lip service to every Sunday." This was, after all, the Christmas issue of *Reader's Digest*!

Once I became a pacifist, I went into it passionately – it became not just an intellectual conviction but a personal self-identification, a way of belonging to a community. I became an evangelist for pacifism. Early in 1970, I walked into Evanston Public Library and saw a book on the new books display with the word WAR in big letters on the cover. It turned out to be the American Anthropological Association's new book *War: The Anthropology of Armed Conflict and Aggression*. This quotation is a good sample of the book and demonstrates its eye-opening quality for a budding pacifist: In one of the articles, "The Uniqueness of Aggression to Humans," Ralph L. Holloway wrote, "Human evolution has been the evolution of a paradox. The evolution of the brain and social structure and symbol systems has also meant an increase in frustration and aggression. The meaning of symbols in an adaptive evolutionary sense is at least twofold: They aid in cognitive optimization and also they mediate the social controls necessary to stem what arises out of the human condition – frustration and aggression. The same symbolism that enhances sentimental bonds between kinsmen and symbolically defined groups outside the biological relationships – that is, clan, tribe, state, nation, ideology – brings in its wake its antithesis, extragroup aggressional tendencies. Role differentiation and intra-group commitments generate frustration and power allocation. Man [sic] is up against himself. He is up against social structure. He is up against culture. These are his costs as well as his gains. The structures, social and symbolic, which permit his adaptations and executions of shared tasks also insure frustration, pain and conflict."

These many years later, I found this quotation in a syllabus I had prepared for a high school unit I taught (in our unique student-participation classes at Evanston Township High School) in war. It is an example of how I tried to convert all my fellow students to the antiwar position! Later, I included that syllabus in my Selective Service application for CO status, trying to prove that I had made public expressions of my beliefs.

The more I became convinced of the immorality of the Vietnam War, the harder it became to read the papers and listen to the news. The My Lai massacre showed up in my diary as an example of the horrors that seemed to me to be an inevitable part of the chaos of war. But, all around me, life seemed to be going on as if no war was happening. Every day on this same little planet, our tax money and our tacit societal permission was being used to end the lives of soldiers and civilians, to injure others and render them homeless, and to blight their land...but for those at home, unlike World War II for my parents and their families, no significant sacrifice, no galvanizing national movement, no threat to our way of life (justified or not) was being experienced. Aside from my little bits of exposure to the rather cultish antiwar circles of Evanston, people were living their lives as if reality didn't include the losses and agonies with which we were directly involved in Vietnam. Something in me felt that this was as bad as the war itself – that we could be so casual and safe. Was there in fact a WAR going on?

My obedient world of certainties began cracking open with that *Reader's Digest* article, became shakier with these meditations on my family's World War II experiences in contrast to the guns-and-butter coziness of middle-class Evanston, and then fell apart completely with the murder of my sister Ellen on March 28, 1970. I date the beginning of my Christian conversion to these events. As I've looked back on it in recent years, and in speeches to various Friends bodies, I have said that the next step was reading the biographies of pacifists through the ages, realizing that many of them were Christian, and then going on to read the Bible for myself. However, in re-reading my diaries for this conference, something jumped out at me: during those years of high school, I listened almost every Sunday to the radio broadcasts of Chicago's First Church of Deliverance, pastored by Rev. Clarence H. Cobbs. This was part of my secret life, as were my diaries, for that matter. My parents would not have approved of me listening to a church, never mind a Black church; religion was a taboo topic in our household. I remember how I'd eagerly look forward to hearing the intercessory prayer "for the sick, the shut-ins, and all those who love the Lord" – somehow I mysteriously felt included in the prayer. Jim Wallis says that, in his rebellious youth, it was the Black church that kept him in Christianity. I'm only now realizing that maybe for me it was a Black church that helped bring me to Christianity!

Ultimately, several years later, after I'd left home involuntarily, graduated from high school, worked for a year in a factory in Pennsylvania, and moved to Canada to be near my father's relatives there, God finished the job. I finally gave my heart to Jesus Christ when I was re-reading the Sermon on the Mount one night in 1974 in my dorm room at Carleton University in Ottawa. As I read the words, "Love your enemies," the sense of immediacy and certainty and trust and presence and aliveness that hit me at that moment was in fact the turning point in my life. I knew it was Jesus himself talking to me. I knew his word was alive and trustworthy, and what is important for this story is that I knew he was telling me that all the competing claims – to kill our enemies, to give our obedience to those who tell us to kill, to follow the world's violent ways unquestioningly – were wrong! I still shake today, my eyes still fill with tears, as I remember the whole new perspective that emerged for me that night.

I still felt the awful contradiction of a comfortable remote-control war that shredded human lives while we watched in comfort. At the same time, I was still trying to figure which end was up in my own life – my parents had kicked me out of our home in Evanston about fourteen months after my sister was killed – but there was joy as well as sorrow and confusion. I knew it was possible to be a joyful, God-centered person without living in denial about what is really going on in this death-worshiping world. But I didn't want to do that alone; I wanted to be with others whose experience of the Gospel cut through all the world's garbage, and Friends seemed to be such a people: New Testament Christians without the clutter. That's why I looked for the closest group of Friends I could find, and became involved with Ottawa Friends Meeting, my first spiritual home.

By this time, the war was muddling to a close, even as I was finally granted I-A-O status after an initial denial. It was hard for me to see what impact the war had had on Ottawa Meeting (that being my first exposure to Friends United Meeting Quakers), but several people in the meeting were US expatriates driven north by their antiwar commitment. Others had spent much of their adult lives working for peace and reconciliation in various ways. As my initial relief at finding Friends wore off and was replaced by a more open-eyed participation, I saw that most of the people in the meeting did not seem (in my youthful judgmentalism) to be passionate about faith and peace issues, nor were they making the explicit links between the Bible and pacifism that I was making. However, I stuck with the meeting because of a few Friends who saw some hope in me and worked with me to confirm my best ideals while gently sanding my rough edges. It also helped that for a while I was simultaneously active with the meeting and with a progressive evangelical Bible study which filled in the gaps for me. While I was in Ottawa, I also spent a summer with Voice of Calvary Ministries in Mendenhall, Mississippi, in a project to develop Black Christian leadership and economic institutions, in a placement arranged through the American Friends Service Committee. There in Mississippi I became aware of the national network of left-wing evangelicals who have provided my sense of theological identification ever since.

Since then, I've also had to patch together those sorts of diverse Quaker and non-Quaker resources in several other places where I've lived, particularly in Boston and Charlottesville. I've been happiest among Friends when I've found those links being made within the Quaker community, because I'm not willing to give up the spiritual home that took me in when I was seeking so desperately, and I'm not willing to give up that biblical anchor which goes even deeper in me than Friends do.

Back to the Vietnam aftermath: With the benefit of twenty-four years of hindsight, I have been thinking about why FUM Friends would or would not make the kind of links between war and the Bible that I as an idealistic new convert would have assumed or demanded. Almost from the start, I was aware that FUM included such diverse elements as Canadian Yearly Meeting with its firm ideas about the right ways of being Quaker, including the idea held by many that all doctrine is negotiable at best...and other Friends who were practically fundamentalist on the Christian scale. But as a new Quaker who was probably closer to the fundamentalists than to those of negotiable doctrine, I assumed right away that we would all be solidly united on the immorality of war, and specifically the war in Vietnam. Perhaps naively I assumed that following Jesus as singlemindedly as George Fox called us to do, and holding each other accountable in the process, would lead to the heroic consistency in the face of evil that my new-found idealism yearned for. I did not know what I do now, that FUM Friends vary in their comfort level with the peace testimony and its practical application in wartime, and that the level of commitment to the peace witness very roughly correlates (with some glorious exceptions) to a theologically more liberal identity.

In my recent unscientific survey of 31 Friends, most of whose names were mentioned in the FUM Triennial minutes of the war years, the biggest impression I got concerning those Friends whose theologies were more conservative (and therefore more likely to be in FUM only, not in a united FUM-FGC Yearly Meeting) – an impression which I confess disappoints me – can be summed up in the words, "Was there really a war going on?"

I would like to research the impression that I have that leadership for peace in the more conservative "silent majority" of FUM came from Friends whose views had been formed long before Vietnam came along, perhaps even before World War II. These people were also willing to exercise a teaching ministry that stated clearly what the norms are for Friends. This is important particularly in dealing with young people; there is a stage in faith development where the admiration of a role model is more effective than theory, but someone, whether pastor or another person, must be willing to step forward and, in that admired role, give a clear message about peace and other discipleship issues. Everyone here who has a gift of teaching and cares about the future of the peace testimony among Friends ought to be available at every opportunity to tell your story to those who might admire you or see you as a role model, *whether or not you welcome such admiration or such a role*!

Keith Sarver, who was for many years the superintendent of California Yearly Meeting, one of the most conservative in FUM at the time, wrote to me:

"... My personal experience was more traumatic during the Second World War than was the Vietnam War. That was because I was a new Christian and a new, inexperienced pastor during that time. Soon after I was converted I attended a Quarterly Meeting in Iowa Yearly Meeting and heard two men speak about the Friends position on war and was convinced that very day that I could not serve in the military, and I certainly could not take the life of another person. I had previously registered for the draft and when it was learned in the community that I had become a conscientious objector that spelled trouble. There were former friends in the community who would no longer speak to me. The draft board was informed of my intention to go to school to prepare for the ministry and without even asking me to meet with them they sent to me a 4-D classification.

"We went to Chicago and after school started I got a part-time job with Railway Express at 95 cents per hour. When I went to collect my first paycheck I was met by a union steward who wanted to know why I was not having anything taken out of my check for War Bonds. I told him I could not in good conscience buy war bonds and he informed me that I could not work there....I then went to work for the school at thirty cents per hour toward our school expenses.

"The Lord opened the way for us to take a pastorate in Watseka, Illinois, which we did not want to do, but when we were convinced that the call was from the Lord, we went. There was a large American flag fastened on the wall immediately behind the pulpit and I quietly expressed my discomfort with the location and when the church was redecorated the chairman of the trustees left the flag down. There were boys from the church in the military and their names were listed in a board on the wall. I never mentioned this but it became a center of controversy [,] but when I pointed out from the discipline what the Friends' testimony had been and still was for me, even some of the parents accepted the rightness of our position as the Friends' testimony and there was no longer outward opposition."

One pastor in Iowa Yearly Meeting still remembers Keith Sarver's influence. This pastor was about thirty, fresh from his own military experiences, and full of the confidence of youth. He remembers a gathering where Sarver was present, at which the young man pointed out the errors in the Friends' peace position. After listening to him, Sarver simply said, in words that still echo today for that pastor, "Perhaps you're misinformed."

Keith Sarver was one of the originators of the suggestion that the Friends Faith and Life movement extend its focus to issues of peace. The proposal he co-authored with Norval Hadley, dated October 28, 1974, on behalf of the Superintendents and Secretaries group, resulted in the New Call to Peacemaking collaboration among all of the peace churches. Although Vietnam is not mentioned in the memorandum, it does say that "We recognize the fact that Friends have been divided in recent years by some actions taken to implement the concern for peace. These divisions exist within all Yearly Meetings. What we yearn for are positive and practical approaches, stemming from spiritual faith, which will be supported by Friends generally."

Here and there in the pastoral Quaker world there were other pastors who had been teaching and preaching a similar strong biblical peace stand for years, long before Vietnam sneaked onto the scene. I use the verb "sneaked" deliberately, because I wonder what would have happened if the Vietnam War (whatever its moral corruption was otherwise) had been initiated with an open and honest national debate and declaration of war. In the case of World War II, Friends United Meeting (called Five Years Meeting of Friends in those days) mounted a careful, well-organized, quarterly-meeting-by-quarterly-meeting campaign to reach potential soldiers with the message of peace and alternative service, even though it was a far more "popular" war than Vietnam ever was. As it was, Vietnam's gradual escalation and Johnson's guns-and-butter policies somehow obscured the urgency to mobilize and implement the church's peace teachings in the same well-organized way.

On a much more random and sometimes seemingly naive basis (when perhaps a prophetic insight somehow penetrated the cultural fog), the connection between the Bible and reality was made. One Friend, Robert Garris (Superintendent of his Yearly Meeting during much of the war) wrote to me, "Western Yearly Meeting was home to the Nelson family, who were members of Courtland Avenue Friends Church in Kokomo, one of our more conservative churches. One of the sons sailed on the *Phoenix,* which attempted to carry supplies to citizens of both North and South Vietnam. This created quite a stir among many, including Friends. When asked where he got the idea to give aid to the enemy the young man said that he was taught in Sunday School at Courtland Avenue Friends to 'love his enemies' and this was his way of expressing the love of Jesus." In connection with the same family, Bob Garris mentioned Marjorie Nelson's service as a civilian doctor in Vietnam under the American Friends Service Committee.

Equal energy in an opposite direction was expressed at a session of Indiana Yearly Meeting, discussing the *Phoenix* case, according to another correspondent, Dan Whitley: "I was just visiting this session, because I was not yet a member of IYM. I remember distinctly someone standing up and saying that we should oppose the *Phoenix*, and have nothing to do with it. This person said that the North Vietnamese were atheists and communists and should be killed. I was appalled that something like that would have been uttered on the floor of a Yearly Meeting. IYM was terribly divided over the *Phoenix* issue."

The voyages of the *Phoenix* were heavily covered in our *Quaker Life* magazine, including the article, "A *Phoenix* Sailor Answers Your Questions," with Henry Harris, in June 1967. The editorial slant was clearly pro-*Phoenix*, but, as Dan Whitley said, there was certainly controversy in the grassroots, as evidenced in this letter to the editor from White Lick Meeting (Mooresville, Indiana) of Western Yearly Meeting, printed in August 1967:

"... Certain groups within the framework of the Religious Society of Friends, but not sponsored by the Religious Society of Friends, have undertaken certain acts to aid the civilian population of North Vietnam.

"This action is drawing adverse publicity in our nation's press on behalf of the entire membership of the Religious Society of Friends, as well as being publicly proclaimed by our Federal Government as being unlawful and subject to prosecution under the Trading with the Enemy Act.

"Therefore, this Meeting wants it known that it stands opposed to any and all such activities by any group, until such time as the Government of North Vietnam allows representatives of the American Friends Service Committee to personally supervise the distribution of aid of any kind, and our Federal Government sanctions this assistance as in past conflicts."

One specific aspect of the controversy, the public image of Friends as the result of A Quaker Action Group's actions, was addressed in *Quaker Life* in an interestingly nuanced signed column by regular columnist Eugene Coffin, who later became more famous as Nixon's pastor. Here are some excerpts from his August 1967 column entitled "The Quaker Image":

"Local churches or Meetings in every state are subjected to severe criticism because of the activities of some Friends whose dedication is to put Christian love into action by aiding the victims of war no matter on what side of the 38th parallel they may be. It has been more newsworthy just to mention aid to the North Vietnamese.

"What should Friends' attitude be in this sort of situation? First of all, our local Meetings should be fully informed about such activity, its motivation and means to carry out the concern before arriving at a judgment about it. When a story about Quakers comes from national news services, local press representatives should be requested to check with the Friends in the area before printing such a story. Most news people will cooperate if approached in the right spirit. This will give an opportunity for interpretation that would make for accuracy.

"Friends also need to realize that the way of the cross is the road upon which the church travels and there are risks to be taken for the sake of Christ. It is because, in far too many instances, the church has taken the highway of conformity instead of the way of the cross that we find ourselves sterile and static. There are occasions in 1967 when we 'must obey God rather than men' and accept the consequences from men and sustaining Grace from God."

Those yearly meetings and local meetings which were both in Friends United Meeting and Friends General Conference tended to be more supportive of the peace position. The war-related minutes adopted by New England Yearly Meeting during those years are uniformly in favor of a nonviolent solution to the war. In 1965, Friends said, "We urge the prayerful consideration of peaceful alternatives leading to negotiation and planned withdrawal of military forces beginning with a cessation of the bombing of North Vietnam." The mild and conciliatory language of 1965 and 1966 is replaced by these words in 1967 (minute 61):

> "The love and fellowship which New England Friends feel manifested in our Yearly Meeting sessions, and which we strive to express to all ..., stand in sharp contrast to our feelings of horror and guilt at what is happening in Vietnam. Indeed, the suffering brought upon Vietnam is so unbearable that we cannot hold it in our consciousness in our daily lives; nevertheless its dark shadow lies continually over us.
>
> "For three hundred years we have known and testified that war is morally indefensible, irreconcilable with Christian faith, and rationally unjustifiable. We have, further, striven to live in ways that remove the occasion for war and have urged our members not to participate in war or in preparation for it. We have never recognized any group of people as our enemies, and we reaffirm this practice now."

Clarabel Marstaller of Durham Meeting in Maine writes, "One issue that came up in New England was the proposal to carry funds to Canada which might go to North Vietnam for relief. The liability to Yearly Meeting officers was too much to win approval for the project." Of course, expressions of unity at Yearly Meeting level, whatever their legitimacy in expressing the Church's teaching voice, do not guarantee unity at the grassroots. One pastor in New England recalls being called one holiday morning to provide pastoral care to a family in his meeting which was being torn apart by the conflict between a pro-war father and an antiwar daughter. In that situation of crisis counseling, the pastor did not mention to the father that his daughter was probably influenced by some of the pastor's own attempts to express an antiwar position.

Concerning New York Yearly Meeting, George Rubin writes, "Our Yearly Meeting supported all the statements that came from FUM and I do not recall any great friction or polarization within yearly meeting regarding the war. There were some who radicalized their position with civil disobedience and were arrested. Our Yearly Meeting set up a Fund for Suffering to help those who took this position due to religious conscience. In our local Monthly Meeting (Westbury, NY) we sent a delegation to Whittier Meeting to ask to have Pres. Nixon read out of the Society of Friends....We also had a member of our meeting who was adamant in his support of the war."

David Finke has provided me much documentation of the cooperation of FUM-oriented Friends in Chicago-area Quaker opposition to the war and to the draft. Such Friends as Don Stanley (pastor of Chicago Monthly Meeting during some of the war years), and Victor Guthrie, Walter Bibler and Grace Bibler of the same meeting, were among those taking active roles. Meanwhile, much of the energy in that city's peace movement, as we have heard from other speakers, came from 57th Street Meeting in Chicago, which is affiliated with both Illinois Yearly Meeting (Friends General Conference) and Western Yearly Meeting (FUM).

While many Friends in united (FUM-FGC) meetings expressed their opposition to the war in Christian terms, Friends also recall a spirit of alienation from established teachings, doctrines and leaders. To my mind the spiritual basis of opposition to war, which is crucial to the integrity of our testimony, was only weakly understood by some. Dan Whitley, whose Friends activities during the war included his education at Guilford College and Earlham School of Religion, a pastorate at Noblesville Meeting in Indiana, and service with Baltimore Yearly Meeting, recalls:

"In the early 70's there was a time when the Selective Service System had in fact expired. We thought we had a chance to do away with the SSS entirely. I was lobbying hard to get the extension of the SSS defeated. I remember going to Senator Spong's office. He was from Virginia. I had an interview with his legislative aide, and was waiting in the corridor when a couple of Mennonites came up to speak with me. They wanted to see this aide for the same purpose, and I invited them to join me. Since it was my appointment, I went first. I remember giving the aide the usual argument against the SSS: how it provided cannon fodder for the war in Vietnam, how it hurt Blacks and other minorities, how it caused an economic drain on our country, etc. Every argument I had was countered rather effectively by the aide. At one point one of the Mennonites interjected the following: 'Sir, our Lord Jesus Christ said not to kill, and if your Senator votes for the draft, he will be voting for killing and will have to answer to Jesus Christ some day for that vote.' You could have heard a pin drop! He then made the same arguments I had made. But he had stated his position as a Christian very clearly, something that I failed to do."

According to Whitley, "Most Quakers I hung out with were very ideological. Our antiwar activities were filled with anger, and sometimes hatred, toward anyone who had anything to do with the war in Vietnam." That hatred, when it happened, was probably aimed more at the Pentagon and the government generally than at the soldiers, but when Friends themselves went into the military, they and their families sometimes experienced rejection from other Friends. A Baltimore Yearly Meeting Friend who had a son in the war wrote to me, "One Friend called [her son] a 'baby-killer.' We felt very much alone at meeting, but continued to attend. On the whole, Friends were not very Friendly." A staff member at Friends United Meeting, who was a member at Nettle Creek Friends in Hagerstown, Indiana, also had a son in Vietnam. She recalls having to face the disapproval of other FUM staff at the same time as she worried every day whether her son would return home alive.

Whitley's letter mentions another Friend whose name has come up at this conference, and whose spirit was far more positive: "One person that I felt really came at the whole issue of the Vietnam war with a Christian heart was Larry Scott. I am sure you knew Larry. He and I became friends. I first met Larry when he was preaching in the Capitol rotunda. I carried his briefcase for him when we went into the Capitol building, and the guard asked him to open it. There was a Bible and a few burlap bags for sackcloths in the briefcase. The guard let us pass, and Larry said, "They let the most dangerous thing into the building they could – more powerful than a bomb!"

Of the FUM-only Yearly Meetings in the USA, perhaps Nebraska Yearly Meeting was the most united against the war. As Kay Mesner writes, "I think probably we [in Central City Friends Meeting] focused on more local activities because we are so far removed geographically from most of FUM. Our Meeting has always been tolerant and accepting and supportive of those people who felt moved to serve their country in a military way. But we were also clearly opposed to the Vietnam War.

"The differing viewpoints did affect our Monthly Meeting, and we did lose one very active family and some others as a result. On a Yearly Meeting level, I can't recall much friction. Friends were pretty much in opposition to the war, I think."

Despite these divisions in the constituency, such leaders as Bob Garris did what they could to support the peace witness and in particular the conscientious objectors in their meetings. In Western Yearly Meeting, a Friend who was a retired military officer had won a seat in Congress. Despite his pro-war views, he respected the conscientious objection position, and Garris deliberately built a relationship between this Congressman and the young Friends of the Yearly Meeting. This relationship proved invaluable when CO applications were denied. As Garris writes, "The 'Quaker grapevine'…shared the word that local draft boards were more receptive to persons regarding CO status after a phone call from Washington."

Several letters I received made clear that the staff leadership at FUM in Richmond, Indiana, agonized about the war and cared very much about a peaceable dissenting response. Programmatic responses included staff support for draft counseling, and a volunteer program to provide alternative service for conscientious objectors. FUM General Secretary Lorton Heusel served on the Friends Coordinating Committee on Peace, at one time as its presiding officer. He and others also personally participated in vigils at home and at such places as the White House and the Capitol. Herbert Huffman, Harold Smuck and Alan Inglis are also mentioned in my correspondence as staff members who supported expressions of Vietnam-era peace witness, and of course there were Friends such as Sam Levering of North Carolina Yearly Meeting who were a constant support on the Board and commission and committee level to these staff members. Bob Garris recalls that, after the war came to a close, the Social Concerns Committee of Wider Ministries Commission of FUM (now World Ministries) "established a fund for relief of persons who had suffered as a result of the war. Hugh Barbour, then at Earlham College, clerked the task group and I was a part of the group."

Quaker Life, the monthly periodical of Friends United Meeting, printed many essays, news items, editorials and letters to the editor relating to Vietnam. The editorial voices of Xen Harvey and Fred Wood, editors during the years I sampled the magazine, were uniformly supportive of the peace testimony, but the same is not true of all the writers. D. Elton Trueblood, for example, seemed to be for peace in the abstract but argued for "... our responsibility to assist the tortured peoples of South Vietnam." Readers' attitudes varied, as well: In connection with the *Phoenix* controversy, I have already given one example of a meeting which opposed non-governmentally approved humanitarian aid to North Vietnam. However, by 1967, readers' reaction was running in favor of the editorial position, although there seem to have been surprisingly few letters on either side. At one point, in May 1967, editor Xen Harvey expresses distress at the falling off of the numbers of letters about the war, suggesting, "We feel so emotional about President Johnson's policy in Southeast Asia, either for it or against it, that we hardly trust ourselves to discuss it." As an incentive to restart the dialogue, the issue offers a thoughtful memorandum to all Friends from Sam Levering of FUM's Board on Christian Social Concerns, entitled "Friends Witness on Vietnam." Other editorials express cautious admiration of the *Phoenix* and, by the time October 1969 came around, a passionate denunciation of the war, period. All along, there is plenty of news coverage of the American Friends Service Committee, A Quaker Action Group, and activities of various yearly and local meetings.

To the extent that FUM responses during the war depended on unity in the constituency, the record is less clear. Here it is worth quoting Lorton Heusel, at some length:

"Rather than identifying Vietnam as the culprit that caused the social turmoil and tension within the Quaker family, I would say that Vietnam served as a catalyst, accentuating and agitating existing tensions and polarizations within the larger society as well as within the Quaker community....

"As on many issue of faith and practice, Friends honestly held to different points of view. To try to come to some sense of the meeting across the chasms rooted in long history, deep fears and fierce loyalties, required hours and hours of discussion in open forum, interspersed with seasons of open worship in an effort to sift out human opinion and to discern divine will, purpose and intention for our common faith community. I became so weary of efforts to hammer out statements or to write letters to elected officials, and yet, in retrospect, these efforts to shape a corporate witness did provide a means for Friends to work across differences to try to find some common ground. The tendency, then as now, was to stereotype. Generally, those on the right side of the spectrum tended to be more concerned for evangelism and church growth than they were about social issues. Anti-AFSC sentiment was strong, particularly as related to the *Phoenix* and other similar efforts of the peace-oriented Friends to confront power nonviolently. The media stories of Quaker efforts to send food or medical supplies to 'the enemy' were seen as too radical, and threatened to alienate prospective converts. Vietnam brought into focus the divergent tracks on which Friends were traveling, tracks that seemed to be taking us in opposite directions at the same time. And yet, here we were, all under the great umbrella of Jesus' call to be 'friends' and 'to love one another as I have loved you.'

"I think it was during the Nixon presidency, the General Board [of FUM] approved a statement or a letter that was sent to him. Again, I cannot recall the year or the content but I do know that it was rather pointed and challenged some of the policies his administration was pursuing. A day or so later, two ESR [Earlham School of Religion] students, both from EFA [Evangelical Friends Alliance] Yearly Meetings, came to see me. Both were extremely troubled; both were Nixon supporters and deeply rooted in Republican political views and loyalties. They doubted that FUM had the wisdom to advise the president on matters of foreign policy. This led to a consideration of the church's role as a prophetic agent in a secular culture. Because we have differing views should we sit on our hands while our tax dollars are being used to slaughter the innocent? Or can we hammer out a corporate witness that bridges our differences and says to those in power roles: 'THIS IS WRONG!' Does not silence convey consent? The young students questioned whether FUM General Board had spent enough time in prayer to assume a prophetic role. That may have been true but I felt proud of the effort and confident of its rightness....

"...I am persuaded that much of the senseless and indiscriminate violence in American society today has its roots in what we became during those Vietnam years, preoccupied with self-interest, insensitive to the values of human lives other than our own, and experimenters with new weaponry using Asians as guinea pigs."

However hard the process was of putting FUM on the record during the Vietnam years, the results did give Friends a clear message consistent with the historic teachings of Friends. The 1966 Triennial sessions issued "An Appeal to End the War in Vietnam Now" over the signature of presiding clerk Oscar O. Marshburn. (Oscar Marshburn was the uncle by marriage of the president who would take office two and a half years later, Richard Nixon.) The appeal was directed toward all parties to the conflict but its first specific recommendation was the ending of the bombing of North Vietnam.

About half of the responses to my survey went something like this: [not an actual quotation] – "We were opposed to the war, but a few in our meeting supported it. We joined one or two demonstrations but did little else." Or, "I was so involved with X activity in those years that I paid little attention to the war." I realized that, for some of those Friends, there did not seem to be a war going on at all, certainly not one which was costing our so-called enemy the demographic equivalent of 10,000,000 American lives. If we combine the numbers of the apathetic Friends with the numbers of those who were actually in favor of our military involvement, how much of the Friends Church in the USA would we find had been compromised? And how has that influenced the strength and health of the Quaker teaching voice in FUM today?

It is certainly not enough to point out that FUM has always upheld the peace testimony in its minutes, with specific applications to our conflicts and tensions with Russia, Cuba, Iraq, Iran and other "enemies" of the day, and that every general secretary has supported this testimony. The debates in the letter pages of *Quaker Life* reflect the deep divisions which continue. As Lorton Heusel pointed out, these divisions predated the war. Our increased readiness in the future to meet the demands of social faithfulness might depend on a closer attention to them, especially since these divisions within Friends may parallel, perhaps in different proportions, divisions which exist in the larger society.

Some of these divisions are more social than theological. A lot of harm has been done by the elitist condescension with which some Friends regard others. This is often but not always apparent in the ways urban and university Friends communicate with rural Friends, or the ways ecumenical and seminary-educated Friends' leaders relate to those of a revivalist or Bible-college background, or National Public Radio contributors relate to those who prefer "hot country" radio. The reverse is also true since, at least in the USA, anti-intellectualism has a long and inglorious tradition. Unprogrammed Friends who regard programmed Friends as second-class without any appreciation for the evolution of their customs, and pastoral Friends who assume the theological worst about nonpastoral Friends without any evidence to go on, are both diminishing the power of our united witness to the world. Isn't it great we can practice and improve our communication skills right within our own family?...Because beyond Friends, in my neighborhood, at least, it is those who listen to country and western music who also seem more likely than typical Quakers to want to "kick Saddam's butt." To build relationships across these social and cultural lines is both effective and righteous.

Some divisions, however, may be irreducibly theological. For myself, I continue to respect the passion of my original conversion to Quaker Christianity, and especially my yearning for a faith that is so biblically radical and miraculous that it allows me to reject all violence and all false distinctions among human beings. I hungered – and still hunger – for a Gospel with both spiritual intimacy and ethical consequences.

If my discovery of Friends was a valid response to this hunger, then the primary need which these divisions over peace point to is a continuing need for conversion even among long-time Friends. There is also an urgent need to begin a conversation among all Friends on the most faithful and effective integration of evangelism and discipleship. But I want this conversation to take place among Friends who are themselves deeply convinced of this integration! Friends who have lost the biblical basis of peace should at least wrestle with the implications of the fact that this basis is the official teaching of the largest branch of Friends in the world, and this teaching has unbroken links with the very origins of the Quaker movement. Their failure to honor this link, and its replacement by secular or non-Christian bases for peace, caused the peace testimony to fall into disrepute among many Friends.

At the same time, I want to challenge every evangelical Friend everywhere to make a fresh commitment to a Savior who is able to break the demonic cycle of violence wherever his Lordship is truly acknowledged. Can I really say Jesus is my Lord if there are no ethical consequences when I face such evils as violence and social oppression? And even if I manage to trick myself into saying "Yes," I still may have to answer for the disrepute into which the Gospel falls when too many seekers of goodwill see too many examples of such Christian inconsistency.

To present this call to conversion seems to me to be an essential part of a stronger, more centered, well-poised peace witness for the wars of these new times, and I'm referring to the culture wars, and the low-intensity wars against poor people everywhere, not just dramatic military conflict. As we face each new battle, no matter how gradually it is initiated, or with whatever trickery, I hope and pray that Friends will be empowered to say clearly and sacrificially to the whole world, in the words of New England Yearly Meeting in 1967, "We have never recognized any group of people as our enemies, and we reaffirm this practice now."

Many thanks to the Friends who wrote to me in response to my survey letter, and who answered my questions in personal interviews. All quotations of written expressions from individuals are from their letters to me unless another source is given in the text above.

Additional Statement and Comments

Daniel E. Ensley

Marion Anderson

Carlie Numi

Tom Rodd

Carl Stieren

A War Story

Daniel E. Ensley

I was born in Japan and raised on a series of Air Force bases until my father retired and moved to Wisconsin. My earliest memory of the Vietnam War was of me saying to a classmate's older brother, "Who are you going to believe, our government or theirs?" After two years of college, I volunteered for the draft in the summer of 1969. My goal was to go to OCS (Officer Candidate School) and then marry the girl I was dating at the time.

One day during basic training I was sent back from rifle practice and told to report to the First Sergeant. He asked me, "What did you do, steal a car, knock some one up, rape a girl; what?"

When I told him I had done nothing like that, I was told to report to G2. At G2 (military intelligence), I found that my proof of citizenship was not satisfactory. On return, the First Sergeant again asked, "What did you do?"

The reply, "I was born in Japan," provoked the response, "You goddamned gook."

From that time, I was referred to as either "the goddamned gook" or "the fucking enemy." This began to bother me. I remembered my father, who had been an attorney for the Air Force, proudly telling me about investigating and prosecuting war crimes in Germany and Japan. Reports of our atrocities at home and abroad and the facile way they were excused were disquieting, but I was still with the program.

I went to advanced training and learned to calculate the trajectories of artillery shells. I found out about "H&I" zones (harassment and interdiction): broad areas were marked off on the map and shells could be fired into them indiscriminately, whomever they might hit – man, woman or child; combatant or not – it didn't matter.

After I graduated, I couldn't get a security clearance – citizenship problems. Everyone admitted that I was a citizen (as provided in the Constitution) saying: "It's just red tape." After much delay, the problem was solved by having me take the oath of citizenship to become a naturalized citizen. This caused delay, and since I no longer had a girlfriend, I withdrew my application to OCS.

Because I had a brother in Vietnam, I was sent to Germany. While there a soldier in the unit next to mine attempted to commit suicide by slashing his wrists. He was my rank, my age, and had the same job; his name was PFC Bloom. He was called a coward in front of the unit, and told that he didn't have the guts to do it right.

Shortly afterward, he was allowed to go on guard duty at the only station where you were alone with a loaded weapon. He wasn't there when they went to relieve him after the first two hours. They told us that they thought he had gone AWOL when they sent us out on a search party to "look for his weapon."

I was the third or fourth person to arrive at the body. He had shot himself in the stomach and bled to death. The ground was scuffed up in a circle around the body and I was struck by how absolutely dead he looked.

I threw it off, went to breakfast right afterwards, and had a nervous breakdown a couple of months later. After a dispute with my superiors, which I won, I got orders for Vietnam.

I got a month's leave before I had to report. It was Christmastime of 1970. I was not in very good shape psychologically. My friends and classmates were home from school and, by this time, the antiwar movement had even reached the town where Joe McCarthy was buried, Appleton, Wisconsin. I read *Johnny Got His Gun* and talked a little bit about the war with my friends.

Then I had a vision, or a hallucination. In it, I saw a man in uniform lying on the ground beneath the trees in a park-like forest.

I knew the artillery shells were about to land at any moment.

This terrified me; I thought I was losing my mind. I went to see a psychiatrist at Fort Sherman, Illinois. I told him about my experiences in Germany and the recent vision. He said, "And that's who you're killing; you're killing Bloom!"

I was really shocked by this revelation and eventually decided to apply for a conscientious objector discharge. I was told at Oakland, California, that I would have to wait until I got to Vietnam, because you weren't allowed to apply for such a discharge from an overseas replacement station. Confronting authority was very difficult for me and I began to stutter so much that I could barely talk. By this time, I was enraged at the army first and the war second. I believed I had an obligation to try to stop the killing.

At that time, I developed something (you couldn't call it a philosophy) I called "Wrench Theory." The Army was a big green machine running amuck, indiscriminately killing. Throwing a wrench in the works would slow it down; enough wrenches would stop it. I had been, up to that point, a tool of the Army, a wrench.

I met with someone from CCCO; I do not know if he was a Quaker. He said, "It would be against the law for me to advise you to do this, but if you go AWOL, until you're dropped from the rolls as a deserter here, you can apply for your discharge at whatever post you turn yourself back in at. It would be against the law for me to advise you to do this, but you would not be 2,000 miles away from a civilian lawyer if you did it that way. It would be against the law or me to advise you to do this, but they have a very nice stockade at Fort Meade, Maryland, and it is only a few miles from your congressman's office."

Despite his unwillingness to give me any advice, I decided to take a short vacation. I called my church, but received no assistance. I ended up living in Chicago with some activists who worked at a downtown antiwar office mailing out "People's Peace Treaties." I met with a young Quaker who helped me to prepare my application for discharge. I turned myself in at Fort Meade and after a few adventures (including a small riot), I was discharged.

Quakers are good at taking responsibility. You are willing

to take responsibility for the fact that some draft counselors were insensitive, for the fact that some veterans were insulted, for the fact that to some, the antiwar movement did not appear to be neutral. Never mind that you weren't giving orders.

I don't know that I would have survived without the help from CCCO. I don't know that I would have survived the long prison sentence that might have been imposed if other people hadn't clogged the courts, the jails and the stockades. I don't know if I would have survived the guilt that would have resulted from "killing PFC Bloom."

So, take responsibility for saving my life.

On the wall of my home are minutes of welcome from the Fox Valley Monthly Meeting of the Religious Society of Friends to my children, Maxwell Altair Ensley-Field and Mira Wynn Ensley-Field.

Take responsibility for them. Take responsibility for helping to end the war, you were a big part of it.

Thank you!

Leafleting a Meeting of the Joint Chiefs of Staff

Marion Anderson

By 1970, I had been organizing against the war full-time for five years. First, in Washington where I was an organizer of the televised National Teach-In which was watched by about ten million Americans, and then in Michigan as chairman of Michigan Clergy and Laymen Concerned About Vietnam. We had organized and gotten staff in every major Michigan city. We had set up draft counseling centers, helped soldiers on a base publish and distribute the antiwar paper *The Broken Arrow*. We spoke to innumerable community groups, and put on vigils and demonstrations throughout Michigan.

But as my young sons said to me, "Mom, you keep working and the war keeps going on."

They were right: by that fall, the war in Vietnam had been going on for what seemed like forever. The heavy American involvement began in 1965, soon after President Johnson was elected on the promise to "Not let American boys do what Asian boys should be doing." The growing unpopularity of the war had forced Johnson from the office he had coveted all of his life, and Americans had elected Richard Nixon with his "secret plan to end the war." The war continued to escalate. We had troops in Vietnam, Laos and Cambodia and had witnessed the massacre at My Lai.

Desperation at home was rising rapidly. People felt that no matter how much they protested, marched, leafleted and lobbied, this unconstitutional war only got worse, killing ever more Vietnamese, and more Americans.

That summer, Senator J. William Fulbright, Chairman of

the Senate Foreign Relations Committee, put into the *Congressional Record* a remarkable statement called *We Have Not Shaken Hands With The Troops; We Have Led Them*. It had been written by the military's elite: Vietnam veterans who were graduates of West Point, Annapolis, and the Air Force Academy.

When I saw this statement in the *Congressional Record*, I determined to print 10,000 copies and take them to Washington, to hand out at a march which was being largely organized by Vietnam veterans. Thousands of people from Michigan were going, by car, chartered bus and plane.

My husband and I took a morning flight to Washington. I was not dressed in people's idea of hippie attire – jeans, T-shirt, sneakers and long hair. Instead, I looked like every military officer's wife, in a navy coat with gold buttons, a red and white silk scarf, and white gloves. My deliberately straight appearance challenged those who insisted that all those against the war were either naive students, nutty hippies, or weird Communist sympathizers. In fact, I was typical of the people the military believed they were defending, the well dressed, the white, and the middle class.

We arrived at the Washington National airport and caught a taxi into Washington. Jim got out at the Archives to work on some of his research.

After he got out of the cab, I thought to myself, "I didn't come here just to go on one more march. I've been on a million marches. I came here to see the Joint Chiefs of Staff." So I said to the taxi driver, "Please take me to the Pentagon."

On the way across the Potomac river, I told him what we were there for. He, like a majority of Blacks in D.C., was very sympathetic. When we arrived I said, "I am not sure how long I'll be here. Will you wait?"

Leaving our suitcases in the cab, I entered the Pentagon. "Where are the Joint Chiefs of Staff meeting?" I asked the first officer I saw.

"They are in the E Ring, but I don't know the room number," he responded, pointing.

I walked on, carrying my 8½ x 11 inch box of copies of *We Have Not Shaken Hands With The Troops; We Have Led Them.*

As I continued down the corridors past one guard after another, I kept asking where the Joint Chiefs were meeting. Of course, I had no picture ID around my neck like everyone else in this area, but the box of literature I was carrying probably obscured this fact.

The people I asked kept getting higher in rank. First sergeants, then second lieutenants, then captains. When the only people in the halls and offices were colonels and generals, I figured I was getting close.

Finally a general gave me the precise number of the room where the Joint Chiefs' meeting was taking place. I walked by a bored Black guard, past a blond secretary, and a general sitting in an anteroom at his desk, and then there I was, in the meeting of the Joint Chiefs of Staff.

Conversation ceased. Stunned, they sat there.

I said, "I have something for you," and handed each of them a copy of *We Have Not Shaken Hands With The Troops; We Have Led Them.*

Then one of them must have given a signal because the blond secretary teetered in on four inch heels, every golden curl lacquered firmly into place à la Marie Antoinette and clutched my arm in a most unladylike vise.

"What are you doing here?" she hissed, dragging me out of the room.

"I am passing out a statement of graduates of West Point, Annapolis, and the Air Force Academy," adding with some satisfaction, "They are *your* boys, not ours."

She was clearly appalled at this monstrous breach of security that a mere citizen, a member of the infamous anti-war movement, could have penetrated deep into the core of the Pentagon into the holy of holies where the Joint Chiefs of Staff were meeting.

She dragged me up to the guard. "Did you let *her* in here?" she demanded.

The guard, bored as ever, shrugged. "I don't know," he said.

I was thinking, "I wonder if they are going to put me into a dungeon in the basement of the Pentagon. What will the taxi driver with our luggage do? What will Jim do? He has no idea where I am." But apparently they didn't want one more *cause célèbre,* so she released me into a main corridor.

It was Friday at 5:00 p.m., and the rush of people to get out of the Pentagon could have knocked a person down. All of the offices quickly emptied. So I decided, this being a golden opportunity to leaflet, to go into every office I could find, leave copies on the desks, and post others on the mirrors in the ladies' rooms.

Then I left the Pentagon, climbed into the cab, rejoined my husband, and went to the March.

"Nobody Would be Killed" – A Comment

Carlie Numi

I only began attending and joined Meeting in the past ten years; so during the US-Vietnam War I did not see the war or the anti-war movement through the Quaker prism.

I first went to Vietnam in 1963 with International Voluntary Services. When I returned to the US the second time in 1968 I was engaged by the Methodist Church to speak about the war to middle America. I soon felt called to speak to what I felt was a void in the discourse about the war. That was to focus on the Vietnamese people and the effect of the war on them as the reason we needed to end the war.

They seemed virtually nonexistent in America's mind's eye except as perhaps a malevolent force determined to kill US soldiers. For example, in a discussion in about 1970 someone suggested the US fight the war by placing war ships off the coast of Vietnam and shooting rockets onto the land – "That way NO ONE will be killed," she asserted.

Later, during a visit to the Vietnam Memorial in Washington in the 1980's I heard a mother respond to her child's question with "these are the names of EVERYONE who died in the Vietnam War."

You might understand that my stomach tightened a bit when, at this conference, I heard more than one mention of "the list of war dead" to describe the list of US MILITARY killed in the US-Vietnam War.

Suggestion for a Panel Discussion

Tom Rodd

For me, in the last fifteen years, I have been haunted in my work in politics and government by the fact of being an "ex-convict" and "draft resister," "coward" and "traitor." It's an easy attack for opponents in hard-fought mainstream political campaigns. Moreover, it's a vulnerability I bring to all such activities, whether it arises as an issue or not.

I don't like being handicapped in this way; it's frustrating – but I soldier on. (I live in a "socially conservative," rural state.) On the other hand, by being "out of the closet" as a former antiwar activist, I set a good example and say that this is still my country, and in fact – we were right.

Do others experience this sort of disenfranchisement, second-class citizen status and, if so, how do they deal with it?

A larger question – is there a general historical disenfranchisement of the antiwar Vietnam era protest movement? Could it, will it ever be made more historically legitimate? Sometimes I feel that the war was so traumatic and the right wing has been so effective in this area that the truly best and brightest of a generation have been crippled in their ability to function as full citizens as well as in other ways. It pisses me off and it makes me sad to feel this way.

Another Country

© 1998 by Carl Stieren

The idea was to stay legal until they came to get you. By that time you would be gone. So I took the Greyhound bus from Toronto back to Chicago in January, 1968, to face my pre-induction physical exam. You know, the one where the doctor says, "Turn your head and cough!" Then you would cross the border to Canada, look for work, and wait for your induction papers to arrive – a process which could take two months. Two months – long enough for at least one last visit to family and friends in a country you'd never set foot in again.

It seemed like a bad dream. As an undergraduate in chemistry at the Illinois Institute of Technology, I had a student deferment. Somehow I just couldn't bring myself to request one again. It seemed as if I was saying, "Don't draft me to fight in Vietnam. I'm going to be part of the military-industrial complex that runs the society based on the war. Draft some poor soul from the ghetto!" So I did nothing.

Sure as rain, my pre-induction physical notice arrived. By that time, I'd been through the agony of making the decision: "Should I go to jail or go to Canada?" There were some compelling arguments for going to jail. One young Friend, who had been in jail, had met with us at Fifty-Seventh Street Meeting in Chicago and said it was the only honest thing he could do. But I wasn't sure I wanted to spend the rest of my life in the United States. And if I went to jail, I might get a passport when I got out, but I might be refused admission to Canada as a convicted felon. But if I went before my induction notice arrived, Uncle Sam would not stop me at the border. And simply refusing to obey the American draft laws did not get you deported from Canada.

Yes, there was a military tradition in my family – and it had all ended in tragedy. My great uncles had been Reserve Army Officers – a great cachet in Bismarck's Germany. My father, Hans Georg Stieren, born in 1900, lied about his age – he was only 17– and joined the Imperial German Army. He went off to fight for his country. There was horrible trench warfare – once he told me how he had dug up trenches that had been filled in after previous fighting and he found the decayed body of a French soldier. Father also led the charge when there was no one left in his unit to do so – and won the Iron Cross for it. Then he was captured by soldiers from New Zealand only months before the war ended.

In a prison camp in Britain, he and other German POWs tried to tunnel out – and were discovered. The British put the prison tents on platforms so they could shine their lights underneath. That winter was one of the coldest on record, and the cold bitter wind whipped through and my father's toes froze. The camp doctor wanted to amputate them, but my father said no. He recovered. But when he walked out of that prison camp, he weighed 90 lbs. – and he was five feet ten and a half. "No one benefited from that war except the war profiteers – people on all sides suffered," Father said.

After the war, back in Germany, he was fed by Quakers as a hungry student in Danzig. *"Quaekerspeise,"* they called it. Nothing to write home about, but it sure kept body and soul together. While Father had been pro-peace after World War I, by the end of the Second World War he had become a Cold War Liberal – pro-rearmament and anxious to keep the Communists at bay. But by the time I faced my pre-induction physical, my father had changed his mind. "If American imperialism keeps up, we will have more wars like the one in Vietnam," he said one day. I nearly fell off my chair.

"Why didn't you apply for conscientious objector status?" everyone asks when I tell them this story. The truth is that I did – and was rejected at my appeal to the Justice Department Hearing Officer. The visit to his office was a day to remember. The Clerk of my Quaker Meeting – Downers Grove – went with me. We sat in the Hearing Officer's waiting room, staring at cigarette lighter bookends that were shaped like a pair of Derringers.

It was all downhill from there. He asked me, "Imagine yourself in a city in Central Asia in the year 2,000. Genghis Khan has surrounded the city. His policy is to kill all the men and take all the women into concubinage and the children into slavery. You have about you a group of strong young men. What do you do?"

I answered quite truthfully, "I don't know." His judgment was that I had failed his Ph.D oral exam on pacifism and should therefore be denied conscientious objector status. A letter from Downers Grove Friends Meeting, stating that I had been attending for two years and had been a member for one, counted for nothing.

In those days, you went to the city of your draft board to be examined. When I was 18 and living with my parents in South Holland, Illinois, the nearest draft board was in Thornton. The draft board sent me a round-trip ticket on the Illinois Central train from Thornton to Chicago, where the Induction Center perched ominously – a four-storey brick building with no windows on the south end of the Loop. When I arrived at the train station, the draft board had chosen – not randomly – one member of our group, who read our names off a checklist. He tried to get us marching down West Van Buren Street toward the induction center, with dubious success.

We all filed into an auditorium – there must have been three hundred of us. A soldier with slicked-back blond hair and a clipboard stood up in front and addressed the group.

"Here's the US Army Intelligence Test," he said. "Where it says 'Reason for test,' if it's induction, check induction, if it's pre-induction, check pre-induction. Don't put 'Screw LBJ' or anything like that." (Laughter from the crowd.)

"Don't try to fail it, because if you fail it, you won't get out of the Army – you'll get the worst job in the Army. If you do well, you'll get one of the best jobs in the Army."

"Oh, and here's the Armed Forces Security Questionnaire. If you have ever belonged to, or have gone to a meeting of one of the following 500 subversive organizations, please check Yes. If you know how liberally the word subversive can be interpreted, you'll read the list very carefully before you sign."

I read the list: Veterans of the Abraham Lincoln Brigade was one of the groups on it. Veterans of the Abraham Lincoln Brigade! Those guys fought in Spain against Franco. Anyone in that group would be 50 if not 60! I looked for Progressive Labor, the W.E.B. DuBois Club, or (gulp) the then-nonviolent Students for a Democratic Society. I didn't belong to Progressive Labor or the W.E.B. DuBois Club. I did belong to Students for a Democratic Society. Not a single one of these groups was listed. These guys were a year or two behind the times (30 years if you counted the Veterans of the Abraham Lincoln Brigade!).

Then Mr. Cool said, "You don't have to sign the list. You can take the Fifth. Anybody here want to take the Fifth?"

I raised my hand straight in the air. "And the First!" I shouted. As long as they were still giving out bourgeois civil liberties these days, I would take my share, thank you very much.

Mr. Cool sauntered over to me. "It's your perfect right not to sign the Security Questionnaire," he said, "But if I were you, I would sign the other form giving my local board the authority to have my medical records."

I looked up at him, puzzled. Why would anyone not release medical records? When you're young, everyone is beautiful and healthy – and naive. "I don't have any problem signing that," I said, and whipped off my signature.

"Fine," he replied. "Just give them this Green Slip at Station 20." I was now the only one in the roomful of draft-age men with a Green Slip.

We went through the line. Army doctors were looking in every conceivable part of our bodies. At one point there was a screen, and these guys were coming out from behind with their left fists clenched and their right hands on the muscle of their forearm. *Far out,* I thought, *the Italian-Americans are telling Uncle Sam what they think of this war!* Wrong. They weren't giving the Italian sign to go stuff yourself – they had just had blood samples taken.

Each was holding a cotton ball over the puncture in his arm.

At one point I was walking through in my boxer shorts, carrying all my valuable possessions in a little brown paper bag. Finally we got to get dressed again, and at Station 19 I had my papers stamped saying "Acceptable to the US Army." But I still had to go to Station 20 and turn in my Green Slip.

There at Station 20 was a sergeant showing a young corporal how to man the station.

"What do I do with this, Sarge?" he said, holding up my Green Slip.

"Oh, you just put his whole file in the pile over here and let his local board deal with it," Sarge said wisely.

Then the young corporal thought he'd try to impress the Sergeant. "Have you ever been arrested?" he asked me.

"Yes, once," I replied.

"Where were you arrested and what for?" said the corporal, gleaming that he might have caught a fish for the sergeant to fry.

"It was Cambridge, Maryland, in 1963, for disorderly conduct during a civil rights demonstration," I replied.

"And what was the outcome of the case?" asked the baby-faced corporal.

"We were all convicted and fined a penny. Typical Southern justice," I shot back.

"Hey, take it easy on us Southerners," said the corporal. "Go see the Moral Waivers Section over there." (The Moral Waivers Section in another induction center was to enjoy a brief moment of fame as the Group W Bench in *Alice's Restaurant.*)

At the Moral Waivers section, another soldier with slicked-back blond hair asked me solemnly if I intended to refuse induction – refuse to step across the line when they say "Take one step forward and you're in the Army now."

I said Yes, since that was Plan B. But Plan A was the one I had decided to do – emigrate to Canada where peace, not war, was most prominent in the country's foreign policy.

"Well, you have to fill out this questionnaire." He handed me a fan-fold questionnaire that when held up would have been taller than I was. On it were questions like "Have you ever left the country? If so, give dates, destinations and reasons for trips." And there was also a question, "Do you have a relative (father, mother, sibling, aunt, uncle) who was arrested under the Smith or the McCarran Acts?" (The Smith and the McCarran Acts were the anticommunist acts passed at the beginning of the McCarthy Era during the Cold War.)

It was a blatant attempt to get you to answer the questions on the Armed Forces Security Questionnaire even if you had refused to fill it out. The US Army had figured out that, by this time, red diaper babies were far more common than converts to communism. (A red diaper baby was someone born into a communist family – I went to school with a number of red diaper babies at Swarthmore.)

One of the questions on the form stumped me: "Have you ever had treatment for any form of mental or emotional illness?"

I had gone to see the campus psychiatrist at the Illinois Institute of Technology, and that seemed to me like a fairly normal thing. Even at my age then, it was obvious that these years of your life pushed tremendous pressures at you: university, career, sex, identity, friendship, politics, religion. Since I didn't know what to answer, I left that question blank, intending to go back and answer it when I'd completed the others.

I finally finished, and turned in the form. The soldier at the counter ran his finger down the form and pointed at the question I'd left blank. "Do you refuse to answer this question?" he asked.

"No," I shot back. "I just don't know what to put. What does seeing the campus psychiatrist count as?"

This was more than the soldier could handle. "Just a minute, I'll see if we've got the form.

"That shows you how to fill out this form," he said, and began rustling in the filing cabinet behind him. "No, we don't have that form. All we've got is the one for the previous form." By this time, I really wanted to go home. The only ones left in the whole induction center were me, the two soldiers behind the counter and the Army Doctor.

"I have an idea," I said. "Why don't you look on the form that shows you how to fill out the previous form? I bet there's a question on there about 'mental or emotional disorder.'" The two soldiers behind the counter looked at each other, unsure if this wasn't a trap.

They looked at the form. "Yup, there it is – it doesn't have the same number, though."

I smiled. "That's OK – I'll accept what it says if you will."

They looked at each other again – the expressions on their faces said, *Hey, maybe this is a trap.* They read the explanation, "psychoanalysis, psychotherapy ...."

Well, that was that. "OK," I said, "the answer is 'Yes.'"

At that point they handed my papers back to me and I handed them to the Army Doctor.

"This is highly irregular," he said, stroking his chin. "You've actually had your papers stamped saying 'Acceptable to the US Army' but we can't let you go in without a neuropsychiatric exam. Set him up for an N-P on Friday, Sam."

I was dumbfounded. Now I couldn't leave for Canada until Friday. I spent that night in my old apartment on the near North side. (I had shared a three-storey walk-up with a classmate on Mozart Street, between Shakespeare and Dickens – not a very peaceful neighborhood, alas, because of the gang in blue uniforms that terrorized the community.) That evening, I had read the cover story in the latest *Ramparts* magazine about how the CIA got Che Guevara.

The next day, Friday morning, I returned to the induction center for my neuropsychiatric exam. Sitting next to me in the waiting room were a couple of guys who were talking about dodging the draft by joining the Marines (that sounded to me like a neuropsychiatric problem, all right). I suggested that if they didn't mind a colder climate, our neighbor to the north might welcome them with open arms.

"Oh, no, I'd never give up my US citizenship," they recited together like the Bobbsey Twins.

Finally it was my turn, and another blond soldier with

slicked-back hair and a clipboard opened the door and called my name. I went in and sat on the chair midway in front of the two desks – the psychiatrist behind one and Corporal Clipboard behind the other.

"I see it says here you've been to see a psychiatrist. Why did you go to see your psychiatrist?" he asked.

I hesitated. I'd been pretty lippy until now, and I started to think it might be better to tell them less and make them ask for anything in particular. "Well, I had certain problems when I went, and I solved those, and now I'm working on some other problems...."

The psychiatrist cut me off, "Why are you being so evasive?"

Right. "I'm not being evasive, I'm just telling you what you want to know." I didn't add *in as few words as possible.*

Then the shrink thought it was time to change tactics, "Well, I'm against the War in Vietnam, too," he said.

"No you're not, or you wouldn't be here," I shot back.

The psychiatrist continued undaunted. "What do you think my role is here, actually?"

I couldn't hold this back. In a few hours I would be across the Canadian border. This was my last chance to get in my licks with the US Army.

"Well, I've been thinking about that," I said. "I suppose I could compare you to one of Adolph Eichmann's aides, but that's a bit too extreme. Let's just say your position is analogous to that of a petty civil servant in Mussolini's Italy who doesn't know what the hell is up."

Now the shrink had me on his ground. "That's a pretty paranoid assumption," he said.

I was boiling. "You'd be paranoid if you knew what was happening with US foreign policy!" I shouted.

That didn't faze him. "Well, you know there are some young men who wouldn't be happy in the US Army, and I'm here to find those young men and..."

I was seething. "If you think you care about what's happening to those young men, what about those *525,000* troops in

Vietnam, and what about the 25,000 guys killed, and what about ..."

By this time I was standing up and pointing my "J'accuse!" finger at him, oblivious to the fact that the only ones present were me, him and Corporal Clipboard.

"That's enough," he said, and wrote "paranoid" on my form, with the notation "Do not re-examine for two years."

I never heard from my draft board again. I did go to Canada, and in 1974 became a citizen. The United States – it's a nice place to visit, but I wouldn't want to live there.

A Letter to the Organizer of the Next Event on the Subject of Friends and the Vietnam War

From Chel Avery

Dear Friend:

I know you're out there. You may not recognize yourself in this role yet, but somewhere is a person, or better yet several persons, who will find themselves with the responsibility of planning the next occasion that brings together Friends (and hopefully, as Jeremy Mott keeps reminding me, *friends* of Friends) to explore our experiences during a particular period of excitement in our recent history sometimes called the American War in Vietnam.

How do I know you exist? First, because as soon as I received the assignment to work on this conference, I began interviewing people that I thought could advise me on what should happen and who should be involved. And from the beginning, most people spoke to me in terms not just of a single, one-shot gathering that would raise every question, resolve every dispute, and package up all our conclusions for posterity, but in terms of opening a conversation that has been left dangling for years, and which calls for long and varied exploration.

So from very early on, I thought of this event as the *first* conference on Friends and the Vietnam War, and I have been thinking about you, the planner of the next one, during all the months of my work on this project: What have I found that I can save for you? What mistakes have I made that perhaps you can rectify? What choices have I made, what directions have I agreed to, in the confidence that you will have the opportunity to go down a different path, to explore other roads, the ones not taken this time?

Not everyone I spoke with was encouraging about the plans for this conference. A small but vigorous minority insisted that we had let those years shadow us too much already, and that we should leave them behind and move on. I suspect for some that was a preference coming out of wisdom, and for some a preference triggered by pain long buried that they wanted to continue to avoid.

I was reminded of a time nearly two decades ago when my 80-something grandmother, a former ILGWU organizer, noticed a copy of *Mother Jones* magazine in my home. "They named a magazine for her? She was my friend, my teacher!"

I was thrilled. "Granny, Granny, did you know Emma Goldman, too?"

"Not very well," she answered. "We never saw eye to eye."

I remember that exchange clearly, because it is all I ever learned. The past was past, and my grandmother was only interested in the present. I could never persuade her to tell me stories about what – as I can only piece together from random scraps of information – must have been very hard years.

So, out of my own experience with disappointed inquiries, I want to thank all those who came to this conference, told their stories, and offered their insights, and especially those who took the trouble to put their thoughts in writing, because those years were legendary, and those memories – the painful and the proud – will be treasured by someone when we are past caring anymore.

The other reason I know there will be more such events in the future is from the experience of the conference itself. After five days, which was probably one or two days more than most of us had the stamina for, nonetheless I have received many messages about what else still needs to be discussed. I know that a few participants at this conference were already thinking ahead about organizing another one to address subjects that did not appear, or did not appear enough, on the agenda of this one.

Whether or not these discussions bear fruit, the seeds are planted. So, if you want to reap the benefits of the thoughts that were shared with me, along with all the other materials I have set aside for you, please check the archives of this conference at the Swarthmore College Library Peace Collection. Pay special attention to the conference evaluations, to the stack of pre-conference correspondence from Jeremy Mott (a wealth of ideas and networking information), and to post-conference correspondence with Jeremy and with Peter Blood. I have left these materials there with you in mind.

What did I learn from this conference?

I'll start with the impact on myself, because that will frame all of the rest.

I am at the young edge of the Vietnam generation, half a decade or more behind most of those who came to the conference. I graduated from high school in 1969. If I'd been male, I'd have been assigned a lottery number in the next few months. I had held my own sincere but rather poorly informed doubts about the war since junior high school. Once out in the world, I participated in the moratoriums and showed up at the antiwar rallies, but I was never an organizer. My knowledge of the names and places was sloppy; my understanding never deep. I eventually cut my activism teeth in the early 70's in the women's movement, and to a certain extent with the farmworkers' struggles and other labor issues. But other than showing up at the demonstrations and accepting leaflets that were handed to me, the only conscious antiwar action I ever took was to vote against Nixon in 1972.

Nonetheless, I realized during this conference, I don't think of those years as the "feminist years" or the "grapes and lettuce years." I don't even think of them as the Michigan years or my high school and college years. They are the "Vietnam years." They always have been. The American war in Vietnam is definitional for that segment of my life, despite the superficiality of my own participation. If that is true for me, then it is probably true for much of my generation.

Ironically, I spent the years after high school and through the end of the Vietnam "police action" living with a Vietnam vet. Tom was angry about his experiences, and to some degree scarred by them. In an act more of guts than strategy, he had thrown his purple heart back from his hospital bed into the face of the general who presented him with it. But he never doubted that the government had told him the real truth about the war, and that the protesters were naïve dupes of our enemies.

How did I handle the contradiction between my own rookie opposition to the war, and then going home to a vet who still thought the war necessary? I didn't. Living with contradiction was part of living with a veteran. In those days, none of us had ever heard of post-traumatic stress. But women, talking together in voices always lowered, sometimes observed that the men close to us who had come back from Vietnam were not the same as they were when they went. Something mysterious and terrible had happened to them there, something that changed them.

Knowing this was a secret. We whispered about it, but we never brought it out into the light and tried to understand it. I do not remember any reference to this secret ever being made in the presence of a man.

Looking back on this memory makes me wonder. What else do we know but not recognize that we know?

My favorite presentation title for this conference was the one chosen by Lynne Shivers and Jack Patterson: "If I Knew Now What I Knew Then." But sometimes I wish I had known *then* what I knew then. And that begs the question, what do we know *now* that we don't know we know? Trying to answer that question is something I want from any conference of this kind – the opportunity to test our truths and find out what it is we know that we haven't yet named.

To a certain extent, I still carry Tom's experience with me. I have not been in touch with him since 1980, but some long impression of his memories has bled into me, and I have my own flashbacks at odd moments. They are not my own trauma. This was not the case of a vet taking his pain out on other people through abuse. They are *his* memories. But they still haunt *me*.

Only a small number of veterans were present at the conference, but without their contributions I doubt I would have recognized this conference as being about the "Vietnam years" as I knew them.

We spent much time at this event discussing whether or not peace activists ever spit on returning vets or otherwise reviled them. Periodically, someone would intelligently conclude that even if such incidents might have happened rarely (and hopefully not by Friends), they were not the norm, and that reports of such events were magnified to discredit the peace movement and to drive a wedge between veterans and antiwar protesters. But the question could not be laid to rest. It kept coming back again. Why couldn't we finish with it? What does it mean, and what about it is so hard to let go of?

I would ask that at another time we discuss instead what is the relationship today between Friends who witnessed for peace during the Vietnam War and Friends who were in the military? Is there anything still unsaid that we need to say to each other? Are there subjects we find difficult to discuss? Where do we go from here?

One of the prevailing themes to emerge from the floor of this conference had already been named by the end of the first evening: Vietnam era peace activists share with Vietnam vets the fact that many of them still carry wounds from those years, long residues of unhealed pain. This observation remained on the floor, frequently referred to, throughout the days of the conference. When our First-day morning worship was structured around the theme of healing, it seemed that Ben Richmond had been rightly guided in his selection of a theme, and that the timing could not have been more suitable.

It was not until after the conference ended that I had the time to reflect on the fact that I did not really understand the nature of these wounds. They were mentioned often, but not explained, at least not from the conference floor. I sought out several participants to explain for me what they understood to be the source of those injuries. My own peacework, in post-Vietnam years, had frequently left me tired, burnt out, or with relationships shredded and empty at the end of a long campaign, but I couldn't say I'd ever experienced any peacenik's version of post-traumatic stress.

Was it the sense of betrayal felt by young people raised in an era of post-World War II optimism and patriotic pride, when they discovered that their country and its government did, in fact, harbor corruption, and that all their efforts could not fully put it right?

Well, yes, I was told. But there was more. There was the

impact of years of constant attention to horror and pain in the world, much of it not publicly acknowledged. It was knowing things, terrible things, denied by the government and not reported in the press, and being branded as an unpatriotic kook (or worse) by those who would not listen. It was for some, for the CO's and for the various practitioners of civil disobedience, long struggles with an unsympathetic bureaucracy that held their futures in dangerous uncertainty.

There is more, I think, that I still do not understand. Perhaps the wounds are all individual and unique. Perhaps the discussions about them that did not happen through the microphones in Thomas Great Hall did happen over lunch tables and in the nighttime colloquies on folding chairs under the Rockefeller Arch. But I am puzzled by a widely shared experience that was so frequently named and so little explained. (Is this a gender communication thing? Is it about the structure of the conference itself?)

I suspect – and others have said the same – that people who came to this conference are, for the most part, the best healed of the Vietnam generation of peace activists and objectors to military service. They are the ones who built on the learnings of those years to create lives that are constructive and consistent with their convictions.

What about the people of similar demographics who did not choose to come? Are there any generalities that can be made of them whatever? Or is that an unfair question, given that they were not gathered together to speak for themselves and draw their own conclusions?

And there were many who would have come if they could. During the long period of registration for the conference, I received one or two envelopes a week from individuals who had taken the trouble to fill out the form and to respond to all of the short answer questions, and who then appended a note saying, "I can't come. But I wanted you to know about me." Please hold these Friends in the Light, and invite them to the next one.

From the beginning of the planning, there was one question I asked of every person I interviewed, especially any male who was of conscription age during the Vietnam years: "Yes or no – if I were to ask you about the impact of your Vietnam-era experience on your faith, or on your spirituality, would that be a meaningful question?"

The answer was *always* an emphatic "Yes."

Even with this preview, however, I was amazed by how much of the discussion at the conference was in the language of religion, rather than in the language of politics. Perhaps the language was influenced by the conference design and by the composition of the participants. Nonetheless, it was a powerful statement that those years were something more than what they are sometimes accused of being: a time when Friends drifted in the direction of secular, political activism and away from our religious roots. Indeed, even if that was the case, it was also, for some who are now among our vital core of energy and leadership, an occasion for deepening into their religious roots.

Once and only once, in the context of a workshop, I heard a Friend talk about how his activism during those years distanced him, for a while, from his religion. I doubt very much that it was an isolated experience, and I wonder why I did not hear more such personal history. I would like for us to have further discussion about how such distancing happens, and what, if anything, we might do in response.

We were soundly critiqued in the evaluations for the absence of some whose presence was missed. For each particular name there is a different story, but for categories of people, there is more to be said.

We should have had a better balance of women to men speakers. The ratio we had did not seem so far off in the early stages of planning, when we thought we would be emphasizing the response of Friends to the challenge of military conscription, but when we expanded our scope to include the larger varieties of Friends' witness during those years, the absence of more women speakers became notable. For the next event, let me refer you (the organizer) to post-conference correspondence with Peter Blood, in which a longer list of names of potential women presenters is begun.

We had no Friends of color, and for this I spent whole nights sweating. We knew from the start that it would be difficult to locate non-white Friends who were deeply enough involved in some aspect of the Vietnam experience to fill speaking slots, and many of those who were asked declined. (The next gathering, perhaps, might go beyond the boundaries of Quakerism, making such contributors easier to recruit.)

I kept a frighteningly large number of presentation slots open until I finally received one "Yes," right before I would either have had to fill those slots or leave town. Unfortunately, the single African American speaker canceled shortly before the conference, which is perhaps poetic justice for what would have been tokenism at best. The very little wisdom I have to offer for next time is in urging you to act proactively and energetically from the very earliest planning stages if you want ethnic variety in the group.

On the other hand, finding Vietnamese participation for this conference should not have been as difficult, and the absence of such voices represents my own oversight in not acting quickly enough. We had good consultation, initiated by Lady Borton, and the AFSC Asia Desk could also have served as an advisory resource. I urge the next planners to think about Vietnamese participation and *work it into the budget* early in the game, in discussion with the above-named advisers.

I was surprised at how many people expressed a disappointment at the small numbers of young people who came to the conference. There was a real hunger for the presence of youth. While I did not make an all-out effort to recruit large numbers of young adults to participate, I did search long and hard for someone to represent the "next generation" in the three-generation panel. I did this with the help of contacts at Quaker colleges and of young people who had spent time at Pendle Hill. It was much more difficult than any of us anticipated.

Here is what I learned: young people today do not have the flexibility in their summer schedules that I remember my peers having at that age. If they are not involved in summer internships or service projects, they are in jobs which they cannot get away from. The good news is that there are definitely some college-age and slightly older Friends who *are* interested in this topic. I don't know what it will take to make it easy for them to participate, but if that is a goal, it should probably be considered from the beginning in the scheduling, budgeting and programming of an event.

Several people noticed the disproportionate weight that the "Philadelphia view of the world" held at this conference. In addition, I had hoped that the Vietnam War, which all of us went through, would present an occasion to bring together a more balanced mix of the various flavors of American Quakerism. (Even our ad in *Quaker Life* brought responses primarily from FGC Friends who subscribe to that FUM periodical.)

Of the various factors involved in the demographics we did get, I am sure geography was one, and I hope that a future event will be located considerably further west. So when I urge you to check the Swarthmore Library, I am not assuming that will be a short trip for you. Call me if you need help finding a place to stay.

Finally, I wish to name one more surprise I experienced in this conference. Discussion was so polite! I know certain deep controversies are still with us: Did we "secularize" too much in our activism during those years? What did we sacrifice? Did we fail to do enough? What is our response to the directions taken by the AFSC? To the actions of [fill in the name of your favorite controversial Friend]?

Some participants have said to me that yes, they pulled their rhetorical punches. I don't think some of the same people would have been as conversationally gentle in 1968 as they were in 1998, and perhaps there is a discussion to be had about the benefits and costs of *that*. At the same time, some participants have expressed gratitude that the conference was a "safe" place to discuss hard subjects. Peter Woodrow has reminded me that Vietnam-era activists possess a wealth of group process skills – a resource that could be tapped in developing creative structures for the exchange of ideas. This is something to look at as decisions are made about discussion topics for any future events – which might take a very different form from this one.

I am grateful to our plenary speakers for some wonderful in-depth and insightful work on the events and meanings of our Vietnam War years' experience. And in response to those presentations, new questions and thoughts arose – in the voices of those who lived through those times and have the benefit of three decades' hindsight. I look forward to hearing what the perspective of another two or three years, or even ten years' consideration of these insights and questions can add to our understanding. Finding the best way to plumb those depths will be your job.

This conference roughly mapped a territory (some of it first-hand, some of it by standing at the boundaries and looking out at ground we weren't covering, marking distant mountains and rumored monsters on the horizon). We plowed the surface of some of that ground. I hope the organizers of the next event will look back at our map, make your best guess about where the archeological treasures lie buried, and organize some serious excavation.

And I hope you will invite me to come.

Peace,

Chel Avery

Presenters & Panel Participants

Marion Anderson is Director of Employment Research Associates in East Lansing, Michigan. She attends Red Cedar Meeting in East Lansing.

Chel Avery was formerly a staff member at Pendle Hill, and is now Director of the Conflict Resolution Studies Program at Bryn Mawr College. She is a member of Goshen (PA) Monthly Meeting.

John Bach lives in Gunnison, Colorado, on Lucky Cat Dog Farm, with 26 Alaska huskies and other animals, and from which he leads dog sled tours.

Bruce Birchard, formerly a staff member of the Friends Peace Committee and the American Friends Service Committee, has been General Secretary of Friends General Conference since 1992. He is a member of Central Philadelphia (PA) Monthly Meeting.

Charlie Bonner grew up in Philadelphia, served with the Marine Corps in Vietnam, and has served as National President of Veterans for Peace. He is a member of Lancaster (PA) Friends Meeting.

Gordon Browne now lives in northern Vermont, and is a member of Plainfield (VT) Monthly Meeting. In addition to a long career as a teacher and writer, he has served as Executive Secretary of the Friends World Committee for Consultation, Section of the Americas.

Max Carter is Director of the Quaker Center at Guilford College, Greensboro, North Carolina, where he is also a member of New Garden Friends Meeting.

Bronson Clark, an Ohio native, was Executive Secretary of the American Friends Service Committee from 1969 to 1975. He now divides his time between Rockport, Maine and Chapel Hill, NC.

Garret Colman-Snyder is a student at Colgate University.

William A. Eagles is a member of New Garden Friends Meeting in Greensboro, NC. He and his wife Catherine have two sons. He is a former member of the Quaker House Board of Overseers. He attended the Raleigh Meeting during the early days of Quaker House.

Daniel E. Ensley is an attorney in Menasha, Wisconsin. He is a member of Fox Valley (WI) Monthly Meeting.

Chuck Fager is a writer, editor and publisher in Bellefonte, Pennsylvania. He is a member of State College, PA (Philadelphia-Baltimore) Friends Meeting.

David Finke is a member of 57th Street Meeting in Chicago, now sojourning with Columbia (MO) Meeting, where he currently resides. He was Peace Secretary for the American Friends Service Committee's Midwest Office in 1967-73. He is a founder of the Quaker Volunteer Service and Witness Network.

Peter Goldberger is an attorney in Ardmore, PA. In addition to his other practice, he is co-counsel to the Central Committee for Conscientious Objectors, and has represented numerous tax resisters before the IRS.

David Hartsough is Director of Peaceworkers, in San Francisco, California.

Kathleen Hertzberg served in England with the Friends Ambulance Unit during World War II, and later emigrated to Canada with her husband Fritz. She served as Chairperson of the Canadian Friends Service Committee for seven years during the Vietnam War. She now lives in Pickering, Ontario.

Ken Maher is a technical writer in Rochester, New York, where he is also Clerk of Rochester Monthly Meeting.

Johan Maurer was born in Norway and joined Friends in Canada. He is now General Secretary of Friends United Meeting in Richmond, Indiana, and Editor of *Quaker Life*.

Jeremy Mott was born and still lives in Ridgewood, New Jersey, where he is a member of Ridgewood Monthly Meeting. He left Harvard College in 1965 to work to end the Vietnam War, and later served 16 months in prison for draft resistance.

Jack T. Patterson is Co-Director of the Conflict Resolution Program of the New York office of the American Friends Service Committee, where he also heads the Expatriates Dialogues Program.

Tom Rodd is an attorney. He lives in Moatsville, West Virginia. he is a member of Monongalia Meeting in Morgantown, West Virginia.

Arthur O. Roberts taught religion and philosophy from 1953 to 1987 at George Fox College in Newberg, Oregon, where he remains Professor at Large. He is also editor of *Quaker Religious Thought,* and serves as Mayor of Yachats, Oregon.

Lou Schneider was Executive Secretary of the American Friends Service Committee from 1974-1980. He lives in Glenmoore, Pennsylvania, and is a member of Downingtown (PA) Meeting.

Daniel A. Seeger is Director of Pendle Hill. He is a member of Birmingham Meeting (PA)

Lynne Shivers is a member of Central Philadelphia (PA) Monthly Meeting. In addition to writing, she teaches English at a community college and leads nonviolence training workshops.

Carl Stieren lives in Ottawa, Ontario.

Beth Taylor is Director of Undergraduate Writing in the English Department at Brown University. She attended Cheltenham, Southampton, and Wrightstown Friends Meetings, and spent the Vietnam War at George School and Smith College. She is writing a book on the young men she lost one way or another to the war in Vietnam, and teaching a course called "Writing Vietnam" at Brown.

Anne Morrison Welsh is a writer in Black Mountain, North Carolina. She is Clerk of Swannanoa Valley Friends Meeting.

Jay Worrall III is a member of Langley Hill Monthly Meeting in McLean, Virginia. He has worked in social science research, as a program manager for the American Correctional Association, as Executive Secretary to the Quaker US/USSR Committee, and as a carpenter.

Liz Yeats worked with the American Friends Service Committee in several capacities during the Vietnam War, and more recently spent eight years on the staff of Friends General Conference. She is now settling into a new life in Austin, Texas.